ACOUSTICS
WAVES AND OSCILLATIONS

ACOUSTICS
WAVES AND OSCILLATIONS

(SECOND EDITION)

S.N. SEN
Ex-Senior Professor of Physics
University of North Bengal
India

PUBLISHING FOR ONE WORLD

NEW AGE INTERNATIONAL (P) LIMITED, PUBLISHERS

New Delhi • Bangalore • Chennai • Cochin • Guwahati • Hyderabad
Jalandhar • Kolkata • Lucknow • Mumbai • Ranchi
Visit us at **www.newagepublishers.com**

Published by New Age International (P) Ltd., Publishers
First Edition: 1990
Second Edition: 2010

Branches:

- No. 37/10, 8th Cross (Near Hanuman Temple), Azad Nagar, Chamrajpet, **Bangalore**-560 018. Tel.: (080) 26756823, Telefax: 26756820, E-mail: bangalore@newagepublishers.com
- 26, Damodaran Street, T. Nagar, **Chennai**-600 017. Tel.: (044) 24353401, Telefax: 24351463 E-mail: chennai@newagepublishers.com
- CC-39/1016, Carrier Station Road, Ernakulam South, **Cochin**-682 016. Tel.: (0484) 2377004, Telefax: 4051303. E-mail: cochin@newagepublishers.com
- Hemsen Complex, Mohd. Shah Road, Paltan Bazar, Near Starline Hotel, **Guwahati**-781 008. Tel.: (0361) 2513881. Telefax: 2543669, E-mail: guwahati@newagepublishers.com
- No. 105, 1st Floor, Madhiray Kaveri Tower, 3-2-19, Azam Jahi Road, Nimboliadda, **Hyderabad**-500 027. Tel.: (040) 24652456, Telefax: 24652457, E-mail:hyderabad@newagepublishers.com
- RDB Chambers (Formerly Lotus Cinema)106A, 1st Floor, S.N. Banerjee Road, **Kolkata**-700 014. Tel.: (033) 22273773, Telefax: 22275247, E-mail:kolkata@newagepublishers.com
- 16-A, Jopling Road, **Lucknow**-226 001. Tel.: (0522) 2209578, 4045297, Telefax: 2204098 E-mail: lucknow@newagepublishers.com
- 142C, Victor House, Ground Floor, N.M. Joshi Marg, Lower Parel, **Mumbai**-400 013. Tel.: (022) 24927869. Telefax: 24915415, E-mail: mumbai@newagepublishers.com
- 22, Golden House, Daryaganj, **New Delhi**-110 002. Tel.: (011) 23262370, 23262368, Telefax: 43551305. E-mail: sales@newagepublishers.com

ISBN : 978-81-224-2680-9

Rs. 195.00

C-10-02-4311

Printed in India at Mohanlal Printers, Delhi.
Typeset at Inhouse.

PUBLISHING FOR ONE WORLD
NEW AGE INTERNATIONAL (P) LIMITED, PUBLISHERS
4835/24, Ansari Road, Daryaganj, New Delhi-110002
Visit us at **www.newagepublishers.com**

Dedicated to
my wife Uma
my sister Jyotsna
and
my daughters Madhusri and Suparna

PREFACE TO THE SECOND EDITION

In view of the potential importance of Acoustics in both theoretical and practical applications in various branches of physics, the book has been thoroughly revised in this edition. The subject of ultrasonics is one of the most important aspect of acoustics for its theoretical and experimental investigation. Consequently the generation and detection of ultrasonics has been presented in detail. A separate chapter has been included regarding the hypersonics velocity in viscous liquid as revealed from Brillouin spectra. As such the new edition will be helpful specially for postgraduate and research students.

I am thankful to New Age International (P) Ltd., Publishers to bring out the revised second edition of the book within a short period.

S.N. Sen

PREFACE TO THE FIRST EDITION

I was engaged in giving a course of lectures in acoustics to the first year students of the B.Sc. (Honours) in Jadavpur University the need was felt for a comprehensive textbook covering the syllabus in honours course in the subject as prescribed by different Indian Universities. Though there are, at present, a number of books in acoustics, the subject has been dealt with from purely mathematical point of view in some, and greater stress has been laid on the physical interpretation of the subject-matter in others. The science of acoustics has been one of the oldest branches of physics but during the First and Second World Wars it underwent a fast development mainly due to its manifold practical applications and to the rapid growth in the subject of ultrasonics. Both in theory and in experimental technique it has advanced to a great extent. In this treatise, an attempt has been made to present the subject-matter by explaining its physical basis with necessary mathematical formulation supplemented by experimental details wherever possible. Existing literature and standard texts have been consulted for the preparation of the book. I am thankful to Mr. Pradip Kumar Chakraborty for neatly typing the manuscript. In the second edition a new chapter entitled "Hypersonic Velocity in Viscous Liquid as Revealed from Brilliouin Spectra" has been added.

I hope that the book will be useful to the honours and postgraduate students of our universities.

S.N. SEN

CONTENTS

1.	**INTRODUCTION**		**1 - 3**
2.	**SIMPLE HARMONIC MOTION**		**4 - 16**
2.1	Phase of simple harmonic vibration	...	6
2.2	Energy of a particle in simple harmonic vibration	...	7
2.3	Composition of simple harmonic vibrations	...	8
2.4	Experimental observation	...	13
2.5	Fourier's theorem	...	13
2.6	Partial Fourier series	...	16
3.	**THEORY OF FORCED VIBRATION AND RESONANCE**		**17 - 28**
3.1	Damped vibration	...	17
3.2	Logarithmic decrement	...	18
3.3	Special cases of damped vibration	...	20
3.4	Forced vibration	...	21
3.5	Phase of forced vibration	...	23
3.6	Amplitude resonance	...	23
3.7	Velocity response	...	25
3.8	Energy of forced vibration	...	28
4.	**THEORY OF COUPLED OSCILLATION**		**29 - 41**
4.1	Two oscillators coupled together	...	29
4.2	General equation	...	29
4.3	Normal modes of vibration	...	32
4.4	General solution	...	32
4.5	Special cases	...	34
4.6	Examples of coupled oscillation	...	37
4.7	Analogy with electrical coupled circuits	...	41
5.	**VIBRATION IN AN EXTENDED MEDIUM**		**42 - 49**
5.1	Plane waves	...	42
5.2	Velocity of wave propagation	...	43
5.3	Energy of a plane wave of sound intensity	...	45
5.4	Power of a source emitting plane wave	...	46
5.5	Elastic vibration in solids	...	47

6. VIBRATION OF STRINGS **50 - 81**

6.1 Transverse vibration of strings ... 50
6.2 Reflection: Formation of stationary waves ... 51
6.3 Experimental verification of the laws of vibrating string: The sonometer ... 53
6.4 General solution of the wave equation in string ... 54
6.5 Methods of producing vibrations in strings ... 55
6.6 Special cases in the vibration of strings ... 75
6.7 Energy of the vibrating string ... 80

7. VIBRATION OF BARS AND TUNING FORKS **82 - 96**

7.1 Transverse vibration of bar ... 82
7.2 Boundary conditions ... 84
7.3 Solution of the general equation ... 85
7.4 Conditions at ends ... 85
7.5 Energy of a vibrating bar ... 88
7.6 Tuning forks ... 90
7.7 Temperature effect on frequency ... 91
7.8 Electrically maintained tuning fork ... 92
7.9 Determination of frequency of tuning fork ... 93

8. VIBRATION OF MEMBRANES AND RINGS **97 - 114**

8.1 Case of stretched membranes ... 97
8.2 Rectangular membrane ... 97
8.3 Initial conditions ... 100
8.4 Discussion of the result ... 101
8.5 Square membrane ... 102
8.6 Energy of a vibrating membrane ... 103
8.7 Case of circular membrane ... 104
8.8 Kinetic energy of the vibrating membrane ... 106
8.9 Potential energy of the vibrating membrane ... 107
8.10 The kettledrum ... 107
8.11 Vibration of rings ... 110

9. VIBRATION OF AIR COLUMNS **115 - 122**

9.1 Vibration of air columns in cylindrical pipe ... 115
9.2 End correction ... 117
9.3 Examples of vibrating air column: Organ pipes ... 118
9.4 High frequency pipes: Galton's whistle ... 120
9.5 Vibrations in air cavity: Helmholtz resonator ... 121

10. TRANSMISSION OF SOUND **123 - 136**

10.1 Velocity of sound in a gas ... 123
10.2 Effect of pressure, temperature and humidity on the sound velocity in a gas ... 124
10.3 Velocity of sound in open air ... 126
10.4 Velocity of sound contained in tubes ... 127
10.5 Velocity of sound in resonance air column ... 131
10.6 Velocity of sound in different gases and vapours at different temperatures ... 132
10.7 Velocity of sound in a liquid ... 132
10.8 Velocity of sound in a solid ... 134

11. REFLECTION, REFRACTION, INTERFERENCE AND DIFFRACTION OF SOUND **137 - 152**

11.1 Reflection at the boundary of two media ... 137
11.2 Phase change on reflection ... 139
11.3 Reflection of sound wave from a plate of finite thickness ... 139
11.4 Formation of echoes ... 140
11.5 Refraction of sound ... 142
11.6 Interference of sound ... 144
11.7 Combination tones ... 144
11.8 Objective and subjective existence of combination tones ... 147
11.9 Diffraction of sound ... 147
11.10 Diffraction through a slit ... 148
11.11 The case of circular aperture ... 150
11.12 The diffraction grating ... 151
11.13 Experimental arrangement ... 151

12. RECEPTION AND TRANSFORMATION OF SOUND **153 - 171**

12.1 The human ear ... 153
12.2 Theories of hearing ... 154
12.3 Sensation of loudness: Waber-Fechner Law ... 154
12.4 Analysis of note: Ohm's Law ... 155
12.5 Intensity and loudness level: The Bel ... 155
12.6 Sensitive flames and jets ... 156
12.7 Transformation of sound ... 156
12.8 Electromagnetic receiver (Moving Iron Type) ... 156
12.9 Electrodynamic receiver ... 158
12.10 Piezoelectric phenomena ... 158
12.11 Use of Piezoelectric property of the crystal ... 159

12.12 Piezoelectric receivers ... 161
12.13 Magnetostriction receiver ... 162
12.14 Microphones ... 162
12.15 Thermal receiver: Hot wire microphone ... 165
12.16 Underwater receiver: Hydrophone ... 166
12.17 Loudspeakers ... 166
12.18 Maintenance of sound by heat ... 169
12.19 Travelyan's rocker ... 169
12.20 Singing flames ... 170
12.21 Singing arc ... 171
12.22 Gauge tone ... 171

13. SOUND MEASUREMENT AND ANALYSIS 172 - 184

13.1 Measurement of intensity ... 172
13.2 Measurement of frequency ... 177
13.3 Doppler's principle ... 179
13.4 Measurement of phase ... 181
13.5 Musical sound ... 181
13.6 Intensity, pitch and quality ... 181
13.7 Consonance and dissonance ... 182
13.8 Musical scale ... 183
13.9 Musical interval ... 183
13.10 Diatonic scale ... 183
13.11 Analysis of musical notes ... 184

14. ACOUSTICS OF BUILDINGS 185 - 192

14.1 Position of the speaker ... 185
14.2 Loudness ... 185
14.3 Reverberation ... 185
14.4 Theoretical consideration ... 187
14.5 Determination of time of reverberation ... 189
14.6 Determination of absorption coefficient ... 189
14.7 Optimum time of reverberation ... 190
14.8 Noise ... 190
14.9 Other considerations ... 192

15. RECORDING AND REPRODUCTION OF SOUND 193 - 200

15.1 Recording in discs ... 193
15.2 Wire or tape recording ... 197
15.3 Recording of sound in film ... 198

16. ULTRASONICS **201 - 221**

16.1 Generation of ultrasonic waves ... 201
16.2 The piezoelectric method ... 202
16.3 The quartz crystal ... 202
16.4 Design of ultrasonic crystal ... 203
16.5 Power for ultrasonic generation ... 203
16.6 Generation of ultrasonic vibration by magnetostriction ... 204
16.7 Magnetostriction oscillator ... 205
16.8 Detection of ultrasonic waves ... 206
16.9 Velocity of ultrasonic waves ... 207
16.10 Absorption and dispersion of ultrasonic waves ... 211
16.11 Propagation of ultrasonics through liquid helium ... 217
16.12 Application of ultrasonics ... 219

17. HYPERSONIC VELOCITY IN VISCOUS LIQUIDS AS REVEALED FROM BRILLOUIN SPECTRA **223 - 228**

17.1 Introduction ... 223

PROBLEMS **229**

INDEX **235**

1

INTRODUCTION

Energy is familiar to us in many ways such as light, heat, kinetic and potential, electrical and magnetic energy. In the same way sound is also a form of energy. Just as it is customary to regard light and heat as radiation in visible, ultraviolet and infrared sections of electromagnetic spectrum, sound can also be regarded as mechanical vibrations having frequencies ranging from a few cycles to ultrasonic vibrations. Human ear is sensitive to mechanical vibrations ranging from a few cycles per second to approximately 20000 c/s and this range is called the audible range. Above this frequency, the vibrations are called ultrasonic vibrations. An important difference, however, exists between the vibrations producing light and those producing sound. Light vibrations are transverse, that is vibrations are perpendicular to the direction of propagation but in case of sound, the vibrations are longitudinal, that is they take place in the same direction as the direction of propagation.

The prime criterion for the production of sound is that the body producing the sound must be in a state of vibration. In some cases, these vibrations can easily be seen as a blurred outline of the sounding body whereas in other cases it may be necessary to use some amplifying device to reveal the vibrations and it has been established beyond any doubt that unless a body is in a state of vibration no sound can be produced.

Propagation of sound

If an electric bell is suspended within a belljar which is being gradually evacuated by connecting it to a vacuum pump, it is found that when the belljar is almost completely evacuated the ringing sound of the bell becomes almost inaudible. This simple experiment demonstrates that a material medium is absolutely necessary for the propagation of sound from one place to another. This communication is generally made by the air of the atmosphere. The vibrations produced by a sounding body are taken up by the medium which begins to vibrate in synchronism with the vibrations of the material body. Besides air and other gases, the solid material bodies are also capable of transmitting sound. Sound is also propagated through a liquid as is observed when two persons diving under water can speak to one another and can be distinctly heard. These experiments show that sound can only propagate through material medium and it is immediately stopped if an evacuated space intervenes between the source and the receiver. With regard to propagation of sound and that of light, another difference exists. Whereas a material medium is absolutely essential for the propagation of sound, light energy can pass through vacuum. This fact clearly demonstrates that though both light and sound are due to some form of vibration, there lies an important difference between their nature and mode of propagation. As it is now established that sound is a form of wave motion, we shall now define the terms which are of frequent occurrence in connection with wave motion.

Period (Time Period). The period of vibration is the time from the instant when the vibrating point passes through any position to the instant when it next passes through the same position moving in the same direction; is denoted generally by T.

Frequency. The frequency of vibration (f) is the number of vibrations performed in unit time. Thus frequency is the reciprocal of time period,

$$f = \frac{1}{T}$$

Amplitude. The amplitude of vibration is the maximum displacement by the vibrating point in the course of its motion from its mean position.

Phase. The phase of a vibrating point at any instant is the state of its displacement and motion at the instant in question with reference to a certain fixed point.

Velocity. The passage of sound from the source to the receiver is not instantaneous which means that sound travels with a finite velocity. We shall find later on that sound travels with different velocities in different media. Within wide limits, the velocity of sound is approximately independent of frequency and intensity.

Wavelength. The distance through which the wave travels during one complete vibration of the vibrating particle is called wavelength. Consequently, if the particle makes f vibrations per second where f is the frequency, we get the relation

$$v = f\lambda$$

where λ is the wavelength.

Noise and musical sound

All sounds can be divided roughly into two broad classes, noise and musical sound. There is no sharp line of demarcation between musical sound and noise, for some noises have more or less a musical character and also some musical sounds are not completely free from noise. Musical sounds are generally characterised by their regularity and smoothness and it is natural to infer that they are produced by periodic vibrations, whereas noises are characterised by irregular or nonperiodic vibrations. All musical sounds are characterised during their steady continuance by three features: (a) pitch, (b) intensity, and (c) quality.

(a) **Pitch.** The pitch of a musical sound is a general feature which is recognised by every one. It solely depends upon the period or frequency of vibration constituting the sound; the greater the frequency the higher the pitch. Pitch is generally specified in two distinct ways: (a) scientifically by the statement of period or frequency of vibration or by the logarithm of frequency and (b) musically by assigning to the sound in question its position in a certain accepted series of sounds constituting the musical scale.

(b) **Intensity and loudness.** The intensity of sound waves is a physical quantity which is proportional to wave energy passing per unit time through unit area and the intensity is generally proportional to the square of the amplitude. Loudness on the other hand corresponds to the degree of sensation depending upon the intensity of the sound and the sensitiveness of the ear. Though the loudness of a sound depends upon the intensity producing it and increases and decreases with the intensity, it is rather difficult to define the relation between the two in a precise manner. The intensity of sound is a purely physical quantity and has an objective existence whereas loudness corresponding to the degree of sensation is not wholly physical but, in part at least, has a subjective existence and depends upon the ear and the hearer. We shall discuss the relation between the two later.

(c) **Quality.** The third characteristic property which distinguishes a musical sound from others having the same pitch and intensity is called the quality. Thus the different musical instruments will produce musical sounds of different qualities. This characteristic difference in the character of musical sound has been ascribed to the fact that very few sounds can be regarded as pure which means that the sound should consist of a single frequency. An example of a pure sound is furnished by a tuning fork – whereas musical sounds emitted by different instruments such as a piano or violin consist of a large and varying number of overtones in addition to fundamental frequency. These overtones produce to the ear the sensation of different musical sounds. An analysis of the wave form of a particular sound will reveal the different overtones which are present in a particular musical note.

Having thus presented the fundamental concepts in the theory of vibration, we shall, in the subsequent chapters, describe the main principles and applications of the theory of sound production, propagation and reception. Apart from the purely academic point of view, the science of acoustics has large and varied practical applications and the development in this old branch of physical science has been due largely to the wartime researches carried on with specific objectives. The branch of acoustics termed ultrasonics has developed to such a great extent that it requires a separate volume for the fuller treatment of the subject. The object of the present treatise is thus to present in simple and logical terms the development of the subject up to the present time and discuss the future possibilities.

2

SIMPLE HARMONIC MOTION

Any kind of motion which repeats itself after a definite period is known as periodic motion. The movement of the moon round the earth and that of the earth and other planets round the sun are familiar examples of periodic motion. The vibrations which produce sound are also a kind of periodic motion. The simplest kind of periodic motion is the simple harmonic motion with which we will be concerned in our present discussion. It has been shown by Fourier[1] that a periodic motion can be analysed into a series of simple harmonic motions having frequencies which are multiples of that of the given motion. We consider a very simple example. Let particle *A* move along the circumference of a circle with a constant velocity as shown in Fig. 2.1 and let

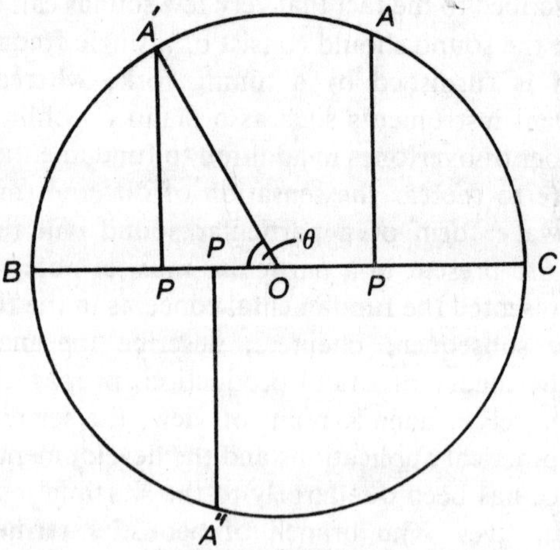

Fig. 2.1

the centre of the circle be *O* and let a perpendicular *AP* be drawn from the particle on the diameter *BC* of the circle. Then as the particle moves along the circumference of the circle, the point *P* (the foot of the perpendicular) moves along the diameter. As particle *A* moves and completes one rotation along the circumference, the point *P* makes *A* to and fro motion along the diameter and this motion of *P* is called a simple harmonic motion. From this it is clear that the requisite conditions for the point *P* to execute a simple harmonic motion are the following:

(a) The force acting on *P* must be proportional to the displacement of the particle from the centre *O*.

(b) The force is acting along the diameter and it must always be directed to the centre of the circle.

The medium in which the body is executing the simple harmonic motion exerts forces of reaction on it; but for the present, we shall neglect the effect of such forces. Consequently, the equation of simple harmonic motion can be written subject to the conditions (a) and (b). If m denotes the mass of the particle, x the displacement from the position of rest and S the force per unit displacement.

$$m \frac{d^2x}{dt^2} = -Sx \tag{2·1}$$

if we write

$$\omega^2 = \frac{S}{m} \tag{2·2}$$

$$\frac{d^2x}{dt^2} = -\omega^2 x$$

or

$$\frac{d^2x}{dt^2} + \omega^2 x = 0 \tag{2·3}$$

Let us assume that $x = A \cos \omega t + B \sin \omega t$, where A and B are constants.

then $\frac{dx}{dt} = -A\,\omega \sin \omega t + B\,\omega \cos \omega t.$

and $\frac{d^2x}{dt^2} = -\omega^2\,[A \cos \omega t + B \sin \omega t].$

$= -\omega^2 x.$

and so equation (2.3) is satisfied by this value of x, and hence $x = A \cos \omega t + B \sin \omega t$ is the solution of equation (2.1) and ω denotes the angular frequency of vibration where $\omega^2 = S/m$. If further we put $A = a \cos \theta$ and $B = -a \sin \theta$ where $\tan \theta = -B/A$ and $a^2 = A^2 + B^2$

then $x = a \cos \theta \cos \omega t - a \sin \theta \sin \omega t$

$$= a \cos(\omega t + \theta) \tag{2.4}$$

where the constants A, B, a and θ are arbitrary. Thus the motion is periodic because the values of x and (dx/dt) recur when ωt increases by 2π. The maximum displacement a of the particle is called the amplitude of vibration and the time period T called the period, is given by

$$T = \frac{2\pi}{\omega} = 2\pi \sqrt{\frac{m}{S}} \tag{2.5}$$

Thus it is seen that the time period T is independent of amplitude or the oscillations are isochronous. From equation (2.4) it is seen that the velocity of the particle is given by

$$v = \frac{dx}{dt} = -a\,\omega \sin(\omega t + \theta). \tag{2.6}$$

and the acceleration of the particle,

$$\alpha = \frac{d^2x}{dt^2} = -a\,\omega^2 \cos(\omega t + \theta)$$
$$= -\omega^2 x. \tag{2.7}$$

If f is the number of vibrations per second, i.e., the frequency of oscillations, we obtain

$$f = \frac{1}{T} = \frac{\omega}{2\pi} = \frac{1}{2\pi}\sqrt{\frac{S}{m}} \tag{2.8}$$

2.1 PHASE OF SIMPLE HARMONIC VIBRATION

The idea of phase is very important in the theory of simple harmonic vibration. If two particles start at the same instant of time from a particular point called the reference point and move with different angular velocities, then after a certain time the particle with higher velocity will gain over the particle with lower velocity by an angle which is called the gain in phase. In Fig. 2.1, let the initial position of the particle be at A' whereas the reference line from which all displacements are counted is the diameter BC. So the particle A' is given an initial gain in phase by the angle θ and so the angle θ is known as initial phase difference; when the particle has come over to A in time t moving with the angular velocity ω, then the total angular displacement of the particle is $(\omega t + \theta)$ and so the angle introduced in equation (2.4) is a constant for the particular problem and has to be identified with the initial phase difference or it is also sometimes designated as epoch. To illustrate graphically, the displacement velocity and acceleration have been plotted against the angular displacement in Fig. 2.2. We find from these curves that

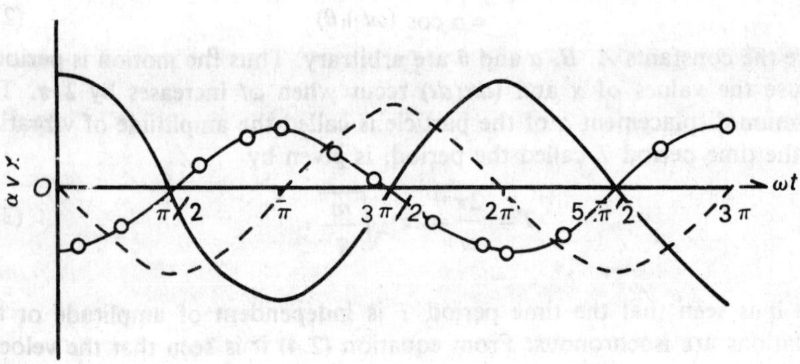

Fig. 2.2

velocity is always 90° or $\pi/2$ radian out of phase with displacement and acceleration 180° or π radian out of phase with displacement. We can see the same result also from our analytical treatment above. The displacement, velocity and acceleration are given respectively by,

$$x = a \cos(\omega t + \theta) \quad v = -a\,\omega \sin(\omega t + \theta) = a\omega \cos(\omega t + \theta + \pi/2)$$

and $$\alpha = -a\omega^2 \sin(\omega t + \theta) = a\omega^2 \cos(\omega t + \theta + \pi).$$

2.2 ENERGY OF A PARTICLE IN SIMPLE HARMONIC VIBRATION

The kinetic energy of a particle is given by

$$E = \frac{1}{2} m v^2$$

From equation (2.6) $v = -a\,\omega \sin(\omega t + \theta)$.

So $$E = \frac{1}{2} m\, a^2 \omega^2 \sin^2(\omega t + \theta).$$

Since the sum of potential energy (V) and kinetic energy of the particle (i.e., the total energy) is constant, at any instant, when one form is maximum the other must be zero. Thus the maximum value of E gives the total energy at any instant and so $E + V = 1/2\, ma^2\, \omega^2$. So the potential energy is given by

$$V = \frac{1}{2} m\, a^2 \omega^2 - \frac{1}{2} m\, a^2 \omega^2 \sin^2(\omega t + \theta)$$

or $$V = \frac{1}{2} m\, a^2 \omega^2 \cos^2(\omega t + \theta) \qquad (2.9)$$

The average value of $\sin^2(\omega t + \theta)$ over the complete period is 1/2 and also that of $\cos^2(\omega t + \theta)$ is 1/2. Hence the average kinetic energy $= \frac{1}{4} ma^2$ $\omega^2 =$ average potential energy.

So the total energy becomes $\frac{1}{2} m\, a^2 \omega^2$

$$\text{The potential energy} = \frac{1}{2} m\, a^2 \omega^2 \cos^2(\omega t + \theta)$$

$$= \frac{1}{2} m\, \omega^2 x^2$$

$$= \frac{1}{2} m \frac{S}{m} x^2$$

$$= \frac{1}{2} S x^2 \qquad (2.10)$$

2.3 COMPOSITION OF SIMPLE HARMONIC VIBRATIONS

If a particle is simultaneously acted upon by a number of forces each of which, when acting upon the particle, would cause it to execute a simple harmonic vibration then the resultant motion will be considered as equivalent to a motion as if each force produces its own effect.

CASE 1: Vibrations of same frequency and different amplitudes

Let the two vibrations be represented by

$$x_1 = a_1 \cos(\omega t + \theta_1)$$
$$x_2 = a_2 \cos(\omega t + \theta_2) \tag{2.11}$$

The resultant displacement is the vector sum of individual displacements. If x is the resultant displacement then $x = x_1 + x_2$ (2.12)

Let x be represented by the equation

$$x = A \cos \omega t - B \sin \omega t \tag{2.13}$$

where the values of A and B are to be determined. We get from equations (2.11) to (2.13)

$$a_1 \cos(\omega t + \theta_1) + a_2 \cos(\omega t + \theta_2) = A \cos \omega t - B \sin \omega t.$$

or
$$a_1 \cos \omega t \cos \theta_1 - a_1 \sin \omega t \sin \theta_1 + a_2 \cos \omega t \cos \theta_2 - a_2 \sin \omega t \sin \theta_2 = A \cos \omega t - B \sin \omega t.$$

Equating the coefficients of cos ωt and sin ωt,

$$A = a_1 \cos \theta_1 + a_2 \cos \theta_2$$
$$B = a_1 \sin \theta_1 + a_2 \sin \theta_2. \tag{2.14}$$

If
$$A = r \cos \epsilon \text{ and } B = r \sin \epsilon$$

then
$$r = \sqrt{A^2 + B^2} \text{ and } \tan \epsilon = B/A$$

and
$$x = r \cos \epsilon \cos \omega t - r \sin \epsilon \sin \omega t.$$
$$= r \cos(\omega t + \epsilon).$$

The resultant motion is therefore simple harmonic with amplitude r and phase angle ϵ.

Hence $r = \sqrt{A^2 + B^2}$

$$= \sqrt{a_1^2 + a_2^2 + 2\, a_1\, a_2 \cos(\theta_1 - \theta_2)} \tag{2.15}$$

and $\tan \epsilon = \dfrac{a_1 \sin \theta_1 + a_2 \sin \theta_2}{a_1 \cos \theta_1 + a_2 \cos \theta_2}$

Thus it is seen that the resultant effect of two simple harmonic vibrations is the same as if the two motions are acting along the two sides of the parallelogram and the resultant effect is represented by the diagonal in magnitude and in direction.

CASE 2: Any number of simple harmonic vibrations of same frequency but differing in phase acting simultaneously on a single mass.

The resultant displacement can be represented by x

where $x = \Sigma\, a \cos(\omega t + \theta)$

$= \cos \omega t\, \Sigma\, a \cos \theta - \sin \omega t\, \Sigma\, a \sin \theta.$

$= r \cos(\omega t + \epsilon).$

and therefore, $r = [(\Sigma\, a \cos \theta)^2 + (\Sigma\, a \sin \theta)^2]^{1/2}.$

and $$\tan \epsilon = \frac{\Sigma\, a \sin \theta}{\Sigma\, a \cos \theta} \quad (2.16)$$

The resultant vibration can be obtained by combining two vibrations and finding the resultant and then combining this resultant with the third vibration and so on.

CASE 3: A large number of simple harmonic vibrations of the same amplitude but differing progressively in phase and acting in the same straight line. This case is an extension of case 2 in which there are n component vibrations and the change of phase is θ from one to the other and may be obtained from the relation in case 2.

$$\Sigma\, a \sin \theta = a\,[\sin 0 + \sin \theta + \sin 2\theta + \ldots\ldots \sin (n-1)\theta]$$

$$= a \frac{\sin n\theta/2}{\sin \theta/2} \sin \frac{(n-1)\theta}{2}$$

and $$\Sigma\, a \cos \theta = a\,[\cos 0 + \cos \theta + \cos 2\theta \ldots\ldots \cos (n-1)\theta]$$

$$= a \frac{\sin n\,\theta/2}{\sin \theta/2} \cos \frac{(n-1)\theta}{2}.$$

and r the resultant amplitude is given by

$$r = [\{\Sigma\, a \cos \theta\}^2 + \{\Sigma\, a \sin \theta\}^2]^{1/2}$$

$$= \left[\frac{a^2 \sin^2 n\theta/2}{\sin^2 \theta/2}\{\sin^2 (n-1)\,\theta/2 + \cos^2 (n-1)\,\theta/2\}\right]^{1/2}$$

$$= \frac{a \sin n\theta/2}{\sin \theta/_2} \quad (2.17)$$

CASE 4: Composition of two simple harmonic vibrations of different amplitudes but differing slightly in frequency.

This case is of very common occurrence and hence is of much importance. This problem gives rise to the well-known phenomenon of beats and is also applicable to the thoery of summation and combination tones.

Let the two vibrations be represented by

$$x_1 = a_1 \cos(\omega t + \theta_1)$$

$$x_2 = a_2 \cos\{(\omega + P)t + \theta_2\} \quad (2.18)$$

where P denotes the difference in angular frequency between the two displacements. The second equation can be written in the form

$$x_2 = a_2 \cos(\omega t + \overline{Pt + \theta_2})$$

where $(Pt + \theta_2)$ can be regarded as the phase of the second simple harmonic motion. Thus the case is similar to Case 1 and the resultant amplitude of vibration is given by

$$r = [a_1^2 + a_2^2 + 2\, a_1\, a_2 \cos\{\theta_1 - (Pt + \theta_2)\}]^{1/2} \tag{2.19}$$

$$\text{and } \tan\epsilon = \frac{a_1 \sin\theta_1 + a_2 \sin(Pt + \theta_2)}{a_1 \cos\theta_1 + a_2 \cos(Pt + \theta_2)} \tag{2.20}$$

and thus the resultant amplitude is given by $x = r\cos(\omega t - \epsilon)$ where r and ϵ are given by equations (2.19) and (2.20). The amplitude r becomes a maximum when

$$\cos\{\theta_1 - (Pt + \theta_2)\} = 1.$$

and then $r = a_1 + a_2$; it becomes a minimum when $\cos(\theta_1 - Pt - \theta_2) = -1$ and then $r = (a_1 - a_2)$.

If further, $a_1 = a_2 = a$ and $\theta_1 = \theta_2 = \theta$

then
$$\begin{aligned} r &= [2\, a^2 + 2\, a^2 \cos Pt]^{1/2} \\ &= [2\, a^2\, \{1 + \cos Pt\}]^{1/2} \\ &= [2\, a^2\, 2\cos^2 Pt/2]^{1/2} \\ &= 2\, a \cos Pt/2. \end{aligned} \tag{2.21}$$

$$\text{and } \tan\epsilon = \tan(Pt/2 + \theta)$$

$$\text{or} \quad \epsilon = Pt/2 + \theta \tag{2.22}$$

Thus the amplitude of the resultant note is a function of time and varies between $2a$ and $-2a$ when $\cos Pt/2$ becomes 1 and -1 respectively. When $Pt/2 = 0$ the first maximum will be heard and again when $Pt/2 = -1$ the second maximum will be heard. Hence the time interval t between the successive maxima will be given by

$$Pt/2 = \pi \text{ or } t = 2\pi/P.$$

As P denotes the difference in angular frequency between the two successive notes

$$P = 2\pi n.$$

where n = difference in number of vibrations, i.e. difference in frequency between the two notes

$$t = 1/n.$$

or the frequency of the beats $= n$; the difference of frequency between the successive notes. Hence when two notes of nearly equal frequencies are sounded together a periodic rise and fall of the resultant intensity is always noticed. This phenomenon is known as 'beats' and is of universal occurrence in all cases of vibration whether of mechanical or electrical origin. When two electrical vibrations of radio frequencies are mixed together a difference frequency is obtained and this principle is utilized in the detection of radio frequency signals by a method which is known as 'heterodyne beat' method. The phenomenon of beats has also an important bearing in the theory of combination tones which we shall discuss in greater detail in another chapter.

CASE 5: Vibrations of same frequency but acting at right angles to one another.

If we take one vibration acting in the direction of x - axis and the other along the y - axis, the two vibrations can be represented by

$$x = a \cos(\omega t + \theta_1) \text{ and } y = b \cos(\omega t + \theta_2) \tag{2.23}$$

Eliminating t between the two equations of (2.23), it is possible to get the resultant equation of the curve which the particle will describe under the simultaneous action of two simple harmonic forces.

From equation (2.23) we get,

$$\frac{x}{a} = \cos(\omega t + \theta_1) \text{ and } \qquad \frac{y}{b} = \cos(\omega t + \theta_2)$$

or

$$\frac{x}{a} = \text{cost } \omega t \cos\theta_1 - \sin\omega t \sin\theta_1$$

$$\frac{y}{b} = \cos\omega t \cos\theta_2 - \sin\omega t \sin\theta_2$$

$$\frac{x}{a}\cos\theta_2 = \cos\omega t \cos\theta_1 \cos\theta_2 - \sin\omega t \sin\theta_1 \cos\theta_2$$

$$\frac{y}{b}\cos\theta_1 = \cos\omega t \cos\theta_1 \cos\theta_2 - \sin\omega t \sin\theta_2 \cos\theta_1$$

$$\therefore \frac{x}{a}\cos\theta_2 - \frac{y}{b}\cos\theta_1 = \sin\omega t \{\sin(\theta_2 - \theta_1)\}$$

Similarly, multiplying the first equation by $\sin\theta_2$ and second equation by $\sin\theta_1$ and subtracting one from the other, we get,

$$\frac{x}{a}\sin\theta_2 - \frac{y}{b}\sin\theta_1 = \cos\omega t \{\sin(\theta_2 - \theta_1)\}$$

Squaring and adding

$$\frac{x^2}{a^2} + \frac{y^2}{b^2} - \frac{2xy}{ab}\cos(\theta_2 - \theta_1) - \sin^2(\theta_2 - \theta_1) = 0. \tag{2.24}$$

This is the equation of an ellipse whose positions and dimensions depend upon the amplitudes a and b and the initial phases θ_1 and θ_2.

If $(\theta_2 - \theta_1) = 0$ or π, equation (2.24) takes the form,

$$\left(\frac{x}{a} - \frac{y}{b}\right)^2 = 0$$

which is the equation of two coincident straight lines. If the phase difference is $(\pi/2)$, i.e. $(\theta_2 - \theta_1) = \pi/2$, the equation reduces to the form

$$\frac{x^2}{a^2} + \frac{y^2}{b^2} = 1.$$

which is the equation of an ellipse whose axes coincide with the x and y-axis. If the amplitudes are equal, i.e. $a = b$,

$$x^2 + y^2 = a^2$$

which is the equation of a circle with the centre at the origin and the radius is equal to the amplitude of either simple harmonic motion. The following typical values have been obtained from the previous analysis.

TABLE 2.1

Resume of the results of combination of two sample have monic motions with different phases

Case No.	Phase difference	Resultant equation	Resultant curve
1	$-\pi$	$\left(\frac{x}{a} - \frac{y}{b}\right)^2 = 0$	coincident straight lines
2	$-\pi/2$	$\frac{x^2}{a^2} + \frac{y^2}{b^2} = 1$	ellipse
3	0	$x^2 + y^2 = a^2$ if $a = b$.	circle
4	$\pi/2$	$\frac{x^2}{a^2} + \frac{y^2}{b^2} = 1$	ellipse
5	π	$\left(\frac{x}{a} - \frac{y}{b}\right)^2 = 0$	coincident straight lines

CASE 6: Two vibrations at right angles to one another but ratio of the frequencies is a whole number or nearly so.

Let the ratio of the two frequencies be 2 : 1. Then the component vibrations can be represented by

$$x = a \cos (2\,\omega t + \theta_1).$$
$$y = b \cos (\omega t + \theta_2).$$

If t is eliminated between these two equations, the equation of the resultant curve becomes

$$\left(\frac{x}{a} - \sin (\theta_1 - \theta_2)\right)^2 + \frac{4y^2}{b^2}\left[\left\{\frac{y^2}{b^2} + \frac{x}{a} \sin (\theta_1 - \theta_2) - 1\right\}\right] = 0 \quad (2.25)$$

This is the equation of a curve having two loops, which is the equation of two coincident parabolas.

$$\left[\frac{2y^2}{b^2} + \frac{x}{a} - 1\right]^1 = 0$$

If $(\theta_1 - \theta_2) = \frac{S\pi}{2}$, the equation reduces to

$$\left(\frac{x}{a} - 1\right)^2 + \frac{4y^2}{b^2}\left\{\frac{y^2}{b^2} + \frac{x}{a} - 1\right\} = 0$$

When $(\theta_1 - \theta_2) = 0$ the equation reduces to the form

$$\frac{x^2}{a^2} + \frac{4y^2}{b^2}\left[\frac{y^2}{b^2} - 1\right] = 0$$

When the ratio of the two component frequencies becomes 3 : 1, the resulting solution of the equations becomes complicated and if the assumption is made so that $\theta_1 = \theta_2 = 0$,

$$x = a \cos 3\,\omega t \text{ and } y = b \cos \omega t$$

elimination of t between the two equations gives

$$\left[\frac{4y^3}{b^3} - \frac{3y}{b} + \frac{x}{a}\right]^2 = 0$$

representing two coincident cubic curves.

When $(\theta_1 - \theta_2) = \pi/2$, the equation assumes the form

$$\left(1 - \frac{y^2}{b^2}\right)\left(1 - \frac{4y^2}{b^2}\right)^2 - \frac{x^2}{a^2} = 0$$

which represents a curve with three loops.

2.4 EXPERIMENTAL OBSERVATION

The above theoretical deductions can be verified experimentally and the firs experimental observation was made by Lissajou who used an optical method to observe the combined resultant vibration of two tuning forks vibrating at right angles to one another; one prong of each fork carries a small mirror and a spot of light is reflected successively from the two mirrors onto a screen where the combined motion of the two forks is clearly seen. The modern method of observing these figures which are known as Lissajou's figures (Fig. 2.3) is to use an oscilloscope as has been used by Wood[2]. The vibrations which are to be observed are to be converted into corresponding electrical oscillations and are to be applied to the horizontal and vertical deflecting plates of the oscilloscope. Depending upon the frequency limit of the oscilloscope, vibrations covering a wide range of frequencies can be investigated. The resultant figure appears on the screen of the oscilloscope where it can be viewed or if necessary can be photographed.

2.5 FOURIER'S THEOREM

In all forms of wave motion we may encounter vibrations which may be periodic motion of any type. Unless this complex motion can be resolved into its constituent components of simple harmonic motion the method of analysis becomes difficult. The method of analysing any type of periodic motion into its constituents was first of all enunciated by Fourier which is regarded as one of the fundamental theorems of mathematical physics. The theorem has a special application in the theory of vibration of strings but it has a much wider application in all branches of physics. The thoerem may be stated thus: 'Any single valued periodic function can be expressed as a summation of simple

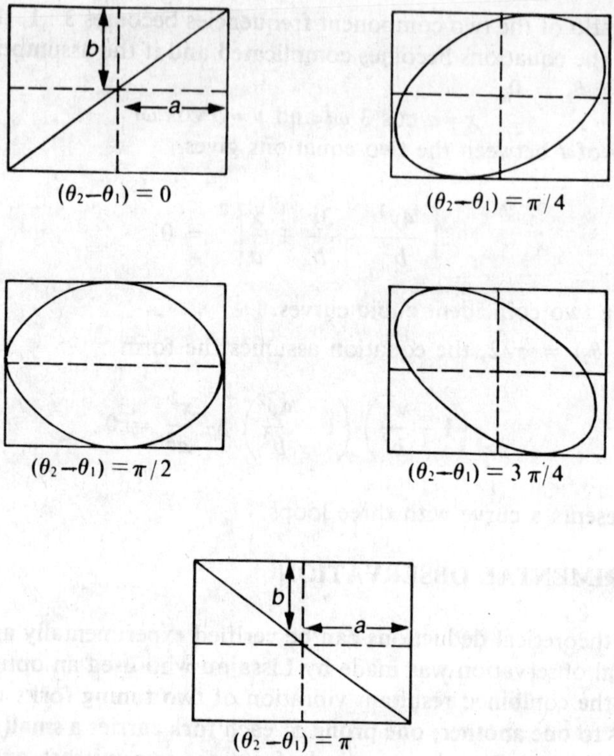

Fig. 2.3

harmonic terms having frequencies which are multiples of that of the given frequency.'

The two conditions which a given wave form must satisfy in order to apply the Fourier's theorem are:

(a) The displacement must be single-valued and continuous which condition is generally fulfilled in case of all mechanical vibrations which means that the displacement must have only one value at any instant of time.

(b) The displacement must be finite which condition is also clearly fulfilled in case of sound. Mathematically, the theorem may be stated thus,

$$f(\omega t) = a_0 + a_1 \cos(\omega t + \theta_1) + a_2 \cos(2\,\omega t + \theta_2.) + \ldots + a_n \cos(n\,\omega t + \theta_n) \qquad (2.26)$$

where $f(\omega t)$ represents any form of displacement of the complex periodic vibration and a_0, a_1, a_2, etc. are amplitudes of constituent simple harmonic motions to be determined from the initial boundary conditions; θ_1, θ_2, etc. are the phases. Equation (2.26) can also be written in the form

$$f(\omega t) = a_0 + \sum_{n=1}^{n=\infty} a_n \cos(n\omega t + \theta_n) \qquad (2.27)$$

Expanding equation (2.26) we get,

$$f(\omega t) = a_0 + a_1 \cos \omega t \cos \theta_1 - a_1 \sin \omega t \sin \theta_1$$

θ_1

$$+ a_2 \cos 2\omega t \cos \theta_2 - a_2 \sin 2\omega t \sin \theta_2$$
$$+ \ldots\ldots + a_n \cos n\omega t \cos \theta_n - a_n \sin n\omega t \sin \theta_n$$

Putting $a_n \cos \theta_n = A_n$ and $a_n \sin \theta_n = B_n$
where A_n and B_n are new constants introduced and putting $a_0 = A_0$ we get,

$$f(\omega t) = A_0 + A_1 \cos \omega t + A_2 \cos 2\omega t + \ldots\ldots + A_n \cos n\omega t$$
$$+ B_1 \sin \omega t + B_2 \sin 2\omega t + \ldots\ldots + B_n \sin n\omega t \qquad (2.28)$$

Multiplying both sides of equation (2.28) by dt and integrating between the limits 0 and T where T is the complete period of vibration.

$$\int_0^T f(\omega t)\, dt = \int_0^T A_0\, dt + \int_0^T A_1 \cos \omega t\, dt + \ldots\ldots \int_0^T A_n \cos n\omega t\, dt$$

$$+ \int_0^T B_1 \sin \omega t\, dt + \ldots \int_0^T B_n \sin n\omega t\, dt. \qquad (2.28)$$

Except the first term, all the terms on the right hand side of the above equation when integrated become zero and consequently, we get

$$\int_0^T f(\omega t)\, dt = A_0 T.$$

$$A_0 = \frac{1}{T} \int_0^T f(\omega t)\, dt \qquad (2.29)$$

In the same way multiplying both sides of equation (2.28) by $\cos(n\omega t)\, dt$ and integrating between the limits 0 to T we get,

or $$\int_0^T f(\omega t) \cos n\omega t\, dt = A_n \int_0^T \cos^2 n\omega t\, dt = A_n\, T/2$$

$$A_n = \frac{2}{T} \int_0^T f(\omega t) \cos n\omega t\, dt \qquad (2.30)$$

In the same way, multiplying both sides of equation (2.28) by $\sin(n\omega t)\, dt$ and integrating between the limits 0 to T we get,

$$B_n = \frac{2}{T} \int_0^T f(\omega t) \sin n\,\omega t\, dt. \qquad (2.31)$$

Hence from the equations (2.29), (2.30) and (2.31) it is possible to get the values of the constants appearing in equation (2.26) and so the complex periodic motion can be analysed into its constituent simple harmonic vibrations. The constant amplitude A_0 is a measure of the displacement of the axis of vibration from the axis of coordinates. If the abscissa of the curve coincides with the axis of the coordinates the constant A_0 vanishes and therefore A_0 represents the mean displacement.

2.6 PARTIAL FOURIER SERIES

Besides the general case treated above there are other forms of Fourier series which can also be sometimes employed. Thus if it is known that the expansion consists of sine terms only or of consine terms only, and extends over half a wave length, a modified form of Fourier expansion can be employed. Thus if y_1 and y_2 are functions of x extending over half the wave length and involving respectively sine and cosine terms, then by the previous theorem

$$y_1 = a_0 + a_1 \cos kx + a_2 \cos 2kx + \,.\,.\,.\,.\,.\; a_n \cos nkx.$$

$$\text{then } a_n = \frac{2}{\lambda/2} \int_0^{\lambda/2} y_1 \cos n\; kx.\, dx. \qquad (2.32)$$

$$y_2 = b_1 \sin kx + b_2 \sin 2\,kx + \,.\,.\,.\,.\,. + b_n \sin nkx$$

$$b_n = \frac{2}{\lambda/2} \int_0^{\lambda/2} y_2 \sin\, nkx.\, dx. \qquad (2.33)$$

In these equations λ and k are related by

$$k\lambda = 2\pi$$

and the value of x lies between 0 and $\lambda/2$. The Fourier theorem may be further extended from expansion in a single dimension to expansion in two dimensions. This theorem is particularly helpful in dealing with the case of vibration of strings and also in case of vibration of membranes as will be seen in later chapters.

REFERENCES

1. Fourier (1822). *Theory de la Chaleur,* (Paris).
2. Wood A.B. (1923). *Proc. Phys. Soc.* (London), 35, 109.

3

THEORY OF FORCED VIBRATION AND RESONANCE

3.1 DAMPED VIBRATION

It has been so far assumed that a vibrating body has a constant amplitude and all effects of dissipative forces involving loss of energy have not been taken into consideration; but in case of all vibrating systems resistive forces come into play which cause a gradual decay of amplitude or 'damping.' If disturbed and left to themselves they oscillate for a time and finally come to rest, the energy given to the initial displacement being used up in doing work against the resistive forces. Experiment has shown that this frictional force varies with the velocity of the vibrating body and for small velocities it will be a fair approvimation if the frictional force is taken to be proportional to the velocity of the body. All vibrating bodies are subject to these frictional forces; otherwise there would not have been any loss of energy and consequently no radiation of sound energy in the surrounding medium.

The equation of motion of a vibrating body of mass m and frictional force $2K$ per unit mass per unit velocity can thus be written, assuming that the frictional force is proportional to velocity as a first approximation, as

$$m\frac{d^2x}{dt^2} + 2\,K.m.\frac{dx}{dt} + Sx = 0 \tag{3.1}$$

The third term is the usual force present due to displacement.

or $$\frac{d^2x}{dt^2} + 2K.\frac{dx}{dt} + \omega^2 x = 0 \text{ where } \omega^2 = \frac{S}{m}$$

Let us assume a solution of the equation

$$x = Ae^{\alpha t} \tag{3.2}$$

where A and α are constants to be determined.

Hence $$\frac{dx}{dt} = A\alpha e^{\alpha t}; \qquad \frac{d^2x}{dt^2} = A\alpha^2 e^{\alpha t}.$$

From equation (3.2) we get,

$$A\alpha^2 e^{\alpha t} + 2K\alpha A e^{\alpha t} + \omega^2 A e^{\alpha t} = 0$$

or $$\alpha^2 + 2\,K\,\alpha + \omega^2 = 0$$

or $$\alpha = -K - \sqrt{K^2 - \omega^2}$$

and $$x = A\,e^{(-K \pm \sqrt{K^2 - \omega^2})\,t}$$

$$x = A_1\,e^{(-K + \sqrt{K^2 - \omega^2 t})} + A_2\,e^{(-K - \sqrt{K^2 - \omega^2 t})} \tag{3.3}$$

if we assume that $\omega^2 > K^2$

then $\quad x = A_1 e^{-(K+i\sqrt{K^2-\omega^2})t} + A_2 e^{-(K-i\sqrt{\omega^2-K^2})t}$

$$= e^{-Kt}[A_1 e^{(i\sqrt{\omega^2-K^2})t} + A_2 e^{(-i\sqrt{\omega^2-K^2})t}$$

if $\qquad \sqrt{\omega^2-K^2} = \lambda$ say,

$$\text{then } x = e^{-Kt}[A_1(\cos\lambda t + i\sin\lambda t) + A_2(\cos\lambda t - i\sin\lambda t)]$$
$$= e^{-Kt}[\cos\lambda t\{A_1+A_2\} + i\sin\lambda t\{A_1 - A_2\}]$$
$$= e^{-Kt}[C\cos\lambda t + D\sin\lambda t]$$

where $C = A_1 + A_2$ and $D = i(A_1 - A_2)$

and $\quad x = e^{-Kt}P\cos(\lambda t - \theta)$

where $\cos\theta = C/P$ and $\sin\theta = D/P$

or $\quad \tan\theta = D/C$

$$\text{or} \quad x = Pe^{-Kt}\cos\{\sqrt{\omega^2-K^2}\,t - \theta\} \tag{3.4}$$
$$= Pe^{-Kt}\cos(\omega' t - \theta)$$

where $\quad \omega' = \sqrt{\omega^2 - K^2}$.

This equation therefore represents a vibration of diminishing amplitude due the presence of the factor e^{-Kt} and of frequency $\sqrt{\omega^2 - K^2}$ and hence, with the progress of time, the vibration will become damped in amplitude for the amplitude of vibration will gradually fall. Since the periodic term cos $(\omega' t - \theta)$ lies between the limits $+1$ and -1, the space time curve of displacement against time lies between $x = Pe^{-Kt}$ and $x = -Pe^{-Kt}$ and the curve is represented in Fig. 3.1

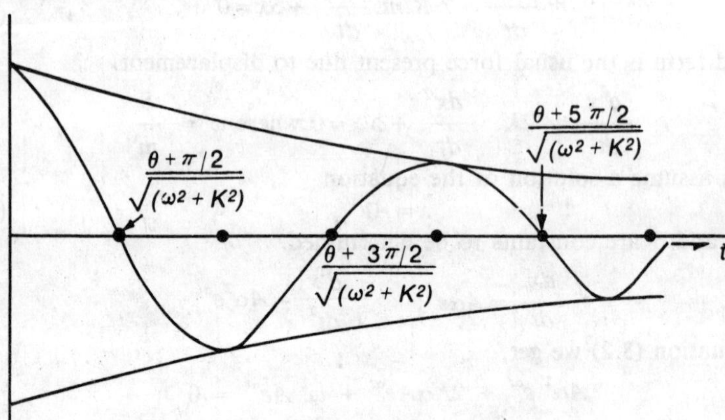

Fig. 3.1

3.2 LOGARITHMIC DECREMENT

The measure of the decay of amplitude is represented by e^{-Kt} where K is called the damping coefficient. If t is measured from the instant when the displacement is maximum and if x_m denotes the displacement at time t then $x_n = Pe^{-Kt}$. The successive maximum displacements will take place when $\omega' t$ changes by integral of π, that is

$$t = S\pi/\omega' \text{ where } S = 1, 2, 3 \text{ etc. Hence}$$

$$x_{n+1} = P\, e^{-K(t+\pi/\omega')}, \text{ and } x_{n+2} = P\, e^{-K(t+2\pi/\omega')},$$

and so on. Hence the ratio of the successive amplitudes will be given by

$$\frac{x_n}{x_{n+1}} = \frac{x_{n+1}}{x_{n+2}} = \frac{x_{n+2}}{x_{n+3}} = \cdots\cdots = e^{K\pi/\omega'} \tag{3.5}$$

If T' denotes the changed period due to damping,

$$T' = \frac{2\pi}{\omega'} \text{ and } \log \frac{x_n}{x_{n+1}} = \log \frac{x_{n+1}}{x_{n+2}} = \quad = \frac{K\pi}{\omega'} = \frac{KT'}{2} \tag{3.6}$$

and this ratio is known as log decrement and is the logarithm of the ratio of successive amplitudes of vibration and is denoted by δ.

Therefore

$$\delta = \frac{KT'}{2} = \frac{\pi K}{\omega'} = \frac{\pi K}{\sqrt{\omega^2 - K^2}}$$

$$\delta^2 = \frac{\pi^2 K^2}{\omega^2 - K^2}$$

$$K^2 = \frac{\omega^2 \delta^2}{\pi^2 + \delta^2} \tag{3.7}$$

We have from equation (3.4)

$$x = P\, e^{-Kt} \cos [\sqrt{(\omega^2 - K^2)}\, t - \theta]$$

or $\quad x = e^{-Kt} [A \cos \omega' t + B \sin \omega' t]$

where the constants A and B are to be determined from the boundary conditions. If when $t = 0$ the displacement is zero, then $A = 0$. If, however, the velocity is $\dot{x}_0$ when $t = 0$, then

$$[\dot{x}] = e^{-Kt} (-K) B \sin \omega' t + e^{-Kt} B \omega' \cos \omega' t$$

and

$$[\dot{x}_0] = B\omega' \text{ and } B = \frac{[\dot{x}_0]}{\omega'}$$

$$x = \frac{[x_0]}{2\pi} T' e^{-Kt} \sin \omega' t. \tag{3.8}$$

as it is assumed that the displacement is zero when $t = 0$ the maximum first amplitude A_1 will be reached when $t = T'/4$. Then from equation (3.8)

$$A_1 = \frac{\dot{x}_0}{2\pi} T' e^{-\omega'\delta/\pi \, T'/4} \sin \frac{\omega' T'}{4}.$$

$$= \frac{\dot{x}_0}{2\pi} . T' e^{-\delta/2}$$

Since $\sin \frac{\omega' T'}{4} = \sin \frac{\pi}{2} = 1$ (3.9)

If A_0 is the maximum amplitude when there is no damping, i.e. $\delta = 0$,

$$A_0 = \frac{\dot{x}_0 T}{2\pi}$$

Where T = time period with no damping. Hence,

$$\begin{aligned}\frac{A_0}{A_1} &= \left(\frac{T}{T'}\right) e^{\delta/2} \\ &= \left(\frac{\omega'}{\omega}\right) e^{\delta/2} \\ &= \sqrt{1 - \frac{K^2}{\omega^2}}\, e^{\delta/2} \\ &\approx \left(1 + \frac{\delta}{2}\right)\end{aligned}$$

as δ is small and $\frac{K^2}{\omega^2}$ is small in comparison with 1. Thus

$$A_0 = A_1 \left[1 + \frac{\delta}{2}\right].$$

This equation is frequently utilised in getting the true throw from the observed throw in a ballistic galvanometer.

3.3 SPECIAL CASES OF DAMPED VIBRATION

CASE 1: Effect of damping on frequency: from equation (3.4) it is seen that the frequency of damped vibration is given by ω' where $\omega' = \sqrt{\omega^2 - K^2}$. Hence the effect of damping is to decrease the frequency. However, in most cases occurring in practice, the difference between ω and ω' is always small, a quantity of the second order and may usually be neglected. Hence the effect of damping on frequency can be neglected in most of the cases occurring in practice.

CASE 2: Damping force is large that is $K >> \omega$.
In case of heavy damping we obtain from equation (3.3)

$$x = A_1 e^{(-K + \sqrt{K^2 - \omega^2})\,t} + A_2 e^{(-K - \sqrt{K^2 - \omega^2})\,t}$$

This equation indicates that the particle does not vibrate, but the displacement after passing its first maximum comes to zero asymptotically. This is the case of dead beat oscillation and is illustrated in the case of a moving coil galvanometer shunted by a low resistance.

CASE 3: When the damping is equal to natural frequency of oscillation.

From equation (3.1) we get

$$\frac{d^2x}{dt^2} + 2K \cdot \frac{dx}{dt} + K^2x = 0 \text{ where } K = \omega. \tag{3.9}$$

If it is assumed that $x = C\, e^{\alpha t}$ where C is also a function of time, we get

$$\frac{d^2C}{dt^2} + 2 \cdot \frac{dC}{dt} (K+\alpha) + C\,(K^2 + 2K\alpha + \alpha^2) = 0$$

and from equation (3.4), $\alpha = -K - \sqrt{K^2 - \omega^2}$.
As, in this case, $K = \omega$ and $\alpha = -K$
the above equation reduces to

$$\frac{d^2C}{dt^2} = 0$$

so that

$$C = At + B$$

where A and B are constants.
Hence in this case

$$x = (At + B)\, e^{\alpha t}$$
$$= (At + B)\, e^{-Kt}.$$

This is the case of critical damping; the motion is aperiodic or nonoscillatory. The amplitude first increases due to the term $(A\,t + B)$, but then diminshes more rapidly due to the term e^{-Kt}.

3.4 FORCED VIBRATION

Uptil this point, we have considered the motion of a particle in which no external force is acting, apart from the frictional forces which damp the amplitude of vibration and ultimately cause the motion to die away. A very important case which frequently occurs in the theory of vibration is that in which the mass is set and maintained in vibration by an external force which may have a frequency different from the natural frequency of the particle or the system, or the two frequencies may be identical. It will be seen from the following analysis that the mass will begin to execute oscillation with a frequency equal to the frequency of the applied force and as such this case is known as forced vibration. The most important and practical case of forced vibration is that in which the system capable of resisted simple harmonic motion is subjected to a force varying harmonically. Let $2\pi/\omega$ be the free period of the system and $2K$ the resisting force per unit mass per unit velocity. Then the equation of resisted motion is

$$m\,\frac{d^2x}{dt^2} + 2\,K.m.\,\frac{dx}{dt} + Sx = 0$$

or

$$\frac{d^2x}{dt^2} + 2K \cdot \frac{dx}{dt} + \omega^2 x = 0$$

cf. equation (3.1)

If now the system is subjected to a force of maximum amplitude E_0 and period $2\pi/P$ the equation of motion becomes

$$\frac{d^2x}{dt^2} + 2K \cdot \frac{dx}{dt} + \omega^2 x = E \cos Pt \tag{3.10}$$

where $E = E_0/m$

Assuming $x = a \cos (Pt - \theta)$

where a and θ are constants to be determined and putting the values of

$$\frac{dx}{dt} \text{ and } \frac{d^2x}{dt^2}$$

in equation (3.10), we have

$$\begin{aligned} - ap^2 \cos (Pt - \theta) - \; & 2\, K\, aP \sin (Pt - \theta) + \omega^2 a \cos (Pt - \theta) \\ = \; & E \cos (Pt - \theta + \theta) \\ = \; & E \cos (Pt - \theta) \cos \theta - E \sin (Pt - \theta) \sin \theta. \end{aligned}$$

Equating the coefficients of cos $(Pt - \theta)$ and that of sin $(Pt - \theta)$, we get

$$\begin{aligned} - ap^2 + a\omega^2 &= E \cos \theta \\ 2\, KPa &= E \sin \theta \\ \tan \theta &= \frac{2\, Kp}{(\omega^2 - P^2)} \end{aligned}$$

and $$a = \frac{E}{\sqrt{(\omega^2 - P^2)^2 + 4\, K^2\, P^2}}$$

$$= \frac{E_0/m}{\sqrt{(\omega^2 - P^2)^2 + 4\, K^2\, P^2}}$$

$$= \frac{E_0}{P\sqrt{4\, K^2\, m^2 + m^2\, (\omega^2/P^2 - 1)^2}} \tag{3.11}$$

$$= \frac{E_0}{P\, z}$$

where $z = \sqrt{4\, K^2\, m^2 + m^2\, (\omega^2/P^2 - 1)^2}$

and z is called the mechanical impedence of the system. Now we have seen in section 3.1 that the solution of equation (3.1) is given by

$$x = Ae^{-Kt} \cos (\sqrt{\omega^2 - K^2}\, t - \theta)$$

and so the complete solution of equation (3.10) is given by

$$x = Ae^{-Kt} \cos \left(\sqrt{(\omega^2 - K^2)}\, t - \theta \right) + \frac{E_0}{m\sqrt{(\omega^2 - P^2)^2 + 4\, K^2\, P^2}} \cos (Pt - \theta). \tag{3.12}$$

We therefore, can think of the motion as made up of two components; the second term represents a simple harmonic vibration of constant amplitude which has the same period as the force ($2\pi/P$) and differs in phase from the force by angle θ representing a retardation. The first term represents a damped vibration decaying at a rate determined by K, a rate which is the same as that of the system when no force is acting. Initially these two vibrations may be expected to produce beats whose frequency is the difference of the frequencies of the two vibrations, that is, difference between $P/2\pi$ and $\omega'/2\pi$. The less the natural damping of the system the more marked and prolonged the beats will be. This beating can actually be recognised. In time, however, the free vibration is damped out and only the forced vibration is left so that the steady state is one in which we have only the vibration given by

$$x = \frac{E_0 \cos (Pt - \theta)}{m\sqrt{(\omega^2 - P^2)^2 + 4K^2P^2}}. \tag{3.13}$$

3.5 PHASE OF FORCED VIBRATION

With regard to θ, the phase difference between the applied force and vibration, we note that

$$E \sin \theta = 2KPa$$

Sin θ is $+ve$, hence θ lies between 0 and π. The vibration is, therefore, less than half a cycle behind the force. Also we have

$$E \cos \theta = a(\omega^2 - P^2)$$

If $\omega > P$ then $\cos\theta$ is $+ve$, $0 < \vartheta < \pi/2$. If, therefore, the period of the system is less than the period of the force, the vibration is behind the force by less than a quarter cycle. If $\omega < P$, θ lies between $\pi/2$ and π. In this case the period of the system is greater than that of the force and the vibration is behind the force by one quarter to one half cycle.

If $\omega = P$, $\cos\theta = 0$, that is $\theta = \pi/2$. In this case the period of the system is identical with that of the force and the vibration is, therefore, in phase quadrature with force, i.e. a quarter cycle behind.

If K is very small, then $\sin\theta = 0$, i.e. $\theta = \pi$ or 0, and further we note that if $\omega > P$, θ will be nearly equal to zero which means that if the period of the system is less than the period of the force, the two will be practically identical in phase. On the other hand, if $\omega < P$ then $\cos\theta$ will be approximately equal to π so that if the period of the system is greater than the period of the force, the two will be almost in opposition. The three cases are represented in Fig. 3.2.

3.6 AMPLITUDE RESONANCE

The amplitude of forced vibration (a) is given by

$$a = \frac{E}{\sqrt{(\omega^2 - P^2)^2 + 4K^2P^2}}$$

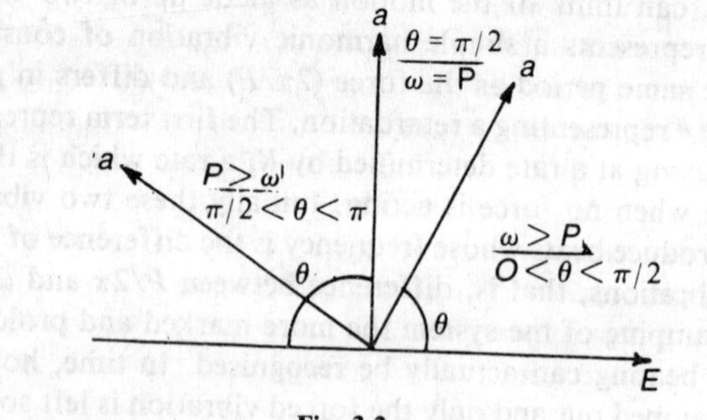

Fig. 3.2

which may be put in the form,

$$a = \frac{E}{P\sqrt{\omega^2 (\omega/P - P/\omega)^2 + 4K^2}} \tag{3.14}$$

If we regard ω/P as indicating the amount of mistuning and if this ratio is fixed, then the quantity $(\omega/P - P/\omega)^2$ has the same value no matter which of these quantities is greater. Since ω^2 and K^2 are constants of the system it follows that, for a given mistuning, a is less when P is greater. The amplitude of the forced vibratioin is, therefore, less for a given ratio of frequencies when the frequency of the force is greater. If we put $s = \omega/K$ where K is the damping factor, then $s = 1$ represents a system very heavily damped while $s = 10$, represents a system very lightly damped. If curves are drawn with P/ω, that is mistuning as abscissa and the corresponding amplitudes as ordinate, we shall get different curves as shown in the Fig. 3.3 for different values of s. The

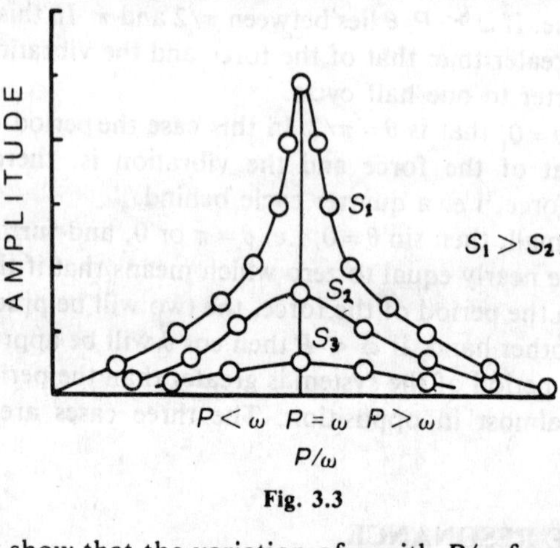

Fig. 3.3

curves clearly show that the variation of a with P/ω for different values of s is not symmetrical. It is observed that for large values of s i.e. for small damping, the curves are steep in nature whereas for small values of s, that is for large damping, the curves are flat. For a given value of mistuning the fall in amplitude is very marked for smaller damping. When $s = 1$, i.e. large damping, the variation of a with P is very small (the curve $s = 1$, being almost parallel to x-axis) but as the value of s increases, that is as the damping gradually falls the rate of fall in amplitude with P is very large. Hence it is concluded that for those systems whose natural damping is very small the amplitude of vibration will fall abruptly if the tuning is not very sharp. Consequently, in a system with small damping the tuning must be very sharp in order to get any vibration at all. The case bears a close analogy with resonance phenomena in an alternating current system where the selectivity of the circuit is determined by analogous term Q which is defined as $Q = PL/R$ where P is the frequency of the alternating current, L the inductance of the system and R its electrical resistance. The importance of natural damping in case of a mechanical system is thus clearly recognised.

The condition for maximum amplitude of forced vibration can next be found. It corresponds to minimum value for the denominator for a; taking ω as constant and P as variable, the condition for minimum value of $(\omega^2 - P^2)^2 + 4K^2P^2$ is

$$\frac{d}{dp}[(\omega^2 - P^2)^2 + 4K^2P^2] = 0$$

$$-4(\omega^2 - P^2)P + 8K^2P = 0$$

or

$$P^2 = [\omega^2 - 2K^2] \tag{3.15}$$

Hence the condition for maximum amplitude of forced vibration is that the frequency of the applied force will be given by equation (3.15) or the period of the force will be given by $\dfrac{2\pi}{\sqrt{\omega^2 - 2K^2}}$. It is to be noted that it is not equal to the natural period of the system which is $2\pi/\omega$ not it is the resisted period which is $\dfrac{2\pi}{(\omega^2 - K^2)^{1/2}}$ but a still longer period, and under this condition the maximum amplitude is given by

$$a_{max} = \frac{E}{[(\omega^2 - \omega^2 + 2K^2)^2 + 4K^2(\omega^2 - 2K^2)]^{1/2}}$$

$$= \frac{E}{[4K^4 - 8K^4 + 4K^2\omega^2]^{1/2}}$$

$$= \frac{E}{2K[\omega^2 - K^2]^{1/2}} \tag{3.16}$$

3.7 VELOCITY RESPONSE

The velocity of the system is given by

$$\dot{x} = -aP\sin(Pt - \theta)$$

The velocity is a maximum when $\sin(Pt - \theta) = 1$, i.e. when $\cos(Pt - \theta) = 0$, i.e.

when $\ddot{x}=0$. The corresponding value of $\dot{x}$ is called the velocity amplitude and is evidently given by

$$\dot{x} = \frac{E}{\sqrt{\omega^2 (\omega/P - P/\omega)^2 + 4K^2}}. \tag{3.17}$$

and for any value of K, this is a maximum when $(\omega/P - P/\omega) = 0$ or $P = \omega$. This is the condition for maximum velocity amplitude which is different from the condition for maximum displacement amplitude [vide equation (3.15)]. Velocity resonance occurs when the frequency of the applied force is equal to the natural frequency of the system. Hence for velocity resonance,

$$\dot{x}_{max} = \frac{E}{2K}$$

or

$$\dot{x}_{max} \propto \frac{1}{K}$$

It is possible to find out how the velocity amplitude varies when the system is mistuned, i.e. when $P \neq \omega$. Let $\dot{x}_P$ denote the velocity amplitude at frequency P; $\dot{x}_\omega$ = velocity amplitude at $P = \omega$, then

$$\frac{\dot{x}_P}{\dot{x}_\omega} = \frac{E}{\{\omega^2 (\omega/P - P/\omega)^2 + 4K^2\}} \cdot \frac{2K}{E}$$

$$= \frac{K/\omega}{[(K/\omega)^2 + 1/4\,(\omega/P - P/\omega)^2]}$$

$$= \frac{1}{\left[1 + \frac{1}{4}\frac{\omega^2}{K^2} \cdot \frac{(\omega+P)^2 (\omega - P)^2}{P^2 \omega^2}\right]^{1/2}} \tag{3.18}$$

Calling R as the percentage response, we observe

$$\frac{R}{100} = \frac{1}{\left[1 + \frac{1}{4}\frac{(\omega+P)^2 (\omega - P)^2}{K^2 P^2}\right]^{1/2}}$$

and further we assume $\omega \approx P$

$$\frac{R}{100} = \frac{1}{\left[1 + \left(\frac{\omega - P}{K}\right)^2\right]^{1/2}} \tag{3.19}$$

In this expression P occurs only in the bracket and the value of the term $\left(\frac{\omega - P}{K}\right)^2$ is the same for a given ratio of ω and P whether ω is greater than P or P is greater than ω. Thus, if we measure the mistuning by the ratio ω/P or by its logarithm, the resulting curve will be symmetrical about the line $P=\omega$. If, as before, we put $s=\omega/K$ and $Y=\log_e(\omega/P)$ where Y is the measure of mistuning then

$\frac{\omega}{P}=e^Y$ and $\frac{P}{\omega}=e^{-Y}$ and consequently

$$\frac{1}{2}\left(\frac{\omega}{P}-\frac{P}{\omega}\right)=\frac{e^Y-e^{-Y}}{2}=\sinh Y.$$

$$\frac{R}{100}=\frac{1}{\sqrt{1+s^2\sinh^2 Y}} \tag{3.20}$$

when $\sinh Y=1/s$, the velocity amplitude falls to $\frac{1}{\sqrt{2}}$ of its value at resonance and the kinetic energy falls to half its value. Thus, as in the case of amplitude resonance, s may be taken as a measure of the sharpness of resonance and we see that sharpness is most marked for large values of s, that is for small damping and large values of ω; since ω/P is considered in the neighbourhood of correct tuning $\omega\approx P$ and $\log(\omega/P)$ is small, i.e. Y is small, so that $\sinh Y\approx Y$, and

$$R=\frac{100}{\sqrt{1+s^2Y^2}} \tag{3.21}$$

The graphical representation of percentage response against mistuning is shown in Fig. 3.4, to get the actual values of velocity amplitude in these cases we observe,

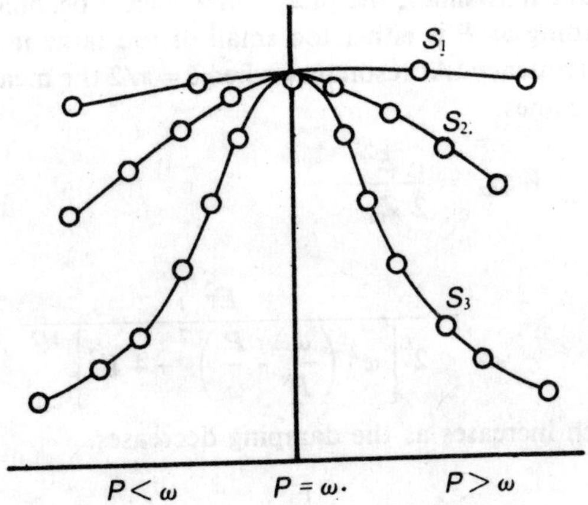

Fig. 3.4

$$\dot{x}_P=\frac{R}{100}|\dot{x}|_{P=\omega}=\frac{R}{100}\frac{E}{2K}=\frac{RsE}{200\omega}. \tag{3.22}$$

3.8 ENERGY OF FORCED VIBRATION

The rate of doing work or the rate of supply or dissipation of energy in the mechanical system is the product of force and velocity and so we get the instantaneous power supplied to maintain vibration as

$$W = \dot{x}\, E \cos Pt.$$

From equation (3.17) $\dot{x} = -\dfrac{E}{Z_m} \sin (Pt - \theta)$.

where $$Z_m = \sqrt{\omega^2 \left(\frac{\omega}{P} - \frac{P}{\omega}\right)^2 + 4K^2}$$

and is called the mechanical impedence.

$$W = \frac{E^2}{Z_m} \cdot \cos\left(Pt - \theta + \frac{\pi}{2}\right) \cos Pt.$$

$$= \frac{E^2}{2Z_m}\left[\cos\left(2pt - \theta + \frac{\pi}{2}\right) + \cos\left(\frac{\pi}{2} - \theta\right)\right]$$

The average value of the first term in the square brackets is zero and as can be shown; consequently the mean power supplied is

$$W = \frac{E^2}{2Z_m} \cdot \cos\left(\frac{\pi}{2} - \theta\right) \tag{3.24}$$

The power is zero when $\theta = 0$ or $\theta = \pi$; we have seen in section (3.5) that if damping constant K is small, the phase difference θ becomes either equal to zero or π according as P is either too small or too large in comparison with ω, the natural frequency. At resonance when $\theta = \pi/2$ the mean power supplied by the force becomes

$$W_{max} = \frac{E^2}{2Z_m}$$

$$= \frac{E^2}{2\left[\omega^2\left(\frac{\omega}{P} - \frac{P}{\omega}\right)^2 + 4K^2\right]^{1/2}} \tag{3.25}$$

a quantity which increases as the damping decreases.

4

THEORY OF COUPLED OSCILLATION

4.1 TWO OSCILLATORS COUPLED TOGETHER

As in the case of electrical coupled circuits we may have two independent oscillators mechanically coupled together. In the electrical case the energy is supplied to the primary circuit and due to magnetic or electric coupling the secondary circuit is energised. In the mechanical case we may have two or more than two oscillators so arranged that the motion of one oscillator effects the others and consequently a part of the energy is transferred from the driver oscillator to the driven. However, the motion of the driven oscillator will also feed back energy to the driver. In the deduction of motion of the coupled system we have followed the analysis given by Morse[1].

4.2 GENERAL EQUATION

Let one of the coupled oscillators have the mass m_1 and its displacement from equilibrium position be x_1. Let the oscillator number 2 has the mass m_2 and its displacement from equilibrium position be x_2 Fig. 4.1. The system as

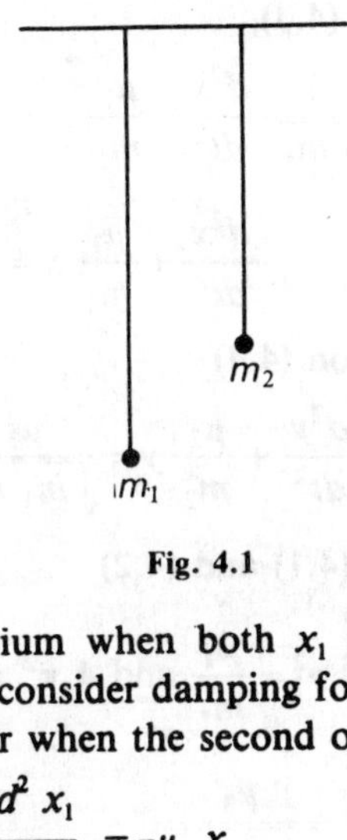

Fig. 4.1

a whole will be in equilibrium when both x_1 and x_2 are zero. As a first approximation we need not consider damping forces. Hence, the equation of motion of the first oscillator when the second one is kept fixed will be

$$m_1 \frac{d^2 x_1}{dt^2} = -\mu_1 x_1$$

and it will vibrate with a frequency

$$\nu_1 = \frac{1}{2\pi}\sqrt{\frac{\mu_1}{m_1}} \tag{4.1}$$

where μ_1 is the restoring force for unit displacement. Similarly, if we clamp the oscillator No. 1 at $x_1 = 0$ the restoring force on m_2 will be $-\mu_2 x_2$ and the frequency of vibration ν_2 will be given by

$$\nu_2 = \frac{1}{2\pi}\sqrt{\frac{\mu_2}{x_2}} \tag{4.2}$$

A displacement of mass m_1 however produces a force on m_2 for this is what is meant by coupling; suppose the force is $\mu_3 x_1$ where μ_3 is the reacting force on the second oscillator due to unit displacement of the first oscillator. Then due to symmetry of the system the force on the mass m_1 due to the displacement x_2 of the second mass will be $\mu_3 x_2$. This constant μ_3 is usually small in comparison with μ_1 and μ_2 and is called the coupling constant. Then the equations of motion of the two masses are given by

$$m_1 \frac{d^2x_1}{dt^2} = -\mu_1 x_1 + \mu_3 x_2 \tag{4.3}$$

The second term on the R.H.S. is positive because it tends to make the displacement larger and, similarly, for the second mass we get,

$$m_2 \frac{d^2x_2}{dt^2} = -\mu_2 x_2 + \mu_3 x_1 \tag{4.4}$$

Putting $x_1 = \dfrac{x}{\sqrt{m_1}}$ and $x_2 = \dfrac{y}{\sqrt{m_2}}$

we get from the equation (4.3)

$$\frac{1}{\sqrt{m_1}} \frac{d^2x}{dt^2} + \frac{\mu_1}{m_1} x_1 = \frac{\mu_3}{m_1} x_2$$

or

$$\frac{d^2x}{dt^2} + \frac{\mu_1}{m_1} x = \frac{\mu_3}{\sqrt{m_1 m_2}} y. \tag{4.5}$$

and similarly from equation (4.4)

$$\frac{d^2y}{dt^2} + \frac{\mu_2}{m_2} y = \frac{\mu_3}{\sqrt{m_1 m_2}} x. \tag{4.6}$$

We have from equations (4.1) and (4.2)

$$4\pi^2 \nu_1^2 = \frac{\mu_1}{m_1} \text{ and } 4\pi^2 \nu_2^2 = \frac{\mu_2}{x_2}.$$

and introducing $4\pi^2 \mu^2 = \dfrac{\mu_3}{\sqrt{m_1 m_2}}$

we get the equations of coupled oscillators as

$$\frac{d^2x}{dt^2} + 4\pi^2 \nu_1^2 x = 4\pi^2 \mu^2 y \tag{4.7}$$

$$\frac{d^2y}{dt^2} + 4\pi^2 \nu_2^2 y = 4\pi^2 \mu^2 x. \tag{4.8}$$

It is clear from the above equations that the motion of the two masses will not, in general, be a simple harmonic one. If one of the oscillators be clamped down, the other will vibrate with a simple harmonic motion. But if both the oscillators are allowed to move, the motion will not be simple harmonic in general. The curves for x and y as functions of time are not sinusoidal. So we shall first enquire whether it is possible to start the two masses in some special way so that the motion is a simple harmonic one even though the motion is in general not so. It is clear that if the motion is to be simple harmonic, both the oscillators must be vibrating with the same frequency. If ν be the resulting frequency, we can assume that

$$x = Ae^{2\pi i\nu t}. \tag{4.9}$$

$$y = Be^{2\pi i\nu t}. \tag{4.10}$$

where A and B are amplitudes of oscillation; substituting the values of d^2x/dt^2 and d^2y/dt^2 as well as that of x and y in equations (4.7) and (4.8) we get,

$$A\,(\nu_1^2 - \nu^2) = B\,\mu^2. \tag{4.11}$$

$$B\,(\nu_2^2 - \nu^2) = A\,\mu^2. \tag{4.12}$$

Eliminating A and B from equations (4.11) and (4.12) we obtain

$$\nu^4 - (\nu_1^2 + \nu_2^2)\,\nu^2 + (\nu_1^2\,\nu_2^2 - \mu^4) = 0$$

and thus

$$\nu = \left[\frac{1}{2}(\nu_1^2 + \nu_2^2) \pm \frac{1}{2}[\,(\nu_1^2 - \nu_2^2)^2 + 4\,\mu^4]^{1/2}\right]^{1/2}$$

$$= \frac{1}{2\pi\sqrt{m_1\,m_2}}\left[\frac{1}{2}(\mu_1\,m_2) + \mu_2\,m_1)\right.$$

$$\left.\pm\frac{1}{2}\sqrt{(\mu_1\,m_2 - \mu_2\,m_1)^2 + 4\mu_3^2\,m_1\,m_2}\right]^{1/2} \tag{4.13}$$

Thus there are two possible frequencies of oscillation of combined system and we shall see how the frequency with which it vibrates depends on how we start the system in motion. Neither of the allowed frequencies is equal to either of the natural frequencies ν_1 and ν_2 of the individual oscillators taken separately. Let us call the frequency involving + sign before the radical as ν_+ and that involving – sign before the radical as ν_- so that

$$\nu_+ = \left[\frac{1}{2}(\nu_1^2+\nu_2^2) + \frac{1}{2}\sqrt{(\nu_1^2-\nu_2^2)^2+4\mu^4}\right]^{1/2} \tag{4.14}$$

$$\nu_- = \left[\frac{1}{2}(\nu_1^2+\nu_2^2) - \frac{1}{2}\sqrt{(\nu_1^2-\nu_2^2)^2+4\mu^4}\right]^{1/2}.$$

4.3 NORMAL MODES OF VIBRATION

We can say that although the general motion of the system is not simple harmonic, nevertheless if the masses are started into motion in just the right way so that the amplitudes of motion of m_1 and m_2 are related by the equation

$$B_+ = \frac{A_+(\nu_1^2-\nu_+^2)}{\mu^2}$$

or

$$B_+ = \frac{A_+\mu^2}{(\nu_2^2-\nu_+^2)} \tag{4.15}$$

then and only then will the system vibrate with simple harmonic motion of frequency ν_+, these ratios between the amplitudes of motion remaining the same throughout the motion; similarly if the motion is started in such a way that the ratio of amplitudes of A and B are related in the way

$$B_- = \frac{A_-(\nu_1^2-\nu_-^2)}{\mu^2}$$

or

$$B_- = \frac{A_-\mu^2}{(\nu_2^2-\nu_-^2)} \tag{4.16}$$

then and only then will the system vibrate with the simple harmonic motion of frequency ν_-. If the motion is started in any other way, there will be no permanent ratio between the displacements of the two masses and the motion will cease to be periodic. These two special simple cases of motion are called its normal modes of vibration.

4.4 GENERAL SOLUTION

If we put

$$C_+\cos\alpha = A_+ \text{ and } C_+\sin\alpha = B_+$$
$$C_-\sin\alpha = A_- \text{ and } C_-\cos\alpha = B_- \tag{4.17}$$

where the angle α has been introduced to unify and simplify the notation, we have then

$$x = C_+\cos\alpha\, e^{2\pi i\nu_+ t}$$
$$y = C_+\sin\alpha\, e^{2\pi i\nu_+ t} \tag{4.18}$$

When the frequency is given by ν_+

or
$$x_1 = \frac{1}{\sqrt{m_1}}\left[a_+ \cos 2\pi \nu_+ t + b_+ \sin 2\pi \nu_+ t\right] \cos \alpha$$

and
$$x_2 = \frac{1}{\sqrt{m_2}}\left[a_+ \cos 2\pi \nu_+ t + b_+ \sin 2\pi \nu_+ t\right] \sin \alpha. \tag{4.19}$$

where a_+ and b_+ are constants.

If the frequency is ν_-

$$x = C_- \sin \alpha \, e^{2\pi i \nu_- t} \text{ and } y = C_- \cos \alpha \, e^{2\pi i \nu_- t}$$

$$x_1 = \frac{1}{\sqrt{m_1}}\left[a_- \cos 2\pi \nu_- t + b_- \sin 2\pi \nu_- t\right] \sin \alpha.$$

$$x_2 = \frac{1}{\sqrt{m_2}}\left[a_- \cos 2\pi \nu_- t + b_- \sin 2\pi \nu_- t\right] \cos \alpha \tag{4.20}$$

and fu. her
$$\tan \alpha = \frac{B_+}{A_+} = \frac{\nu_1^2 - \nu_+^2}{\mu^2} = \frac{\mu^2}{\nu_2^2 - \nu_+^2}.$$

and also
$$\tan \alpha = \frac{\nu_2^2 - \nu_-^2}{\mu^2} = \frac{\mu^2}{\nu_2^2 - \nu_-^2}. \tag{4.21}$$

When the normal modes of vibration are found out the problem of determining the general motion of the system becomes very simple. For it turns out that the general motion can always be represented as the combination of two normal modes of vibration. The general motion can thus be written as

$$\begin{aligned} x &= C_+ \cos \alpha \, e^{2\pi i \nu_+ t} + C_- \sin \alpha \, e^{2\pi i \nu_- t} \\ y &= C_+ \sin \alpha \, e^{2\pi i \nu_+ t} + C_- \cos \alpha \, e^{2\pi i \nu_- t} \end{aligned} \tag{4.22}$$

$$x_1 = \frac{\cos \alpha}{\sqrt{m_1}}\left[a_+ \cos 2\pi \nu_+ t + b_+ \sin 2\pi \nu_+ t\right]$$
$$+ \frac{\sin \alpha}{\sqrt{m_1}}\left[a_- \cos 2\pi \nu_- t + b_- \sin 2\pi \nu_- t\right].$$

$$x_1 = \frac{1}{\sqrt{m_1}}\left[A_+ \cos \alpha \cos (2\pi \nu_+ t - \phi_+) + A_- \sin \alpha \cos (2\pi \nu_- t - \phi_-)\right] \tag{4.23}$$

and similarly

$$x_2 = \frac{1}{\sqrt{m_2}}\left[A_+ \cos \alpha \cos (2\pi \nu_+ t - \phi_+) + A_- \sin \alpha \cos (2\pi \nu_- t - \phi_-)\right]$$

Thus the general equation involves four arbitrary constants A_+, A_-, ϕ_+ and ϕ_- which are initially fixed.

4.5 SPECIAL CASES

(a) Case of loose coupling. We shall deal now with some special cases of coupling. We assume ν_1 is larger than ν_2 and $\mu < (\nu_1 - \nu_2)$. By expanding equation (4.13) and retaining only the first two terms, the rest being neglected, we get

$$\nu_+ = \left[\frac{1}{2}(\nu_1^2+\nu_2^2) + \frac{1}{2}\{(\nu_1^2 - \nu_2^2)^2 + 4\mu^4\}^{1/2}\right]^{1/2}$$

$$= \left[\frac{\nu_1^2+\nu_2^2}{2}\right]^{1/2} + \frac{1}{4}\frac{\{(\nu_1^2 - \nu_2^2)^2+4\mu^4\}^{1/2}}{\left\{\frac{1}{2}(\nu_1^2+\nu_2^2)\right\}^{1/2}}$$

$$\nu_+^2 = \frac{1}{2}(\nu_1^2+\nu_2^2) + \frac{1}{2}[(\nu_1^2 - \nu_2^2)^2 + 4\mu^4]^{1/2}$$

$$= \frac{1}{2}(\nu_1^2+\nu_2^2) + \frac{1}{2}(\nu_1^2 - \nu_2^2) + \frac{1}{2}\cdot\frac{1}{2}\frac{4\mu^4}{(\nu_1^2 - \nu_2^2)}$$

$$= \nu_1^2 + \frac{\mu^4}{(\nu_1^2-\nu_2^2)} \tag{4.24}$$

In the same way it can be shown that

$$\nu_-^2 = \nu_2^2 - \frac{\mu^4}{(\nu_1^2 - \nu_2^2)} \tag{4.25}$$

It is thus evident that ν_+ is just a bit larger than ν_1 and ν_- is just a bit smaller than ν_2.

(b) When the natural frequencies of the two oscillators are equal, case of resonance. Let us consider the case when the two oscillators have the same natural frequency, i.e. $\nu_1 = \nu_2$ and where the friction is negligible. In such a case the feedback of energy from the driving system to the driven system is considerable. If in this problem we use the formula deduced in case of forced oscillation we find it predicts an infinite amplitude of the driven oscillator. This infinite amplitude simply means that the amplitude of motion of the driven is large enough to absorb a large fraction of energy of the driver. If $\nu_1 = \nu_2$, we get from equation (4.13)

$$\nu_+ = [\nu_1^2 + \mu^2]^{1/2} = \nu_1 + \frac{\mu^2}{2\nu_1} \tag{4.26}$$

and similarly $\qquad \nu_- = \nu_1 - \dfrac{\mu^2}{2\nu_1}.$

If μ is smaller than either ν_1 or ν_2

and as $\tan 2\alpha = \dfrac{-2\mu^2}{\nu_1^2 - \nu_2^2}$

$$\alpha = -\pi/4$$

Hence if two oscillators each of frequency ν_1 are coupled together they can oscillate no longer with frequency ν_1 but will oscillate with a frequency either $\mu^2/2\nu_1$ greater or by this amount smaller than ν_1; as $\alpha = -\pi/4$, it is seen from equation (4.20) that if the system is so started so that $x_1 = -x_2\sqrt{m_2/m_1}$ then; the system has only the higher frequency. It is also seen from equation (4.20) that if masses are started so that $x_1 = x_2\sqrt{m_2/m_1}$ then the system has only the lower frequency. If the masses are started in any other way, then the system will vibrate with a frequency which will be a combination of both the frequencies.

If the masses are so started that the initial conditions are $x_1 = x_0$ at $t=0$ and $x_2 = 0$ at $t=0$, i.e. started by putting the mass m_1 aside a distance x_0 while putting x_2 at 0 and then letting both the masses go at time $t=0$, we get from equation (4.23).

$$0 = \frac{\sin\alpha}{\sqrt{m_2}}[a_+] - \frac{\cos\alpha}{\sqrt{m_2}}[a_-]$$

and as $\sin\alpha = \dfrac{1}{\sqrt{2}}$ and $\cos\alpha = \dfrac{1}{\sqrt{2}}$

then $\quad a_+ = a_-$

$$\dot{x}_2 = \frac{\sin\alpha}{\sqrt{m_2}}[-2\pi\cdot\nu_+ a_+ \sin 2\pi\nu_+ t + 2\pi\nu_+ b_+ \cos 2\pi\nu_+ t]$$

$$-\frac{\cos\alpha}{\sqrt{m_2}}[-2\pi\nu_- a_- \sin 2\pi\nu_- t + 2\pi\nu_- b_- \cos 2\pi\nu_- t].$$

and as $\dot{x}_2 = 0$ at $t=0$ and $\sin\alpha = -\dfrac{1}{\sqrt{2}}$ and $\cos\alpha = \dfrac{1}{\sqrt{2}}$

$$-b_+ = -b_- = 0$$

as $x_1 = x_0$ at $t=0$ we get from equation (4.23)

$$x_0 = \frac{1}{\sqrt{2}}\frac{1}{\sqrt{m_1}}[a_+] + \frac{1}{\sqrt{2}}\frac{1}{\sqrt{m_1}}[a_+].$$

Hence $\quad a_+ = \dfrac{x_0\sqrt{m_1}}{\sqrt{2}}.$

$$x_1 = \frac{1}{\sqrt{2}\sqrt{m_1}}\left[\frac{x_0\sqrt{m_1}}{\sqrt{2}}\cos 2\pi\left(\nu_1+\frac{\mu^2}{2\nu_1}\right)t\right]$$

$$+\frac{1}{\sqrt{2}}\frac{1}{\sqrt{m_1}}\left[\frac{x_0\sqrt{m_1}}{\sqrt{2}}\cos 2\pi\left(\nu_1-\frac{\mu^2}{2\nu_1}\right)t\right]$$

$$=\frac{x_0}{2}\left[\cos 2\pi\left(\nu_1+\frac{\mu^2}{2\nu_1}\right)t+\cos 2\pi\left(\nu_1-\frac{\mu^2}{2\nu_1}\right)t\right] \quad (4.28)$$

$$= x_0 \cos 2\pi\,\nu_1\, t \cos\frac{\pi\mu^2}{\nu_1}t.$$

and it can be shown that

$$x_2 = x_0\sqrt{\frac{m_1}{m_2}}\sin 2\pi\nu_1\, t\,\sin\frac{\pi\mu^2}{\nu_1}t.$$

The values of x_1 and x_2 are plotted in Fig. (4.2) as shown. The equations show and it is also apparent from the curves of Fig. (4.2) that if the oscillators are started in the manner described above, and if the coupling is weak the motion is like an oscillation of frequency ν_1 whose amplitude of oscillation itself oscillates with *a*

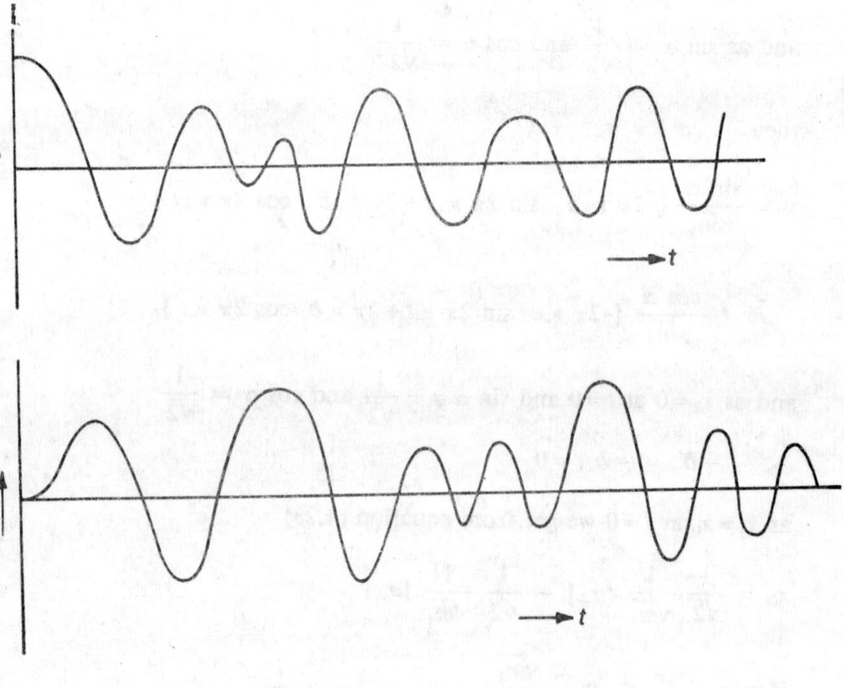

Fig. 4.2

smaller frequency $\mu^2/2\nu_1$. Such a motion is not simple harmonic because the amplitude varies with time. From the equations it can be seen that the resultant motion of either x_1 or x_2 is a combination of two simple harmonic motions whose frequencies differ by a small amount so that at first they reinforce each other but after a while get out of phase and cancel each other and so on. We further note that when the amplitude of motion of m_1 is large that of m_2 is small and vice versa.

4.6 EXAMPLES OF COUPLED OSCILLATION

CASE 1: Two weights on a string. A special case of coupled oscillation which will be of interest is that of two masses m placed on a weightless string of length l stretched between two rigid supports (Fig. 4.3). Suppose the masses divide the string into three equal parts of length $l/3$ and the string is under a tension T_1; let y_1 be the displacement of one mass from the equilibrium position and y_2 that of the other. If y_1 and y_2 are small compared with the length of the string, the angles which the string makes when displaced with its undisturbed position are small so that if θ_1 and θ_2 are the angles we get $\sin\theta_1 = \tan\theta_1$ and $\sin\theta_2 = \tan\theta_2$. Resolving T_1 horizontally and vertically we have the vertical component as

$$T_1 \sin\theta_1 = T_1 \tan\theta_1 = \frac{T_1 y_1}{l/3}$$

and it is negative since the restoring force is in the opposite direction to the displacement. The other vertical component is $T_1 \sin\theta_2$ where θ_2 is the angle as shown on the right in Fig. 4.3.

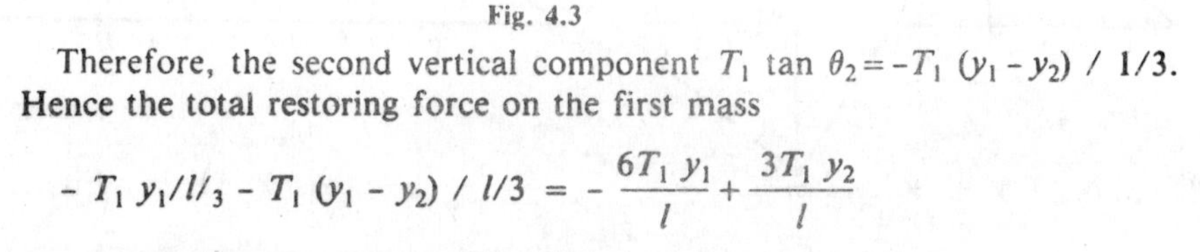

Fig. 4.3

Therefore, the second vertical component $T_1 \tan\theta_2 = -T_1 (y_1 - y_2) / l/3$. Hence the total restoring force on the first mass

$$-T_1 y_1/l/_3 - T_1 (y_1 - y_2) / l/3 = -\frac{6T_1 y_1}{l} + \frac{3T_1 y_2}{l}$$

and, similarly, the total restoring force on the second mass

$$-\frac{6T_1 y_2}{l} + \frac{3T_1 y_1}{l}$$

Hence the equations of motion of the two masses are

$$m\frac{d^2y_1}{dt^2} + \frac{6T_1 y_1}{l} = \frac{3T_1 y_2}{l} \tag{4.30}$$

or $$\frac{d^2y_1}{dt^2} + \frac{6T_1y_1}{lm} = \frac{3T_1y_2}{lm}$$

If we put $4\pi^2 \nu_0^2 = 6T_1/lm$.

then

$$\frac{d^2y_1}{dt^2} + 4\pi^2 \nu_0^2 y_1 = 2\pi^2 \nu_0^2 y_2$$

If we put $n = 2\pi\ \nu_0 = \sqrt{6T_1/lm}$

then equation (4.30) reduces to

$$\frac{d^2y_1}{dt^2} + n^2 y_1 = \frac{n^2}{2} y_2 \tag{4.31}$$

and, similarly, we get for the 2nd mass,

$$\frac{d^2y_2}{dt^2} + n^2 y_2 = \frac{n^2}{2} y_1. \tag{4.32}$$

These equations are not equations of simple harmonic motion but by suitable manipulation they can be adopted to simple harmonic motion.

Normal Modes of Motion

Let us see whether it is possible to find a relation between y_1 and y_2 so that both the above equations may reduce to the same equation of motion for S.H.M. This can be done in two ways: (a) making $y_1 = y_2$, i.e. to start the masses into motion in such a way that the portion of the string between the two masses is horizontal; and (b) making $y_1 = -y_2$, i.e. to start the masses into motion in such a way so that the centre of the string between the two masses is always on the equilibrium line. These conditions are shown in Fig. (4.4). If

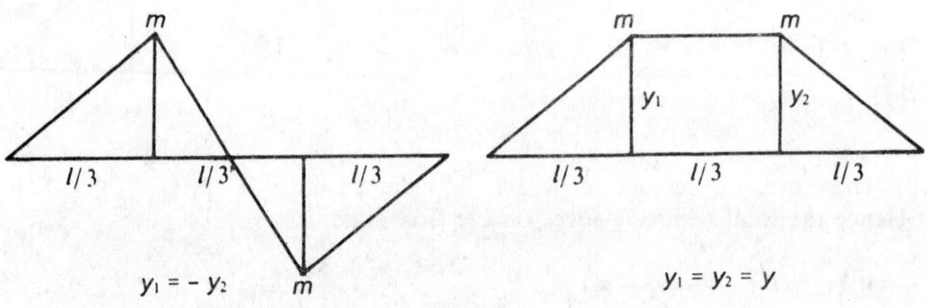

Fig. 4.4

we apply the first condition to equations (4.31) and (4.32), both the equations reduce to the form

$$\frac{d^2y}{dt^2} + \frac{n^2}{2} y = 0 \text{ where } y_1 = y_2 = y. \tag{4.33}$$

$$\therefore\ y_1 = y_2 = y = C\,e^{i\frac{n}{\sqrt{2}}t} = Ce^{\sqrt{2}\,\pi i\,\nu_0 t} \tag{4.34}$$

If we denote this frequency as ν_-

then $2\pi\,\nu_- = \sqrt{2}\,\pi\,\nu_0$

$$\nu_- = \frac{\nu_0}{\sqrt{2}} = \frac{1}{2\pi}\sqrt{\frac{3T_1}{lm}} \tag{4.35}$$

Applying the 2nd condition, i.e. $y_1 = -y_2$,
we get

$$\frac{d^2y}{dt^2} + \frac{3\,n^2}{2}\,y = 0$$

$$\therefore\ y = Ce^{\sqrt{6}\,\pi i\,\nu_0 t}.$$

$$= a\cos\sqrt{6}\,\pi\,\nu_0\,t + ib\sin\sqrt{6}\,\pi\,\nu_0 t$$

If then ν_+ denotes this frequency,

$$\nu_+ = \nu_0\sqrt{\frac{3}{2}} = \frac{1}{2\pi}\sqrt{\frac{9T_1}{lm}} \tag{4.36}$$

Thus it seen that, if the masses are started with exactly similar motions, then the lower frequency only will be presented while if we start them with opposite motion the higher frequency only will be present. In general, however, the system will oscillate with both the frequencies simultaneously and if the oscillations are rapid enough beats will be heard.

CASE 2: Double pendulum. This case is also an illustration of coupled oscillation. A mass M is hung from a fixed point by a string of length a and a second mass m hangs from M by a string of lenth b Fig. 4.5; for simplicity it is suppos-

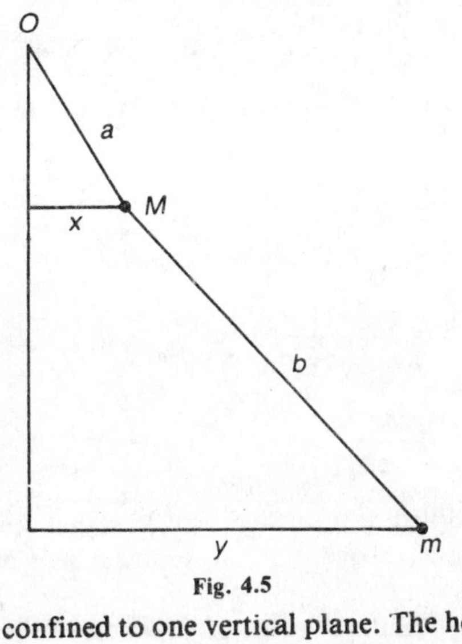

Fig. 4.5

ed that the motion is confined to one vertical plane. The horizontal excursions x and y of masses M and m respectively being supposed small, the tensions of upper and lower strings will be $(M+m)\,g$ and mg respectively. Consequently the equations of motion of the two masses will be,

$$M\frac{d^2x}{dt^2} = -(M+m)\,g\frac{x}{a} + mg\,\frac{(y-x)}{b} \tag{4.33a}$$

$$m\frac{d^2y}{dt^2} = -\,mg\,\frac{(y-x)}{b} \tag{4.33b}$$

To find the possible modes of simple harmonic motion, it is assumed that $x = A\cos(nt+\epsilon)$; $y = B\cos(nt+\epsilon)$. Puting the values of d^2x/dt^2 and d^2y/dt^2 and also that of x and y we get from (4.33a)

$$-M\,A\,n^2 + (M+m)\,g\,\frac{A}{a} - \frac{mg}{b}(B-A) = 0$$

or
$$\frac{MAn^2}{(M+m)^2} - g\left[\frac{M}{(M+m)_a} + \frac{m}{(M+m)_a} + \frac{m}{(M+m)_b}\right]A$$

$$= \frac{m}{M+m}\cdot\frac{g}{b}B$$

Putting $\mu = \dfrac{m}{m+M}$.

$$A\left[(1-\mu)\,n^2 - g\left\{\frac{1}{a} + \frac{\mu}{b}\right\}\right] + \frac{\mu}{b}\,g\,B = 0 \tag{4.34}$$

and, similarly, from equation (4.33b)

$$B\left[n^2 - \frac{g}{b}\right] + \frac{g}{b}A = 0 \tag{4.35}$$

Eliminating A and B from the equations (4.34) and (4.35)

$$(1-\mu)\,n^4 - g\left[\frac{1}{b} + \frac{1}{a}\right]n^2 + \frac{g^2}{ab} = 0 \tag{4.36}$$

which is quadratic in n^2; the conditions for real roots are

$$g^2\left(\frac{1}{a} + \frac{1}{b}\right)^2 > \frac{4\,g^2\,(1-\mu)}{ab}$$

$$g^2\left(\frac{1}{a} - \frac{1}{b}\right)^2 + \frac{4g^2\mu}{ab} > 0 \tag{4.37}$$

Which are always fulfilled. It is further easily seen that the two roots are always positive and hence n is a real quantity. The problem includes a number of special cases.

(a) If the ratio μ is small, the roots of equation (4.36) are $n_1^2 = g/a$ and $n_2^2 = g/b$. In the former case M oscillates like the bob of a simple pendulum of length a while m executes what may be called a forced oscillation of the corresponding frequency.

(b) When the ratio A/B is small, M is practically at rest while m oscillates like the bob of a pendulum of length b.

(c) Since the expression on the L.H.S. of equation (4.37) cannot vanish, the two frequencies can never exactly coincide but they become approximately equal if $a = b$ and μ is small. A curious phenomena then presents itself. The motion of each mass, being made up of two superposed simple harmonic motions of nearly equal period, may fluctuate greatly in extent and if the amplitudes of the two vibrations are equal we have periods of approximate rest i.e. the amplitude of vibration tends towards zero. The motion then appears to be transferred alternately from m to M and from M to m at regular intervals.

(d) If M is small compared with m, and $\mu \simeq 1$ and the two roots of the equation (4.36) are

$$n_1^2 \simeq \frac{g}{(a+b)} \quad \text{and} \quad n_2^2 \simeq \frac{mg}{M} \cdot \frac{a+b}{ab}$$

so that the two masses are nearly in a line with the point of suspension. In this case, m oscillates like the bob of a pendulum of length $(a+b)$. In the 2nd mode, the ratio B/A is small so that m is almost at rest. The motion of M is like that of a particle attached to a string which is stretched between the two fixed points with a tesnion mg.

(e) If $a \simeq \infty$ one root of equation (4.36) vanishes and the other is

$$n^2 = \frac{g}{(1-\mu)\,b} = \frac{g}{b}\left(1 - \frac{m}{M}\right) \text{ which makes } \frac{A}{B} = -\frac{m}{M}.$$ This indicates that if the support of the simple pendulum yields horizontally but without elasticity, the frequency is increased in a certain ratio which is, of course, smaller the greater the inertia of the support.

4.7 ANALOGY WITH ELECTRICAL COUPLED CIRCUITS

The theory of two coupled oscillators just outlined is identical with the theory of coupled circuits in radio engineering or that of electrical circuits in the case of a transformer. The primary coil is identical with the driver oscillator and the secondary coil resembles the driven oscillator and as in the case of a transformer, energy is fed back from the driven to the driver oscillator. The presence of secondary modifies the elements of the primary in that the ohmic resistance of the primary is increased while the reactance is decreased. Thus the natural frequency of the primary circuit is changed as the natural frequency of a mechanically coupled oscillator is affected by the presence of the second oscillator.

REFERENCE

1. Morse, P.M. (1948). *Vibration and sound,* 2nd ed., McGraw-Hill, New York.

5
VIBRATION IN AN EXTENDED MEDIUM

We have thus far considered the case of a particle or a system executing vibration. This case is of special importance in case of a source emitting sound wave or in the case of receiver receiving sound energy. It is of prime importance now to consider how this vibration is propagated along the medium which surrounds the source. That medium may be a solid, a liquid or a gas. It is natural that the generated vibrations will make the medium itself vibrate and the state of vibration will be affected by the physical properties of the medium. In the introductory chapter we have noted that the vibrations will be propagated with a finite velocity and as the vibrations are longitudinal, the displacement will be in the same direction as the direction of wave propagation. When a source is embedded in an elastic medium, sound waves will be produced and will be propagated with a certain velocity which will be dependent upon the density, viscosity and elasticity of the medium.

5.1 PLANE WAVES

We assume a progressive wave to be propagated along the positive direction of x-axis. Then displacement y at a point x from the origin will be given by

$$y = a \sin (\omega t - \theta) \tag{5.1}$$

where a = amplitude of vibration, ω = angular frequency, and θ = phase difference.

For a path difference λ, the phase difference will be 2π, where λ is the wavelength.

Hence λ corresponds to 2π

x corresponds to $2\pi x/\lambda$.

and consequently phase difference $\theta = 2\pi x/\lambda$ and $\omega = 2\pi/T$, where T is the time period. We get from equation (5.1)

$$y = a \sin\left(2\pi \frac{t}{T} - 2\pi \frac{x}{\lambda}\right)$$

$$= a \sin 2\pi \left(\frac{t}{T} - \frac{x}{\lambda}\right) \tag{5.2}$$

$$= a \sin 2\pi \left(ft - \frac{x}{\lambda}\right) \tag{5.3}$$

and as v = velocity of sound $= f\lambda$.

We obtain other forms of equation (5.1) as

$$y = a \sin \frac{2\pi}{\lambda} (vt - x). \tag{5.4}$$

$$= a \sin \omega \left(t - \frac{x}{v}\right) \tag{5.5}$$

Any of these equations from (5.1) to (5.5) can be used to express the displacement in a plane progressive wave proceeding along the + ve direction of x-axis.

Particle velocity. The particle velocity is obtained from equation (5.5) by differentiating, as

$$y = \frac{dy}{dt} = a\,\omega \cos \omega \left(t - \frac{x}{v}\right). \tag{5.6}$$

and so we obtain from equations (5.5) and (5.6)

$$\frac{dy}{dt} = -v\frac{dy}{dx}. \tag{5.7}$$

which gives the particle velocity in terms of wave velocity and slope of the displacement curve.

Acceleration of the particle. We get from equation (5.6) the acceleration of the particle to be

$$\frac{d^2y}{dt^2} = -\omega^2 a \sin \omega \left(t - \frac{x}{v}\right) \tag{5.8}$$

then from equations (5.8) and (5.5)

$$\frac{d^2y}{dt^2} = v^2 . \frac{d^2y}{dx^2} \tag{5.9}$$

Thus the acceleration is equal to the product of the square of the velocity of the wave motion and the curvature of the displacement curve. And equation (5.9) is the general equation which characterises a wave motion. The general solution of equation (5.9) is given by

$$y = F(vt - x) + F'(vt + x). \tag{5.10}$$

where F denotes a function. This equation evidently represents waves travelling in opposite directions with the velocity v where $F(vt - x)$ represents a wave travelling in the positive direction of x-axis and $F'(vt + x)$ represents a wave proceeding in the negative direction of x-axis.

5.2 VELOCITY OF WAVE PROPAGATION

It is clear from the form of equation (5.9) that the velocity of wave propagation is independent of the form of the wave and also independent of the amplitude and frequency of the wave and consequently it is a function of the physical properties of the medium. As the wave passes through a medium, any portion of the medium undergoes alternate compressions and rarefactions which cause a change in the volume and density of the medium. Let us consider a fixed mass of gas which at a pressure P_0 occupies a volume with a density ρ_0. These values define the equilibrium state of the gas which is disturbed or changed by the compression and rarefaction of sound wave. Under the influence of the sound wave the pressure P_0 becomes P_0+P the volume becomes V_0+V. Let us now consider a volume element of the gas of unit cross-section and enclosed by two planes at x and $x+dx$. Hence the original volume V_0 is dx. If y is the longitudinal displacement of the plane at x, then the changed coordinate of the plane at x will be $x+y$ and that of the plane at $x+dx$ will be $x+y+dx+\frac{dy}{dx}\,dx$. The distance between the two planes is now $\frac{dy}{dx}\,dx+dx$, which is also the new volume. Hence change of volume is $\frac{dy}{dx}\,dx$.

$$\text{Strain}=\frac{\text{change of volume}}{\text{original volume}}=\left(\frac{dy}{dx}\right)dx\Big/dx.$$

$$=\left(\frac{dy}{dx}\right)$$

$$K \text{ the bulk modulus}=\frac{\text{stress}}{\text{strain}}=\frac{-P}{(dy/dx)} \tag{5.11}$$

If P_x is the pressure at x, then the pressure at $(x+dx)$ is

$$P_x-\left(P_x+\frac{dP_x}{dx}\,dx\right)=-\frac{dP_x}{dx}\,dx=-\frac{d}{dx}(P_0+P)\,dx=-\frac{dP}{dx}dx.$$

and as the area of cross-section is unity, force $=-\frac{dP_x}{dx}\,dx$. If ρ is the density of the medium, then from Newton's law we have

$$\rho\,dx\,\frac{d^2y}{dt^2}=-\frac{dP_x}{dx}dx$$

as

$$P=-K.\,\frac{dy}{dx} \tag{5.12}$$

then

$$\rho.\,\frac{d^2y}{dt^2}=K.\,\frac{d^2y}{dx^2}.$$

This equation alongwith equation (5.9) gives

$$v^2 = \frac{K}{P} \tag{5.13}$$

Thus the velocity of wave propagation is determined by the density and elasticity of the medium. Equation (5.13) is a general equation applicable in case of solids, liquids and gases provided the appropriate values of bulk modulus are taken.

5.3 ENERGY OF A PLANE WAVE OF SOUND. INTENSITY

The intensity of a plane sound wave is defined as the quantity of energy which crosses per unit area of a plane normal to the direction of propagation and this energy is generally made up of kinetic and potential energies. The kinetic energy can be easily calculated as follows:

From equation (5.5) the displacement y is given by

$$y = a \sin \omega\ (t - x/v)$$

$$dy/dt = a\ \omega \cos \omega\ (t - x/v)$$

and kinetic energy = ½ mass × (velocity)^2.
If ρ is the density of the medium, then the mass of a layer of the medium of unit area and thickness dx is $\rho\ dx$ and

$$\text{the kinetic energy} = \frac{1}{2} \rho\ dx.\ a^2\ \omega^2 \cos^2\omega \left(t - \frac{x}{v}\right) \tag{5.14}$$

Therefore, the kinetic energy of the wave system in a length x and of unit corss-section and hence of volume x, is

$$T = \int_0^x \frac{1}{2} \rho\ a^2\ \omega^2 \cos^2 \omega \left(t - \frac{x}{v}\right) dx = \frac{1}{4} \rho.\ a^2\ \omega^2 x$$

Hence the average energy per unit volume is

$$T = \frac{1}{4} \rho a^2\ \omega^2. \tag{5.15}$$

In calculating the potential energy, we note that the force acting on unit area is P.

As $P = K \dfrac{dy}{dx}$. from equation (5.11) the work done for a further strain

$d\ (dy/dx)$

$$dV = K \left(\frac{dy}{dx}\right) d \left(\frac{dy}{dx}\right)$$

Hence the total work done is $V = \int K\left(\frac{dy}{dx}\right) d\left(\frac{dy}{dx}\right)$

$$= \frac{1}{2} K \left(\frac{dy}{dx}\right)^2 \tag{5.16}$$

As $y = a \sin \omega \left(t - \frac{x}{v}\right)$.

$$\left(\frac{dy}{dx}\right)^2 = a^2 . \frac{\omega^2}{v^2} . \cos^2 \omega \left(t - \frac{x}{v}\right).$$

Hence from equation (5.16) $V = \frac{1}{2} K . \frac{a^2 \omega^2}{v^2} \cos \omega^2 \left(t - \frac{x}{v}\right)$.

as

$$v = \sqrt{\frac{K}{P}}.$$

$$V = \frac{1}{2} \rho\, a^2 \omega^2 \cos^2 \omega \left(t - \frac{x}{v}\right).$$

Integrating as in the case of kinetic energy the average potential energy per unit volume

$$V = \frac{1}{4} \rho\, a^2 \omega^2. \tag{5.17}$$

Hence the total energy per unit volume = Kinetic energy + Potential energy $= \frac{1}{2} \rho\, a^2 \omega^2$. (5.18)

This quantity then represents the energy per unit volume and may be called the energy density. The quantity of energy that flows per unit area per unit time through the wavefront is called the intensity of the wave and may be obtained from equation (5.18) by multiplying it with the velocity of the sound wave. Hence if I denotes the intensity of the wave,

$$I = \frac{1}{2} \rho\, a^2 \omega^2 v \tag{5.19}$$

Thus the intensity is proportional to density of the medium, to the product of squares of amplitude and frequency and the velocity of the sound wave.

5.4 POWER OF A SOURCE EMITTING PLANE WAVE

The energy of the plane sound wave is derived entirely from the source of sound producing it and consequently the intensity of a plane wave of sound as derived is equal to the power of the source emitting the sound wave and equals ½ $\rho\, a^2\, \omega^2\, \nu$. If we push this analogy with the electrical case then we observe that comparing the current with the particle velocity and $(\rho\nu)$ with the resistance, the power term becomes analogous with the expression for the power term in the electrical case. Comparing the electrical resistance with the term $(\rho\nu)$ it is generally called the radiation resistance. If S denotes the area then power radiated through the area S is

$$P_R = \frac{1}{2}\, \rho\, a^2\, \omega^2\, \nu\, S.$$

5.5 ELASTIC VIBRATION IN SOLIDS

Longitudinal Waves in a Solid

CASE 1: Thin bar – The velocity of longitudinal waves in a solid depends upon the dimension of the specimen in which waves are travelling. If the solid is a thin bar of finite cross-section, the analysis for longitudinal waves in a gas is equally valid except that the bulk modulus in case of a gas is to be replaced by Young's modulus Y and the velocity of longitudinal waves is given by

$$\nu^2 = \frac{Y}{\rho} \tag{5.19}$$

CASE 2: Waves in an extended medium – Let us consider the propagation of a plane wave along the x-axis in an extended medium. In case of a bar when the wave proceeds along the x-axis an element along the direction of propagation is elongated and the elements of length in the perpendicular directions are contracted. If α is the extension per unit length along the axis, β and γ contractions per unit length along the y- and z-direction, then if F_x, F_y *and* F_z are the stresses along the three axes

$$F_x = \alpha Y$$

and $$F_y = F_z = 0$$

and $$\beta = \gamma = -\alpha\, \sigma$$

where σ is the Poisson's ratio. However in an extended medium when the wave is travelling along the x-axis there is extension and contraction along the x-axis but no change in y and Z directions. Hence, $\beta = \gamma = 0$. For an isotropic medium, the strains along the x-, y- and z-axis are

$$\left.\begin{aligned} \alpha &= \frac{1}{Y}\,[F_x - \sigma\,(F_y + F_z)\,]. \\ \beta &= \frac{1}{Y}\,[F_y - \sigma\,(F_x + F_z)\,]. \\ \gamma &= \frac{1}{Y}\,[F_z - \sigma\,(F_y + F_x)\,]. \end{aligned}\right\} \tag{5.20}$$

then

$$\alpha\, Y = F_x - \sigma\,(F_y + F_z).$$

$$\gamma Y = F_z - \sigma (F_x + F_y). \tag{5.21}$$

or $Y(\alpha - \gamma) = F_x (1+\sigma) - F_z (1+\sigma)$

and from the second equation in (5.20) we get

$$\sigma \beta Y = \sigma F_y - \sigma^2 (F_z + F_x) \tag{5.22}$$

From the third equation in (5.20) and equation (5.22), we get

$$(\gamma + \sigma\beta) Y = F_z (1 - \sigma^2) - \sigma F_x (1+\sigma). \tag{5.23}$$

From equations (5.21) and (5.23) we get

$$Y(\sigma \beta + \alpha - \alpha \sigma + \gamma\sigma) = F_x (1+\sigma)(1-2\sigma).$$

$$F_x = [\alpha (1-\sigma) + \sigma (\beta + \gamma)] Y/(1+\sigma)(1-2\sigma).$$

Putting $\lambda = \dfrac{\sigma Y}{(1+\sigma)(1-2\sigma)}$. and $\delta = \alpha + \beta + \gamma$.

$F_x = \alpha\lambda\delta + 2n\alpha$ where n = rigidly modulus $= \dfrac{Y}{2(1+\delta)}$.

In the same way

$$F_y = \lambda \delta + 2n\beta$$

$$F_z = \lambda \delta + 2n\gamma$$

In an extended medium, $\beta = \gamma = 0$ and $\delta = \alpha$.

Hence $F_x = (\lambda + 2n)\alpha$

$$= \alpha \frac{(1-\sigma)}{(1+\sigma)(1-2\sigma)} Y.$$

Since α is the extension per unit length if y is the displacement at x and $y + dy$ at $x + dx$, then

$$\alpha = dy/dx$$

or $F_x = Y \dfrac{1-\sigma}{(1+\sigma)(1-2\sigma)} \dfrac{dy}{dx}$.

The resultant force acting on the element in the positive direction is dF_x/dx; then, if ρ is the mass per unit length,

$$\rho \frac{d^2y}{dt^2} = Y. \frac{(1-\sigma)}{(1+\sigma)(1-2\sigma)}. \frac{d^2y}{dx^2}$$

then

$$v^2 = \frac{Y(1-\sigma).}{(1+\sigma)(1-2\sigma)} \frac{1}{\rho}.$$

Putting $K = \dfrac{Y}{3(1-2\sigma)}$ where K is the bulk modulus, and $\sigma = \dfrac{3K - 2n}{6K + 2n}$. we get

$$v^2 = \left[\frac{K + 4n/3}{\rho}\right].$$

CASE 3: A longitudinal wave in a medium compresses the medium and distorts it laterally. Because a solid can develop a shear force in any direction, such a lateral distortion is accompanied by a transverse shear. The modulus of rigidity plays the same role in the propagation of pure transverse waves in a bulk solid as Young's modulus plays for longitudinal waves in a thin specimen. If the transverse strain is defined as $\partial y/\partial x$, the transverse stress at x is $T_x = n\partial y/\partial x$. The equation of transverse motion of the thin element is then given by

$$T_{x+dx} - T_x = \rho\ dx.\ \frac{d^2y}{dt^2}.$$

or

$$\text{or}\ \frac{\partial}{\partial x}\left(n.\ \frac{\partial y}{\partial x}\right) dx = \rho.\ dx.\ \frac{d^2y}{dt^2}.$$

or

$$\text{or}\ n.\ \frac{\partial^2 y}{\partial x^2} = \rho.\ \frac{d^2y}{dt^2}.$$

or

$$\text{or}\ v^2 = \frac{n}{\rho}$$

6

VIBRATION OF STRINGS

We have so far discussed mainly the vibration of a simple point mass, the propagation of vibration through a homogeneous medium and the cases of simple harmonic motion, the resisted motion and the case of two oscillators coupled together. We shall now discuss how these results apply when we are considering the actual sources of sound. The most widely used source of sound in musical instruments is the stringed instruments and so the consideration of the case of a vibrating string is of fundamental importance. A string may vibrate in a number of modes; though the transverse mode of vibration of the string is of prime importance, it is possible to excite longitudinal and torsional vibrations also in the string.

6.1 TRANSVERSE VIBRATION OF STRINGS

Theoretically a string is defined as a body having length only, infinitely thin, able to be bent laterally in transverse vibration without bringing into play the viscous forces in the material. Insofar as natural wires and threads fail in this respect we say they possess stiffness. The type of vibration of the stretched strings and wires with which we are most familiar is that in which the particles of the string are vibrating in a plane perpendicular to its length and this type of vibration is called the transverse vibration. For the purpose of discussing this type of vibration we shall assume the following conditions:

(*a*) A wire or a string whose length is great compared with its diameter.
(*b*) The string is perfectly flexible so the ends of the element are subject to forces of tension directed along the tangent.
(*c*) The magnitude of the tension is constant.
(*d*) The square of the inclination of any part of the string to the initial direction is neglected.

These conditions are fulfilled in case of a long, thin, tightly stretched wire held between massive and well clamped supports. Later on we shall deal with the case of an actual string in which the wire has stiffness and the supports yield horizontally, as the string vibrates. When any point of such wire is displaced from its original position and then released, the string vibrates which is due to transverse motions travelling in opposite directions along the string and successive reflections from the opposite end.

Let the string be stretched along the x-axis under a tension T_1 and let the displacement of the string take place along the xy-plane and let the mass of the string be m per unit length. Let AB represent a small portion of the displaced position of the string (Fig. 6.1). Let θ be the angle which the string makes when displaced with its undisplaced position. As the angle θ is small

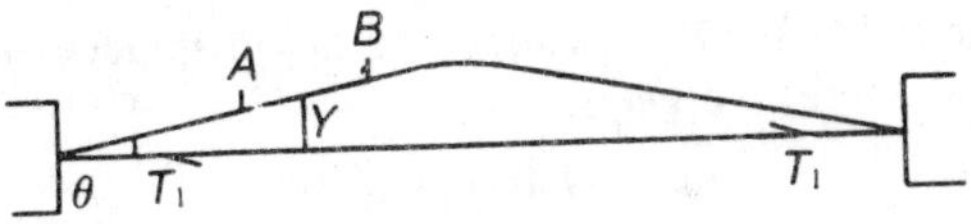

Fig. 6.1

$\sin\theta = \tan\theta = \dfrac{dy}{dx}$. Hence the component of tension acting in the Y direction at A is $T_1 \dfrac{dy}{dx}$.

As the length of the element AB is (dx) the tension at B is

$$T_1 \frac{dy}{dx} + \frac{d}{dx}\left(T_1 \frac{dy}{dx}\right) dx.$$

acting downwards. Hence the resultant tension on AB acting along the y-axis is

$$T_1 \frac{dy}{dx} + \frac{d}{dx}\left(T_1 \frac{dy}{dx}\right) dx - T_1 \frac{dy}{dx} = T_1 \frac{d^2y}{dx^2} dx.$$

As m . the mass per unit length of the string the force acting on the element is $m.\ dx.\ \dfrac{d^2y}{dt^2}$. Hence the equation of motion is

$$m.\ dx.\ \frac{d^2y}{dt^2} = T_1 \frac{d^2y}{dx^2} dx. \tag{6.1}$$

or

$$\frac{d^2y}{dt^2} = \frac{T_1}{m} \cdot \frac{d^2y}{dx^2}. \tag{6.2}$$

This equation characterises a wave motion and comparing with the wave equation in chapter 5 [equation (5.9)], we find that the equation (6.2) can be written as

$$\frac{d^2y}{dt^2} = c^2 \frac{d^2y}{dx^2}$$

where

$$c = \sqrt{\frac{T_1}{m}}. \tag{6.3}$$

and c is called the velocity of transverse vibration in a string. A solution of the wave equation (6.3) is given by

$$y = f\ (ct - x) + F\ (ct + x). \tag{6.4}$$

which represents transverse waves travelling in opposite directions with the same velocity c.

6.2 REFLECTION: FORMATION OF STATIONARY WAVES

As the string is held fixed at both ends, the waves on reaching the end will get reflected and these reflected waves superimposing on the outgoing waves will form what are known as stationary waves. Applying the boundary conditions in equation (6.4) which are: $y=0$ when $x=0$ and $y=0$ when $x=l$, where l is the length of the string (as there cannot be any displacement at the two ends as it is held fixed there) we get

$$0 = f(ct) + F(ct).$$

or

$$f(ct) = -F(ct).$$

then equation (6.4) can be written as

$$y = f(ct-x) - f(Ct+x).$$

and as $y=0$ when $x=l$ we get,

$$0 = f(ct-l) - f(ct+l).$$

or

$$f(ct-l) = f(ct+l) \tag{6.5}$$

calling

$$ct - l = b$$

we get

$$f(b) = f(b+2l). \tag{6.6}$$

Hence from equation (6.6), $f(b)$ is a periodic function which repeats itself at an interval of $2l$ and so the motion of the string is periodic, the period being $T=2l/c$. Hence frequency of vibration is given by

$$N = \frac{1}{T} = \frac{c}{2l} = \frac{1}{2l}\sqrt{\frac{T_1}{m}}. \quad \text{Ref. equation (6.3)} \tag{6.7}$$

If the displacement y varies sinusoidally with time we get

$$y = a \cos \omega \left(t - \frac{x}{c}\right) - a \cos \omega \left(t + \frac{x}{c}\right) \tag{6.8}$$

$$= 2\,a \sin \omega t \sin \frac{\omega x}{c}$$

$$= 2\,a \sin 2\pi\, Nt \sin \frac{2\pi\, Nx}{c}$$

The amplitude term in the equation is $2a \sin \dfrac{2\pi Nx}{c}$ which varies between 0 and $2a$ and sinusoidally with time and also varies with x. When the amplitude becomes zero that is minimum, it is called a node and when the amplitude is $2a$ that is maximum, it is called the antinode. The condition for the formation of nodes is clearly given by $\sin \dfrac{2\pi\, Nl}{c} = \sin s\pi$. where S, is an integer, i.e.

$$N = \frac{Sc}{2l}$$

$$= \frac{S}{2l}\sqrt{\frac{T_1}{m}}. \tag{6.9}$$

So that the number of loops into which the string is divided is S. These vibrations are shown in Fig. 6.2 for different values of S. Thus we are now

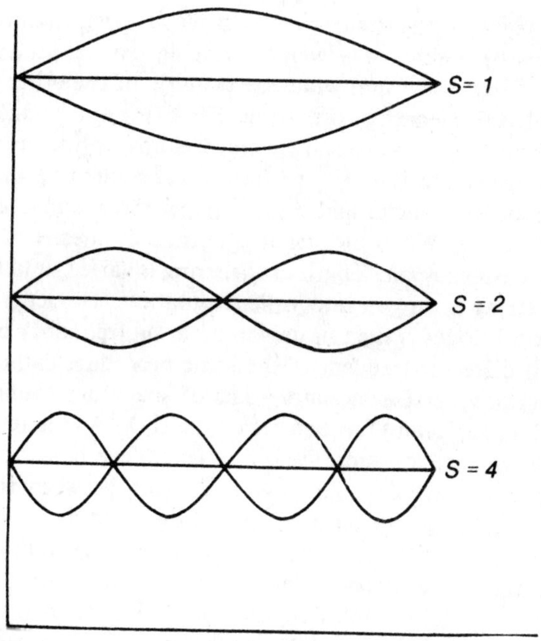

Fig. 6.2

in a position to formulate the laws of vibrating string which were first enunciated by Mersenne in 1638 from his experimental observations.

(a) **Law of Length.** The frequency of vibration of the string varies inversely as the length of the string if the mass per unit length and tension are constant.

$$N \propto \frac{1}{l}.$$

(*b*) **Law of Tension.** The frequency varies directly as the square root of the tension if the length of the string and mass per unit length are constant.

$$N \propto \sqrt{T_1}$$

(c) **Law of Mass.** The frequency varies inversely as the square root of mass per unit length if the tension and length of the string are constant.

$$N \propto \frac{1}{\sqrt{m}}$$

6.3 EXPERIMENTAL VERIFICATION OF THE LAWS OF VIBRATING STRING: THE SONOMETER

The foregoing conclusions regarding the laws of vibrating string can be verified experimentally by means of an instrument which is known as sonometer. It consists essentially of a thin metallic wire stretched over two wooden bridges by means of a weight hanging over a pulley. One of the bridges is kept fixed in position while the position of the other is varied so as to change the effective length of the string. The string and bridges are mounted on a base which is very massive and strong, yielding as little as possible to the forces applied due to tension. The vibrations are excited by means of tuning forks of different frequencies and a small paper rider is placed on the string to indicate resonance. When the string is excited by means of a tuning fork with a definite frequency, the length of the string is varied until the paper rider placed on the string is thrown into violent agitation. The length of the string between the two bridges is then in unison with the frequency of the fork. By taking forks of different frequencies the same procedure can be repeated for the same string and corresponding lengths of string are found which are in resonance with the different frequencies of the fork. As the tension and mass per unit length are kept constant, the law of length can be verified in this way.

In the same way, keeping the length of string between the two bridges constant and changing the tension, the corresponding resonance can be observed for forks of different frequencies and corresponding tension.

In order to verify the law of mass, different strings with different masses per unit length are taken and keeping the tension and length the same, resonance is observed between forks of different frequencies and different strings.

Sonometers are sometimes provided with a second wire of fixed length and tension to provide a standard frequency as a basis for comparison. The above simple experiment is somewhat inaccurate because the effective length of the string is rendered uncertain due to stiffness of the wire and the frequency is further affected by the yielding of the support.

6.4 GENERAL SOLUTION OF THE WAVE EQUATION IN STRING

Referring to the general equation of the string

$$\frac{d^2y}{dt^2} = c^2 \frac{d^2y}{dx^2}$$

we note that the solution of this equation can be written as

$$y = [A \sin mx + C \cos mx] \cos mct + [B \sin mx + D \cos mx] \sin mct,$$

where A, B, C and D are constants. For any continuous length of the string satisfying, without interruption, the differential equation, this is the most general solution possible under the condition that the motion of every point shall be simple harmonic. The most simple as well as the most important problem connected with the present subject is the investigation of the free vibration of a string of finite length l held fixed at both ends. If we take the origin of x at one end of the string the terminal conditions which must be satisfied are

$$y = 0 \quad \text{when } x = 0$$

and also $\quad y = 0 \quad$ when $x = l$ for all values of t.

Then from equation (6.10) $0 = C \cos mct + D \sin mct$ and consequently $C = D = 0$

Therefore $y = A \sin mx \cos mct + B \sin mx \sin mct$

$$= \sin mx \, [A \cos mct + B \sin mct]$$

when $x = l$, $y = 0$

so that $0 = \sin ml \, [A \cos mct + B \sin mct]$.

As A and B cannot be zero,

$$0 = \sin ml.$$

$$\sin S\pi = \sin ml.$$

or

$$m = S\pi/l.$$

where S is an integer.

Therefore, the only harmonic vibration possible under the prescribed condition is

$$y = \sin \frac{S\pi x}{l} \left[A_s \cos \frac{S\pi ct}{l} + B_s \sin \frac{S\pi ct}{l} \right] \tag{6.11}$$

Now we know, *a priori* that whatever the periodic motion may be, it can always be represented as a sum of simple harmonic vibrations. We conclude that the most general solution for a string fixed at $x = 0$ and $x = l$ is given by

$$y = \sum_{S=1}^{S=\infty} \sin \frac{S\pi x}{l} \left[A_s \cos \frac{S\pi ct}{l} + B_s \sin \frac{S\pi ct}{l} \right]. \tag{6.12}$$

Just as in the case of Fourier's analysis, the constants A_s and B_s can be determined from the boundary conditions of the problem.

6.5 METHODS OF PRODUCING VIBRATIONS IN STRINGS

The stretched string may be set into vibration in a variety of ways. All stringed musical instruments are in general excited either by means of plucking or striking or by bowing. The example of plucked string instrument is the harp, that of struck string is the piano and that of bowed string the violin. We shall discuss these cases one by one.

(*a*) Plucked string

This is the simplest method of exciting transverse vibrations in a string. The string is pulled aside by a finger or by a plectrum at a particular point and then let go.

In Fig. 6.3, AB represents the undisplaced position of the string and the axis of x coincides with the length of the string and let the coordinate of A be $x = 0$,

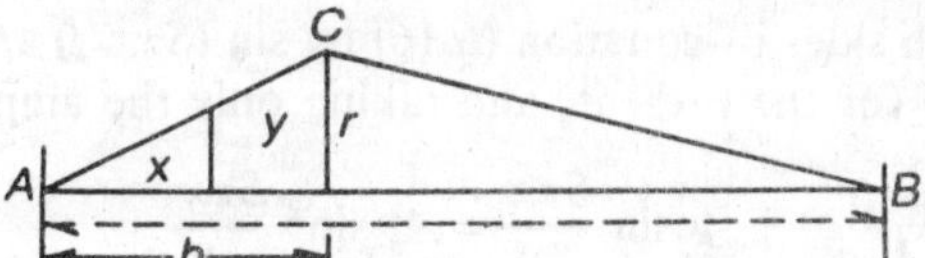

Fig. 6.3.

$y=0$ and those of B be $y=0$ and $x=l$, where l is the length of string. The string is plucked at the point C whose coordinate is $(x=b)$ to a distance $y=r$ and let go. The displacement of the string between $x=0$ and $x=b$ is given by

$$\frac{y}{x}=\frac{r}{b}$$

or $y=\frac{rx}{b}$ between $x=0$ to $x=b$. (6.13)

and between $x=b$ to $x=l$ we get

$$\frac{y}{(l-x)}=\frac{r}{(l-b)} \text{ or } y=r.\frac{(l-x)}{(l-b)} \tag{6.14}$$

The general equation of motion of the string fixed at $x=0$ and $x=l$ is given by equation (6.12), i.e.

$$y=\sum_{S=1}^{S=\infty}\sin\frac{S\pi x}{l}\left[A_s\cos\frac{S\pi ct}{l}+B_s\sin\frac{S\pi ct}{l}\right] \tag{6.12}$$

In the particular case of plucked string, we get the following conditions from which the constants A_s and B_s have to be determined:

(a) $y = 0$ at $t=0$ for all values of x.
(b) $y = rx/b$ from $x=0$ to $x=b$. (6.15)
(c) $y = r.\frac{(l-x)}{(l-b)}$ from $x=b$ to $x=l$.

From condition (a) of equation (6.15) we get

$$\dot{y}=\sum_{S=1}^{S=\infty}\sin\frac{S\pi x}{l}\left(\frac{S\pi c}{l}\right)\left[-A_s\sin\frac{S\pi ct}{l}+B_s\cos\frac{S\pi ct}{l}\right]$$

and as $\dot{y}=0$ at $t=0$

$$0=\text{Sin}\frac{S\pi x}{l}.\left(\frac{S\pi c}{l}\right)B_s.$$

then $B_s=0$

Therefore in case of plucked string we get

$$y=\sum_{S=1}^{S=\infty}\text{Sin}\frac{S\pi x}{l}.\ A_s\cos\frac{S\pi ct}{l}. \tag{6.16}$$

Multiplying both sides of equation (6.16) by sin $(S\pi x/l)$ and leaving aside the summation sign for the present, and taking only the amplitude term,

$$y\sin\frac{S\pi x}{l}=A_s\sin^2\frac{S\pi x}{l}.$$

Integrating both sides with respect to x between the limits $x=0$ to $x=l$

$$\int_0^l y \sin \frac{S\pi x}{l}\, dx = A_s \int_0^l \sin^2 \frac{S\pi x}{l} dx = A_s . \left(\frac{l}{2}\right)$$

$$A_s = \frac{2}{l} \int_0^l y \sin \frac{S\pi x}{l} .\, dx.$$

Putting the values of y from equation (6.15) we get

$$A_s = \frac{2}{l}\left[\int_0^b \frac{rx}{b} \sin \frac{S\pi x}{l} dx + \int_b^l r. \frac{l-x}{l-b} \sin \frac{S\pi x}{l} dx\right]$$

The first term on the R.H.S.

$$= \frac{2r}{l}\left[\frac{x}{b}\left(-\cos\frac{S\pi x}{l}\right)\frac{l}{S\pi}\Bigg|_{x=0}^{x=b} - \int_{x=0}^{x=b}\left(-\frac{1}{b}\right)\frac{l}{S\pi} \cos \frac{S\pi x}{l} dx\right]$$

$$= \frac{2r}{l}\left[\cos\left(\frac{S\pi b}{l}\right)\frac{l}{S\pi} - \left\{-\frac{l^2}{b\, S^2 \pi^2} \sin \frac{S\pi x}{l}\right\}_{x=0}^{x=b}\right.$$

$$= \frac{2r}{S\pi}\left[\frac{l}{b\,S\pi} \sin \frac{S\pi b}{l} - \cos \frac{S\pi b}{l}\right]$$

the second term of R.H.S.

$$= \frac{2r}{l}\left[\left\{-\frac{(l-x)}{(l-b)}\left(\cos\frac{S\pi x}{l}\right)\frac{l}{S\pi}\right\}_{x=b}^{x=l} - \int_{x=b}^{x=l} \frac{1}{(l-b)}\frac{l}{S\pi} . \cos \frac{S\pi x}{l} . dx\right]$$

$$= \frac{2r}{l}\left[\cos\frac{S\pi b}{l}\left(\frac{l}{S\pi}\right) - \left\{\frac{l^2}{(l-b)\, S^2 \pi^2} . \operatorname{Sin} \frac{S\pi x}{l}\right\}_{x=b}^{x=l}\right]$$

$$= \frac{2r}{S\pi}\left[\frac{l}{(l-b)}\frac{1}{S\pi} \sin \frac{S\pi b}{l} + \cos . \frac{S\pi b}{l}\right].$$

Hence $A_s = \dfrac{2r}{S\pi}\left[\left\{\dfrac{l}{bS\pi} + \dfrac{l}{(l-b)}\dfrac{1}{S\pi}\right\} \sin \dfrac{S\pi b}{l}\right]$

$$= \frac{2r}{S^2 \pi^2}\frac{l^2}{b\,(l-b)} . \sin \frac{S\pi b}{l}.$$

and $$y = \sum_{S=1}^{S=\infty} \frac{2r\,l^2}{S^2\,\pi^2\,b\,(l-b)} \sin\frac{S\pi b}{l}.\ \sin\frac{S\pi x}{l}.\ \cos\frac{S\pi\,ct}{l}$$

$$= \frac{2r\,l^2}{\pi^2 b\,(l-b)}.\ \sum_{S=1}^{S=\infty} \frac{1}{S^2} \sin\frac{S\pi b}{l}\ \sin\frac{S\pi x}{l}.\ \cos\frac{S\pi\,ct}{l}.$$

which is the complete solution of the general equation of motion of plucked string.

Interpretation of the formula: We have in the case of plucked string

$$y = \frac{2\,rl^2}{\pi^2\,b\,(l-b)} \sum_{S=1}^{S=\infty} \frac{1}{S^2} \sin\frac{S\pi b}{l}\ \sin\frac{S\pi x}{l}.\ \cos\frac{S\pi\,ct}{l}. \tag{6.16}$$

This relation indicates that the Sth harmonic will disappear when $\sin S\pi b/l = 0$ i.e. when Sb/l is an integer, or those harmonics will be absent which have got a node at C. Thus it is clear that if the string is divided into S equal parts and plucked at any one of these points the Sth harmonic will be absent from the resultant vibration.

Now, from the general equation, we have

$$A_s = \frac{2r\,l^2}{S^2\pi^2 b\,(l-b)} \sin\frac{S\pi b}{l}$$

and if $b = l/2$

$$A_s = \frac{2r\,l^2}{S^2\pi^2\, l/2.\ l/2} \sin\frac{S\pi}{2} = \frac{8r}{S^2\pi^2} \sin\frac{S\pi}{2}$$

and if $S = 2, 4, 6, 8$ etc., then $A = 0$ and $y = 0$.

This equation, therefore, also shows that in case of a string at rest in its equilibrium position it is impossible for a force applied at the middle point of the string to produce any even harmonic. The equation in this case will be of the form,

$$y = \frac{8r}{\pi^2}\left[\sin\frac{\pi x}{l}\cos.\ \frac{\pi ct}{l} - \frac{1}{9}\sin\frac{3\pi x}{l}\cos\frac{3\pi\,ct}{l} + \frac{1}{25}\sin\frac{5\pi x}{l}.\ \cos\frac{5\pi\,ct}{l} - \right]$$

If, after the application of the force at the middle point, this point is damped by touching it lightly, the string will be brought to rest. For odd harmonics cannot persist with a node at the middle point and even harmonics will be absent for the reason given above. Thomas Young proved experimentally that when any point of the string is plucked, struck or bowed, all the overtones or partials which require that point as a node will be absent from the resultant vibration.

The relation for A_s given above indicates that a string plucked in the above manner has the full harmonic series of overtones, the amplitude varying inversely as S^2, i.e. the amplitude of partials falls off rapidly towards the higher harmonics. The quality of the resultant tone depends upon the ratio b/l and varies with the point of plucking.

It must be remembered that the above treatment refers to an ideal string. As we know the stiffness of the string causes a slight departure from the harmonic series. Damping due to internal friction is another factor which has a similar tendency, the effect becoming more and more important at higher frequencies. Since the higher partials are damped most rapidly, the tone of a plucked string improves in quality as it diminishes in loudness. Well known examples of plucked stringed instruments are harp, guitar, mandolin and banzo.

(b) Struck string

When the string is excited by striking, complications arise due to finite time of contact of the striking hammer with the string. The general features of vibration produced by striking are much the same as those in which the string is excited by plucking but the motion is complicated due to the fact that the point of the string which receives the blow of the hammer is displaced before the remainder of the string. The resultant waveform is therefore dependent on a number of factors, including the duration of the blow, the velocity of the hammer and the relative masses of the hammer and the string. During recent years, considerable amount of research work has been carried out in connection with this complex motion. Various theories have been put forward notably those of Helmholtz and Kauffman in which the assumptions made regarding the mode of contact between the hammer and the string are of a somewhat artificial character when compared with the actual conditions experimentally determined. We shall deal however with the case of struck string on the following simplyfying assumptions. It will be assumed that the velocity will be imparted to a geometric point so that the conditions of the problem are as follows:

(a) $y=0$ at all points of the string when $t=0$

(b) $y=\dot{y}_0$ at the interval between $x=b$ and $x=b+db$.

where it is assumed that the hammer strikes the string between $x=b$ and $x=b+db$ and as usual l is the length of the string.

(c) $\dot{y}=0$ at $t=0$ at all other points of the string.

The general equation of vibration of a string fixed at $x=0$ and $x=e$ is given by

$$Y = \sum_{S=1}^{S=\infty} \sin \frac{S\pi x}{l} \left[A_s \cos \frac{S\pi\ ct}{l} + B_s \sin \frac{S\pi\ ct}{l} \right] \tag{6.12}$$

Applying the the first condition $y=0$ at $t=0$ for all points of the string, we get

$$0 = \sin \frac{S\pi x}{l} A_s$$

$$\text{or } A_s = 0$$

Then, in case of struck string, the equation (6.12) reduces to

$$y = \sum_{S=1}^{S=\infty} \sin \frac{S\pi x}{l} B_s \sin \frac{S\pi\, ct}{l}.$$

$$\dot{y} = \sum_{S=1}^{S=\infty} \sin \frac{S\pi x}{l} \left(\frac{S\pi c}{l}\right) B_s \cos \frac{S\pi\, ct}{l}.$$

and as $\dot{y} = \dot{y}_0$ *at* $t = 0$

$$\dot{y}_0 = \sin \frac{S\pi x}{l}. \left(\frac{S\pi c}{l}\right) B_s$$

Therefore, as in the case of plucked string

$$\int_0^l \dot{y}_0 \sin \frac{S\pi x}{l}.\, dx = B_s \int_0^l \frac{S\pi c}{l}.\, \sin^2 \frac{S\pi c}{l}.\, \sin^2 \frac{S\pi x}{l}.\, dx.$$

$$= B_s.\, \frac{l}{2}.\, \frac{S\pi c}{l} = B_s \frac{S\pi c}{2}.$$

$$B_s = \frac{2}{S\pi c} \int_0^l \dot{y}_0 \sin \frac{S\pi x}{l}.\, dx.$$

as $\dot{y} = \dot{y}_0$ at $t = 0$, between b and $b + db$

$$B_s = \frac{2}{S\pi c} \int_b^{b+db} \dot{y}_0 \sin \frac{S\pi x}{l}.\, dx.$$

Assuming $\dot{y}_0$ to be constant

$$B_s = \frac{2}{S\pi c}\, \dot{y}_0 \left[-\cos \frac{S\pi x}{l} \right]_b^{b+db} \frac{l}{-S\pi}.$$

$$= \frac{2l\, \dot{y}_0}{S^2\, \pi^2\, c}. \left[\cos \frac{S\pi b}{l} - \cos \frac{S\pi}{l} (b + db) \right]$$

$$= \frac{2l\, \dot{y}_0}{S^2\, \pi^2\, c}. \left[\cos \frac{S\pi b}{l} - \cos \frac{S\pi b}{l}.\, \cos \frac{S\pi db}{l} + \sin \frac{S\pi b}{l}.\, \text{Sin} \frac{S\pi db}{l} \right].$$

As $\left(\dfrac{S\pi\, db}{l}\right)$ is very small because db is small, we get

$$\sin \frac{S\pi\, db}{l} = \frac{S\pi\, db}{l} \text{ and } \cos \frac{S\pi\, db}{l} = 1$$

$$B_s = \frac{2l\, y_0}{S^2\pi^2\, c}\left[\sin \frac{S\pi b}{l}\right] \cdot \frac{S\pi\, db}{l}.$$

$$= \frac{2\dot{y}_0\, db}{S\pi\, c} \cdot \sin \frac{S\pi b}{l}.$$

If m is the mass per unit length of the string and μ is the momentum delivered by the hammer, then $\mu = m\, db.\, \dot{y}_0$

or $db.\, \dot{y}_0 = \mu/m$

$$\text{Hence } B_s = \frac{2}{S\pi c} \cdot \frac{\mu}{m} \cdot \sin \frac{S\pi b}{l}$$

Thus we obtain

$$y = \frac{2\mu}{\pi\, cm} \sum_{S=1}^{S=\infty} \frac{1}{S} \sin \frac{S\pi b}{l} \cdot \sin \frac{S\pi x}{l} \sin \frac{S\pi ct}{l}.$$

As the general solution for the struck string.

Interpretation

From equation (6.17) we note that as in the case of plucked string the Sth harmonic is absent if the string be struck at one of the nodes corresponding to this harmonic. In the case of plucked string the amplitude of the partials is inversely proportional to S^2, whereas in case of struck string it is inversely proportional to S; so the note is richer in nonintense harmonics and the note is more sonorous.

(c) *A typical example on struck string.* A string is struck by a hard hammer at a point such that $y = 0$ at $t = 0$

$$\dot{y}_0 = \frac{4\mu x}{l} \text{ between } x = 0 \text{ to } x = l/4$$

$$\dot{y}_0 = \frac{4\mu}{l}(l/2 - x) \text{ between } x = l/4 \text{ to } x = l/2.$$

$$\dot{y}_0 = 0 \text{ from } x = l/2 \text{ to } x = l.$$

Show that 4th, 8th, 12th harmonic etc. will be absent from the resultant vibration.

As before, the general equation of the vibration of the string fixed at the ends [see equation (6.12)]

$$y = \sum_{S=1}^{S=\infty} \sin \frac{S\pi x}{l}\left[A_s \cos \frac{S\pi ct}{l} + B_s \sin \frac{S\pi ct}{l}\right].$$

and, as $y=0$ when $t=0$ from the condition given, we get

$$A_s = 0$$

Therefore

$$B_s = \frac{2}{S\pi c}\int_0^l y_0 \sin\frac{S\pi x}{l}\,dx.$$

$$= \frac{2}{S\pi c}\left[\int_0^{l/4} \frac{4\mu x}{l}\sin\frac{S\pi x}{l}\,dx + \int_{l/4}^{l/2}\frac{4\mu}{l}\left(\frac{l}{2}-x\right)\sin\frac{S\pi x}{l}\,dx\right]$$

The first term on the R.H.S. after integration becomes

$$\frac{4\mu l}{S^2\pi^2}\sin\frac{S\pi}{4} - \frac{\mu l}{S\pi}\cos.\frac{S\pi}{4}.$$

and the 2nd term on the R.H.S. becomes after integration

$$\frac{\mu l}{S\pi}\cos\frac{S\pi}{4} - \frac{4\mu l}{S^2\pi^2}.\operatorname{Sin}\frac{S\pi}{2} + \frac{4\mu l}{S^2\pi^2}.\operatorname{Sin}\frac{S\pi}{4}.$$

$$\therefore B_s = \frac{2}{S\pi c}\left[\frac{4\pi l}{S^2\pi^2}.\sin\frac{S\pi}{4} - \frac{4\mu l}{S^2\pi^2}.\operatorname{Sin}\frac{S\pi}{2} + \frac{4\mu l}{S^2\pi^2}.\operatorname{Sin}\frac{S\pi}{4}\right].$$

$$= \frac{2}{S\pi c}\left[\frac{8\mu l}{S^2\pi^2}.\operatorname{Sin}\frac{S\pi}{4} - \frac{8\mu l}{S^2\pi^2}.\operatorname{Sin}\frac{S\pi}{4}.\operatorname{Cos}.\frac{S\pi}{4}\right].$$

$$= \frac{8\mu l}{\pi^3 c}\left[\frac{1}{S^3}\left\{2\operatorname{Sin}\frac{S\pi}{4} - \operatorname{Sin}\frac{S\pi}{2}\right\}\right].$$

$$\dot{y} = \frac{8\mu l}{\pi^3 c}\left[\sum_{S=1}^{S=\infty}\frac{1}{S^3}\operatorname{Sin}\frac{S\pi x}{l}\operatorname{Sin}\frac{S\pi ct}{l}\left\{2\sin\frac{S\pi}{4} - \sin\frac{S\pi}{2}\right\}\right].$$

$$= \frac{8\mu l}{\pi^3 c}\left[\frac{1}{1^3}\left\{2\operatorname{Sin}\frac{\pi}{4} - \sin\frac{\pi}{2}\right\}\operatorname{Sin}\frac{\pi x}{l}\sin\frac{\pi ct}{l}\right.$$

$$+\frac{1}{2^3}\left\{2\sin\frac{\pi}{2} - \sin\pi\right\}\sin\frac{2\pi x}{l}\sin\frac{2\pi ct}{l}$$

$$+\frac{1}{3^3}.\left\{2\sin\frac{3\pi}{4} - \operatorname{Sin}\frac{3\pi}{2}\right\}\operatorname{Sin}\frac{3\pi x}{l}\sin\frac{3\pi ct}{l}$$

$$+\frac{1}{4^3}\left\{2\sin\pi - 2\pi\right\}\operatorname{Sin}\frac{4\pi x}{l}\sin\frac{4\pi ct}{l}$$

$$+ \frac{1}{5^3}\left\{2 \sin \frac{5\pi}{4} - \sin \frac{5\pi}{2}\right\} \sin \frac{5\pi x}{l} \sin \frac{5\pi ct}{l} + \dots \Bigg]$$

$$\text{or } y = \frac{8\mu l}{\pi^3 c}\left[(\sqrt{2}-1) \sin \frac{\pi x}{l} \sin \frac{\pi ct}{l} + \frac{1}{8} 2 \sin \frac{2\pi x}{l} \sin \frac{2\pi ct}{l}\right.$$

$$+ \frac{1}{27}(1+\sqrt{2}) \sin \frac{3\pi x}{l} \sin \frac{3\pi ct}{l}$$

$$\left. + \frac{1}{125}(1+\sqrt{2}) \sin \frac{5\pi x}{l} \sin \frac{5\pi ct}{l} + \dots \right].$$

Hence 4th, 8th, 12th harmonic notes will be absent from the resultant vibration.

(*d*) *Piano string: a detailed treatment.* In the case of piano string, the cause of vibration is the blow of the hammer which is projected against the string and after the impact it rebounds. The hammer used to strike the piano forte string is covered with small layers of cloth for the express purpose of making them yielding and prolonging their contact.

Helmholtz remarks that since the actual yielding of the string must be slight in comparison with that of the covering of the hammer, the law of force called into play during the contact must be nearly the same as if the string was absolutely fixed. In that case, the force would change very nearly as a circular function. We shall, therefore, suppose that initially when $t=0$ and $y=0$, a force $F \sin pt$ begings to act upon the string at $x=b$ and continues to operate for half the period, as Helmholtz assumes that the time of contact is half the period ($t=\pi/p$) of the circular function. After this period, the string is free to execute its natural vibration. The differential equation of motion of the string is given by

$$\frac{d^2y}{dt^2} = c^2 \frac{d^2y}{dx^2}.$$

where $$c = \sqrt{T_1/m}.$$

This is satisfied over both parts into which the string is divided at the point, but is violated in crossing from one part to the other. Any solution of the above equation must satisfy the following conditions at the junction $x=b$.

(*a*) There is no discontinuous change in the value of y.

(*b*) The resultant tension acting at b must balance the impressed force.

Hence we get from the second condition the equation of motion as

$$\rho.\, dx. \frac{d^2y}{dt^2} = T_1 \,\Delta\left(\frac{dy}{dx}\right) + F \sin pt. \tag{6.18}$$

where $\Delta\,(dy/dx)$ denotes the variation of (dy/dx) incurred in crossing the point b in the positive direction. Equation (6.18) is true for all the points subjected to pressure, and hence for the particular point, as $dx \approx 0$, we have

$$T_1 \Delta \left(\frac{dy}{dx} \right) + F \sin pt = 0 \tag{6.19}$$

At all other points of the string the usual conditions hold.

On the assumption that y varies as $\sin pt$ we can assume the following solution for y

$$y = \sin \frac{px}{c} [A \cos pt + B \sin pt] \qquad \text{for } 0 < x < b$$

$$y = \sin \frac{p(l-x)}{c} [A' \cos pt + B' \sin pt] \qquad \text{for } b < x < l. \tag{6.20}$$

where A, B and A' and B' are constants to be determined from the boundary conditions of the problem. As $y = 0$ when $t = 0$ from the condition of the problem. $A = A' = 0$, and

$$y = \sin \frac{px}{c} B \sin pt \qquad \text{for } 0 < x < b$$

$$y = \sin \frac{p(l-x)}{c} B' \sin pt \qquad \text{for } b < x < l \tag{6.21}$$

From equation (6.21) putting $x = b$, and since they are both values of y at $x = b$,

$$\sin \frac{pb}{c} B \sin pt = \sin \frac{p(l-b)}{c} B' \sin pt$$

$$= r \sin pt.$$

where $\sin \frac{pb}{c} B = \sin \frac{p(l-b)}{c} B' = r$ (6.22)

From equation (6.21) we get,

$$\frac{\partial y}{\partial x} = \frac{p}{c} . \cos \frac{px}{c} . B \sin pt.$$

$$\left(\frac{\partial y}{\partial x} \right)_{x=b} = -\frac{p}{c} . \cos \frac{pb}{c} . B . \sin pt.$$

and also $\left(\frac{\partial y}{\partial x} \right)_{x=b} = -\frac{p}{c} . \cos \frac{p(l-b)}{c} . B' \sin pt.$

from the second equation. As from equation (6.22)

$$B = \frac{r}{\sin \frac{pb}{c}} \text{ and } B' = \frac{r}{\sin p \frac{(l-b)}{c}}$$

We get $\left(\frac{\partial y}{\partial x} \right) = \frac{p}{c} . \cos \frac{px}{c} . \frac{r}{\sin \frac{pb}{c}} . \text{Sin } pt.$

and also $$\left(\frac{\partial y}{\partial x}\right) = -\frac{p}{c}.\cos\frac{p(l-x)}{c}.\ \frac{r}{\sin\frac{p(l-b)}{c}}\sin pt. \tag{6.23}$$

$$\Delta\left(\frac{\partial y}{\partial x}\right)_{x=b} = -\left\{\frac{p}{c}r\left[\frac{\cos p(l-b)/c}{\sin p(l-b)/c}+\frac{\cos pb/c}{\sin pb/c}.\right]\sin pt\right\} \tag{6.24}$$

Since from equation (6.19)

$$T_1\,\Delta\left(\frac{\partial y}{\partial x}\right) + F.\sin pt = 0$$

we get,

$$T_1\,\frac{p}{c}.\,r\,\frac{\sin pl/c}{\sin p(l-b)/c.\ \sin pb/c} = F.$$

or $$r = \frac{F}{T_1}.\ \frac{\sin pb/c\ \sin p(l-b)/c}{p/c.\ \sin pl/c.}.$$

$$\therefore\quad y = \frac{F}{T_1}.\ \frac{\sin px/c\ \sin p(l-b)/c}{p/c.\ \sin pl/c}.\ \sin pt \text{ between } 0 < x < b.$$

and $$y = \frac{F}{T_1}.\ \frac{\sin p(l-x)/c\ \sin pb/c}{p/c.\ \text{Sin}\ pl/c.}\ \sin pt \text{ between } b < x < l. \tag{6.25}$$

In addition, we shall have the natural motion of the string; hence in general,

$$y = \frac{F}{T_1}.\ \frac{\sin px/c\ \sin p(l-b)/c}{p/c\ \sin pl/c,}\ \sin pt$$

$$+\sum_{S=1}^{S=\infty}\sin\frac{S\pi x}{l}\left[A_s\cos\frac{S\pi ct}{l}+B_s\sin\frac{S\pi ct}{l}\right]$$

for $x = 0$ to $x = b$. and

$$y = \frac{F}{T_1}\ \frac{\sin p(l-x)/c\ \sin pb/c}{p/c\ \sin pl/c}\ \sin pt$$

$$+\sum_{S=1}^{S=\infty}\sin\frac{S\pi x}{l}$$

$$\left[A_s\cos\frac{S\pi ct}{l}+B_s\sin\frac{S\pi ct}{l}\right]$$

for $x = b$ to $x = l$. (6.26)

Ist stage: The force commences at a time $t = 0$ when $y = 0$; so $A_s = 0$ and

$$\dot{y} = \frac{cF}{T_1} \cdot \frac{\sin px/c \sin p\,(l-b)/c}{\sin pl/c} . \cos pt + \sum_{S=1}^{S=\infty} \sin \frac{S\pi x}{l} \left(\frac{S\pi c}{l} \right) \cos \frac{S\pi ct}{l} . B_s .$$

Since $\dot{y}=0$ at $t=0$

$$\sum_{S=1}^{S=\infty} \sin \frac{S\pi x}{l} . \left(\frac{S\pi c}{l} \right) B_s = -\frac{cF}{T_1} . \frac{\sin px/c \sin p\,(l-b)/c}{\sin pl/c} .$$

from $x=0$ to $x=b$.

$$= -\frac{cF}{T_1} . \frac{\sin p\,(l-x)/c \sin pb/c}{\sin pl/c} .$$

from $x=b$ to $x=l$ (6.27)

Therefore

$$\frac{-S\pi T_1}{Fl} \int_0^l \sin^2 \frac{S\pi x}{l} dx.\ B_s . \sin \frac{pl}{c}$$

$$= \int_0^b \sin \frac{px}{c} \sin \frac{p\,(l-b)}{c} \sin \frac{S\pi x}{l} dx$$

$$+ \int_b^l \sin \frac{p\,(l-x)}{c} \sin \frac{pb}{c} . \sin \frac{S\pi x}{l} dx.$$

or

$$-\frac{S\pi T_1}{2F} . B_s . \sin \frac{pl}{c} = \int_0^b \sin \frac{px}{c} . \sin \frac{p\,(l-b)}{c} \sin \frac{S\pi x}{l} dx$$

$$+ \int_b^l \sin \frac{p\,(l-x)}{c} \sin \frac{pb}{c} \sin \frac{S\pi x}{l} dx.$$

The R.H.S. when integrated becomes $-\dfrac{pcl^2}{p^2\, l^2 - S^2\, \pi^2\, c^2} . \text{Sin} \dfrac{pl}{c} . \text{Sin} \dfrac{S\pi b}{l} .$

$$\therefore \quad B_s = \frac{2F}{S\pi T_1} \frac{pcl^2}{p^2\, l^2 - S^2\, \pi^2\, c^2} . \sin \frac{S\pi b}{l} . \tag{6.28}$$

2nd Stage. The pressure comes after a time $t=\pi/p$ and hence substituting $t=\pi/p$ in equation (6.26)

$$y = \sum_{S=1}^{S=\infty} B_s . \sin \frac{S\pi x}{l} \sin \frac{S\pi^2 c}{pl} \tag{6.29}$$

$$\dot{y} = \frac{cF}{T_1} \frac{\sin px/c \sin p\,(l - b)/c}{\sin pl/c} \cos pt$$

$$+ \sum_{S=1}^{S=\infty} \sin \frac{S\pi x}{l} B_s \cos \frac{S\pi ct}{l} . \left(\frac{S\pi c}{l}\right)$$

from $x = 0$ to $x = b$

and $$\dot{y} = \frac{cF}{T_1} . \frac{\sin p\,(l - x)/c.\ \sin pb/c.\ \text{cost}\ pt}{\sin pl/c}$$

$$+ \sum_{S=1}^{S=\infty} \sin \frac{S\pi x}{l} . B_s . \cos \frac{S\pi ct}{l} \left(\frac{S\pi c}{l}\right)$$

from $x = b$ to $x = l$.

When $t = \pi/p$

$$\dot{y} = \frac{\pi c}{l} \sum_{S=1}^{S=\infty} S.\ B_s.\ \sin \frac{S\pi x}{l} \cos \frac{S\pi^2 c}{pl} + r'$$

where $$r' = -\frac{cF}{T_1} . \frac{\sin px/c \sin p\,(l - b)/c}{\sin pl/c} .$$

from $x = 0$ to $x = b$.

and $$r' = -\frac{cF}{T_1} . \frac{\sin p\,(l - x)/c \sin pb/c}{\sin pl/c} .$$

from $x = b$ to $x = l$. (6.30)

3rd Stage. The string starts its natural motion with an initial displacement given by equation (6.29) and an initial velocity given by equation (6.30). The general solution for displacement of a string fixed at $x = 0$ to $x = l$ is given by

$$y = \sum_{S=1}^{S=\infty} \sin \frac{S\pi x}{l} \left[C_s \cos \frac{S\pi ct}{l} + D_s \sin \frac{S\pi ct}{l} \right] . \tag{6.31}$$

Thus, when $t = 0$ we get from equations (6.29) and (6.31)

$$C_s = B_s \sin \frac{S\pi^2 c}{pl} \tag{6.32}$$

and from equations (6.30) and (6.31), when $t = 0$

$$D_s = B_s \left[1 + \cos \frac{S\pi^2 c}{pl} \right] . \tag{6.33}$$

Putting the value of C_s from equation (6.32), and that of D_s from equation (6.33) becomes,

$$y = \sum_{S=1}^{S=\infty} \sin \frac{S\pi x}{l}.\ B_s \left\{ \sin \frac{S\pi^2 c}{pl} \cos \frac{S\pi ct}{l} + 2.\ \cos^2 \frac{S\pi^2 c}{2pl}.\ \sin \frac{S\pi ct}{l} \right\}$$

$$= 2 \sum_{S=1}^{S=\infty} B_s \cos \frac{S\pi^2 c}{2\ pl} \sin \frac{S\pi x}{l} \sin \frac{S\pi c}{l} \left[t + \frac{\pi}{2p} \right].$$

Thus the amplitude of vibration for the S-th harmonic

$$= 2\ B_s.\ \cos \frac{S\pi^2 c}{2\ pl}$$

which from equation (6.28) becomes

$$= \frac{4F}{S\pi\ T_1}.\ \frac{pcl^2}{p^2\ l^2 - S^2\ \pi^2\ c^2}.\ \sin \frac{S\pi b}{l}.\ \cos.\ \frac{S\pi^2 c}{2pl} \tag{6.34}$$

In order to understand the result deducible from the above expression we must refer back to the hypothesis made above, concerning the law of pressure during contact of the hammer with the string. The hypothesis is founded on the assumption that the impact may be simulated to that of an elastic body upon a hard obstacle. On this assumption, λ is the length of the hammer, μ the mass, $\mu\ k^2$ the moment of inertia about the axis on which it turns, θ the angle through which it turns before it strikes from rest at the time t; θ_0 and $\dot{\theta}_0$ the values of θ and $(d\theta/dt)$ at $t=0$; q is a constant depending upon the elasticity of the material of which the hammer is made; then the pressure during contact is $\lambda\ q\ (\theta - \theta_0)$. Then the equation of motion becomes

$$\mu\ K^2 \frac{d^2\theta}{dt^2} = -\ \lambda^2\ q\ (\theta - \theta_0). \tag{6.35}$$

$$\text{or } \mu\ K^2 \frac{d^2}{dt^2} (\theta - \theta_0) = -\ n^2 q\ (\theta - \theta_0)\ db^2$$

Assuming $(\theta - \theta_0) = A \sin pt$ we get

$$-Ap^2 \sin pt + \frac{\lambda^2 q}{\mu\ K^2} A \sin pt = 0$$

We have

$$p = \frac{\lambda}{K} \sqrt{\frac{q}{\mu}} \tag{6.36}$$

$$\left(\frac{d\theta}{dt}\right)_{t=0} = Ap = \dot{\theta}_0 = A \frac{\lambda}{K} \sqrt{\frac{q}{\mu}}$$

$$A = \dot{\theta}_0 / p$$

$$\therefore \quad (\theta - \theta_0) = \frac{\dot{\theta}_0}{p} \sin pt$$

$$\text{Pressure during contact} = \lambda\ q \frac{\dot{\theta}_0}{p} \sin pt$$

$$= \lambda\, q.\, \frac{\dot{\theta}_0}{\lambda}\, K \sqrt{\frac{\mu}{q}}\,.\, \sin pt$$

$$= q\, \dot{\theta}_0\, K \sqrt{\frac{\mu}{q}} \sin pt$$

and duration of contact $= \dfrac{\pi}{p} = \dfrac{\pi K}{\lambda} \sqrt{\dfrac{\mu}{q}}$

We have then $\dot{\theta}_0\, K \sqrt{q\mu} \sin pt = F.\ \sin pt.$

$$F = \dot{\theta}_0\, K \sqrt{q\mu}.$$

Hence the value of F depends on the velocity of the hammer at the beginning of impact as well as on its weight, material and form. But the value of p which determines the duration of contact depends only on the latter factors and not upon velocity.

Referring to equation (6.34) we note that it vanishes if $\sin s\pi b/l = 0$ or $Sb = ml$ where m is an integer. This shows that if the blow of the hammer is applied at any one of those points which divides the string into S equal parts, all the harmonic components of the tone which would have nodes at these points are extinguished. In general, the quality of the note produced which is determined by the comparative strength of its different component tones is independent of the momentum of the blow (which only affects the value of the coefficient F), but depends on the ratio b/l and c/pl, i.e. upon the place at which the blow is struck and upon the ratio of the duration of contact to the period of the fundamental tone of the string, i.e. $\pi c/2pl$. If we put ν for the latter ratio

$$\nu = \frac{\pi c}{2pl} \quad \text{or} \quad pl = \frac{\pi c}{2\,\nu}$$

Then equation (6.34) becomes

$$\frac{4F}{S\pi T_1}.\ \frac{\pi c^2 l/2\,\nu}{\left(\dfrac{\pi^2 c^2}{4\nu^2} - S^2\, \pi^2\, c^2\right)} \sin \frac{S\pi b}{l}.\ \cos S\pi\nu$$

$$-\ \frac{8Fl}{\pi^2\, T_1}\ \frac{\nu}{S\,(1 - 4\,S^2\,\nu^2)}.\ \sin \frac{S\pi b}{l}.\ \cos S\pi\nu.$$

and $\nu = \dfrac{\pi c}{2pl} = \dfrac{\pi c}{2l}\, \dfrac{K}{\lambda} \sqrt{\dfrac{\mu}{q}}.$

Thus ν depends upon the coefficient of elasticity and becomes very small if q is large, i.e. if the hammer is of a hard unyielding material; but the product

$p\nu$ is seen to be independent of q, so that the above expression for the amplitude becomes

$$\frac{A}{(1-4S^2\nu^2)}\sin\frac{S\pi b}{l}\cos S\pi\nu$$

where A depends upon the weight, form and velocity of the hammer but not upon its elasticity. If we suppose the hammer to be absolutely hard so that q is very large, and ν tends to zero, then the expression for amplitude becomes

$$\frac{A}{(1-4S^2\nu^2)}\sin\frac{S\pi b}{l}$$

(c) Bowed String

This is the case of a string excited by a bow. The motion of the violin string excited by bow has been studied by Helmholtz through his vibration microscope. The mathematical theory has been built up by him by a beautiful combination of mathematics supplemented by experimental data. His experimental observations yielded the following results.

(*a*) When the violin bow bites well, the vibrations are strictly periodic. The note excited has quite the same pitch as the natural note of the string. The vibrations although sustained are in some sense free. They have to depend for the maintenance on the energy drawn from the bow but the latter does not modify the tone.

(*b*) All component tones which have a node at the point of excitation are extinguished.

(*c*) All points of the string ascend and descend alternately. The velocity of ascend is constant and also that of descend though the two are different. The displacement diagram therefore consists of two parts. Two portions AC and CD of any wave are to one another as the two sections of a string which lie on either side of the observed point; hence the motion of the curve is a two-step zig-zag one. In Fig. 6.4, time is reckoned along the abscissa and the

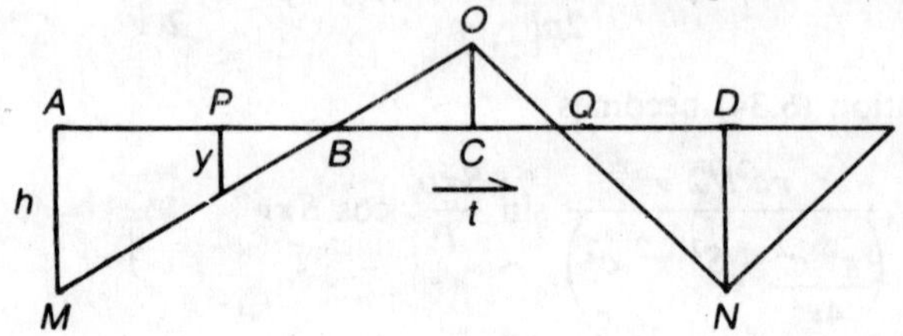

Fig. 6.4

displacement is along the ordinate, so that at A, $t=0$ at C, $t=\tau_0$ and at D, $t=\tau$ when τ is the complete period. Time is reckoned at the instant when the lowest point is at M.

Hence the displacement y between $t=0$ to $\tau=\tau_0$ is given by

$$\frac{y}{BP}=\frac{h}{AB}$$

$$\frac{y}{h} = \frac{BP}{AB}$$

Therefore

$$\frac{h-y}{y} = \frac{AP}{BP} = \frac{t}{BP}$$

and since tan $\angle ABM = -f$ and $BP = -y/f$

$y = ft + h$ between $t = 0$ to $t = \tau_0$ (6.39)

and $y = g(\tau - t) + h$ between $t = \tau_0$ to $t = \tau$

where $g = -\tan \angle DQN$. (6.40)

Hence at $t = \tau_0$, we get both equations (6.39) and(6.40) to be satisfied simultaneously. So we get

$$f\tau_0 + h = g(\tau - \tau_0) + h$$

or

$$f\tau_0 = f(\tau - \tau_0) \tag{6.41}$$

Now, if y is developed in terms of Fourier series, as

$$y = \sum_{S=1}^{S=\infty} \left[A_s \sin \frac{2S\pi t}{\tau} + B_s \cos \frac{2S\pi t}{\tau} \right] \tag{6.42}$$

where the constants A_s and B_s are to be determined from the boundary conditions, from Fourier's analysis we get,

$$A_s = \frac{2}{\tau} \int_0^\tau y \sin \frac{2S\pi t}{\tau} dt$$

$$B_s = \frac{2}{\tau} \int_0^\tau y \cos \frac{2S\pi t}{\tau} dt \tag{6.43}$$

Putting the values of y from (6.39) and (6.40)

$$A_s = \frac{2}{\tau} \left[\int_0^{\tau_0} (ft + h) \sin \frac{2S\pi t}{\tau} dt + \int_{\tau_0}^{\tau} \left\{ g(\tau - t) + h \right\} \sin \frac{2S\pi t}{\tau} dt \right]$$

The first integral on the R.H.S. becomes

$$\frac{\tau}{2S\pi} \left[(-f\tau_0 - h) \cos \frac{2S\pi\tau_0}{\tau} + h + \frac{f\tau}{2S\pi} \sin \frac{2S\pi\tau_0}{\tau} \right]$$

and the second integral on the R.H.S. becomes

$$-\frac{\tau}{2S\pi} h + \{g(\tau - \tau_0) + h\} \frac{\tau}{2S\pi} \cos \frac{2S\pi\tau_0}{\tau} + \frac{g\tau^2}{(2S\pi)^2} \cdot \sin \frac{2S\pi\tau_0}{\tau}.$$

Thus

$$A_s = \frac{2}{\tau} \left[\frac{\tau}{2S\pi} \left\{ \cos \frac{2S\pi\ \tau_0}{\tau} (-g[\tau - \tau_0]) + g[\tau - \tau_0] \right.\right.$$

$$+ \frac{\tau}{2S\pi} (f+g) . \sin \frac{2S\pi}{\tau} \tau_0 \Big] \Big]$$

$$= (f+g) \frac{\tau}{S^2 \pi^2} . \sin \frac{S\pi \tau_0}{\tau} . \cos \frac{S\pi\tau_0}{\tau} .$$

and in the same way, performing the integration on B_s it can be shown that

$$B_s = - \frac{(f+g) \tau}{S^2 \pi^2} \sin^2 \frac{S\pi\tau_0}{\tau} .$$

Hence from equation (6.42) we get,

$$y = \sum_{S=1}^{S=\infty} \frac{(f+g) \tau}{S^2 \pi^2} \sin \frac{S\pi\tau_0}{\tau} \left[\cos \frac{2S\pi\tau_0}{\tau} \sin \frac{2S\pi t}{\tau} - \cos \frac{2S\pi t}{\tau} \sin \frac{S\pi\tau_0}{\tau} \right]$$

$$y = \sum_{S=1}^{S=\infty} \frac{(f+g) \tau}{S^2 \pi^2} \sin \frac{S\pi\tau_0}{\tau} . \sin \frac{2S\pi}{\tau} \left(t - \frac{\tau_0}{2} \right)$$

$$= \frac{(f+g) \tau}{\pi^2} \sum_{S=1}^{S=\infty} \frac{1}{S^2} \sin \frac{S\pi \tau_0}{\tau} \sin \frac{2S\pi}{\tau} \left(t - \frac{\tau_0}{2} \right) . \quad (6.44)$$

In equation (6.44), y denotes the distance of the determinate point of the string from the position of rest. If x denotes the distance of the point from the beginning of the length of string l fixed at the extremities, then the general solution of the vibration of the string is given by

$$y = \sum_{S=1}^{S=\infty} \sin \frac{S\pi x}{l} \left[C_s \cos \frac{2S\pi}{\tau} \left(t - \frac{\tau_0}{2} \right) + D_s \sin \frac{2S\pi}{\tau} \left(t - \frac{\tau_0}{2} \right) \right] \quad (6.45$$

and comparing equations (6.45) and (6.44)

$$C_s = 0$$

$$D_s \sin \frac{S\pi x}{l} . \sin \frac{2S\pi}{\tau} \left(t - \frac{\tau_0}{2} \right) = \frac{(f+g)}{\pi^2} . \tau . \frac{1}{S^2} \sin \frac{S\pi\tau_0}{\tau} . \sin \frac{2S\pi}{\tau} \left(t - \frac{\tau_0}{2} \right)$$

$$\therefore \quad D_s = \frac{(f+g) \tau}{\pi^2} . \frac{1}{S^2} \frac{\sin S\pi\tau_0/\tau}{\sin S\pi x/l} . \quad (6.46)$$

Putting $S=1$ and $S=2$ in equation (6.46)

$$D_1 \sin \frac{\pi x}{l} = \frac{(f+g) \tau}{\pi^2} \frac{1}{1^2} . \sin \frac{\pi\tau_0}{\tau} .$$

and $$D_2 \sin \frac{2\pi x}{l} = \frac{(f+g) \tau}{\pi^2} \frac{1}{2^2} . \sin \frac{2\pi\tau_0}{\tau} .$$

$$\therefore \quad \frac{D_1 \sin \pi x/l}{D_2 \sin 2\pi x/l} = \frac{4 \sin \pi\tau_0/\tau}{2 \sin \pi\tau_0/\tau . \cos \pi\tau_0/\tau}$$

$$\therefore \quad \frac{D_2}{D_1} \cos \frac{\pi x}{l} = \frac{1}{4} . \cos \frac{\pi\tau_0}{\tau} \tag{6.47}$$

As the observation shows, when $x = \frac{l}{2}$, $\tau = \tau_0$

$$D_2 = \frac{1}{4} D_1 \tag{6.48}$$

and as $x = 0$, $\tau_0 = 0$ and $\frac{l}{x} = \frac{\tau}{\tau_0}$

$$\frac{l - x}{l} = \frac{\tau - \tau_0}{\tau} \tag{6.49}$$

If further $f\,\tau_0 = g\,(\tau - \tau_0) = 2r$ say

then $\qquad f = \frac{2r}{\tau_0}$ and $g = \frac{2r}{(\tau - \tau_0)}$

and as $\frac{l}{x} = \frac{\tau}{\tau_0}$, $(f+g) = \frac{2r\, l^2}{\tau\,(l - x)\, x}$.

$$\therefore \qquad r = \frac{(f+g)\, \tau\, (l - x)\, x}{2l^2}.$$

Calling the value of $r = P$, when $x = l/2$.

$$P = \frac{(f+g)\,\tau}{8} \text{ and hence } r = \frac{4P\,(l - x)\, x}{l^2}.$$

$$\therefore \qquad (f+g) = 8P/\tau$$

Then from equation (6.46), since $x/l = \tau_o/\tau$

$$D_s = \frac{(f+g)\,\tau}{\pi^2} \frac{1}{S^2}$$

so that

$$y = \sum_{S=1}^{S=\infty} \sin\left(\frac{S\pi x}{l}\right) \frac{8P}{\pi^2} . \frac{1}{S^2} \sin \frac{2S\pi}{\tau}\left(t - \frac{\tau_0}{2}\right).$$

$$= \frac{8P}{\pi^2} \sum_{S=1}^{S=\infty} \frac{1}{S^2} \sin \frac{S\pi x}{l} . \sin \frac{2S\pi}{\tau}\left(t - \frac{\tau_0}{2}\right) \tag{6.50}$$

which gives the complete expression for the motion of the string. We shall now determine the nature of the motion.

(1) When $t=\tau_0/2$, $y=0$ for all values of x, i.e. all parts of the string pass through their positions of rest simultaneously.

(2) From that time the velocity f of the point x is

$$f = \frac{2r}{\tau_0} = \frac{8P}{\tau_0} \cdot \frac{x\,(l-x)}{l^2}.$$

Since
$$\frac{x}{l} = \frac{\tau_0}{\tau},\ f = \frac{8P\,(l-x)}{l\tau} \tag{6.51}$$

and this velocity lasts from $t=0$ to $t=\tau_0$ as long as $t < \tau_0$ and

$$y = ft = \frac{8P\,(l-x)\,t}{l\tau} \tag{6.52}$$

(3) From this point, y returns with the velocity between $t=(\tau_o-\tau)$

$$g = \frac{2r}{\tau-\tau_0} = \frac{8Px\,(l-x)}{l^2\,(\tau-\tau_0)}$$

and since

$$\frac{l-x}{l} = \frac{\tau-\tau_0}{\tau}$$

$$g = \frac{8P}{l^2}\,\frac{l}{\tau}\,x = \frac{8Px}{l\tau} \tag{6.52}$$

and hence after a time $t=(\tau_0+t_1)$

$$y = \frac{8P}{l\tau}\,(l-x)\,\tau_o - \frac{8Px}{l\tau}\,t_1$$

$$= \frac{8Px}{l\tau}\,(\tau-t) \tag{6.53}$$

The deflection in one part of the string is given by equation (6.52) and that in the other part by equation (6.53). Both equations show that the form of the string is a straight line passing through $x=0$ in equation (6.52) and $x=l$ in equation (6.53), the two extremities. The point of intersection is given by

$$y = \frac{8P\,(l-x)\,t}{l\tau} = \frac{8Px}{l\tau}\,(\tau-t)$$

$$(l-x)\,t = x\,(\tau-t)$$

$$lt = x\tau$$

$$x = lt/\tau \tag{6.54}$$

Hence, the abscissa x of the point of intersection increases in proportion to time. The point of intersection or the highest point of the string passes therefore with a constant velocity from one end of the string to the other and during this interval describes a parabolic arc for which $y = 8Px\ (l - x)/l^2$. Thus the foot of the ordinate of the highest point moves backwards and forwards with a constant velocity on the horizontal line AC. The highest point B describes in succession two parabolic curves ABC and CDA. The string is always stretched along the two lines AB and BC or along AD and DC (Fig. 6.4).

When the string excited by the bow speaks well, the upper partial tones are produced and their intensity diminishes as $1/S^2$. All the partials excepting those having a node at the point of bowing are present. Little crumples on the vibration of figures usually perceived arise from damping and disappearance of the above mentioned tones.

Helmholtz's observations indicate that the note produced by bowing has the same pitch as the natural note of the string. The vibrations apparently forced by the bow may still be regarded as free. Although the energy for maintenance comes from the bow, the note is determined by the string. The intermittent dragging action of the bow serves to maintain the natural vibration of the string in the short intervening periods.

The foundation for the mechanical theory of vibration of bowed strings has been laid by the work of Raman and his associates. One of the outstanding questions which has not been cleared up is the manner in which the overtones of the bowed string are influenced by the position of the bowing point. The problem is complicated by other variable factors which influence the character of overtones, i.e. by bowing pressure and speed and width of the region of contact between the bow and the string. Raman has found in these investigations that the vibration curve of a point in the string departs slightly from two-step zigzag. One of the motions being uniform and the other fluttering; Young's theorem is verified, the amplitude of a partial being zero for bowing at its node and the phase of that partial passes discontinuously from $\pi/2$ to $-\pi/2$ as the bowing point passes that node.

Wolf-note. When the pitch of the note elicited from the string coincides with the fundamental or with an important harmonic of the wood or air of the body one would expect a large reinforcement of the former, the energy being furnished by the increased bowing pressure needed to maintain the same amplitude of the string. Under this circumstance, a quite special and undesirable effect is produced in which the control of the string seems to pass out of player's hands. The howling effect produced at this pitch has been given the name 'wolf-note'.

6.6 SPECIAL CASES IN THE VIBRATION OF STRINGS

If we take the effect of damping of the medium on the vibration of the string we get the equation of motion of the string as

$$\frac{\partial^2 y}{\partial t^2} + 2K.\frac{\partial y}{\partial t} = c^2.\frac{\partial^2 y}{\partial x^2} \tag{6.55}$$

The boundary conditions of the problem are:

(1) $y=0$ when $x=0$ or $x=l$
where l is the length of the string
(2) $y=f(x)$ when $t=0$
(3) $\dot{y}=0$ when $t=0$

If we assume the solution of the equation (6.55) as

$$y=e^{\alpha x+\beta t}$$

then
$$\frac{\partial y}{\partial t}=\beta e^{\alpha x+\beta t} \tag{6.56}$$

$$\frac{\partial^2 y}{\partial t^2}=\beta^2 e^{\alpha x+\beta t}$$

$$\frac{\partial^2 y}{\partial x^2}=\alpha^2 e^{\alpha x+\beta t}$$

Hence, substituting these values in equation (6.55)

$$\beta^2+2K\beta=\alpha^2 c^2$$

$$y=e^{\alpha x-(K\pm\sqrt{C^2\alpha^2+K^2})t}$$

$$=e^{-Kt}\, e^{\alpha x\pm\sqrt{C^2K^2+K^2}\,t} \tag{6.57}$$

Hence, the particular solutions of equation (6.55) are

$$\begin{aligned} y&=e^{-Kt}\sin\alpha x\cos\sqrt{c^2\alpha^2+K^2}\,t\\ &=e^{-Kt}\sin\alpha x\sin\sqrt{c^2\alpha^2+K^2}\,t\\ &=e^{-Kt}\cos\alpha x\cos\sqrt{c^2\alpha^2+K^2}\,t\\ &=e^{-Kt}\sin\alpha x\cos\sqrt{c^2\alpha^2+K^2}\,t \end{aligned} \tag{6.58}$$

As from the first boundary condition $y=0$ when $x=0$ the last two solutions of equation (6.58) are discarded; then the solution which satisfies the first boundary condition is given by

$$y=e^{-Kt}\sin\alpha x\cos\sqrt{c^2\alpha^2+K^2}\,t$$

and as $y=0$ when $x=l$, we get $\sin\alpha l=0=\sin S\pi$ where S is an integer.

Therefore
$$y=e^{-Kt}\sin\frac{S\pi x}{l}\cos\sqrt{\frac{S^2\pi^2c^2}{l^2}+K^2}.\,t$$

or in general

$$y=e^{-Kt}\sum_{S=1}^{S=\infty}A_s\sin\frac{S\pi x}{l}\cos\sqrt{\frac{S^2\pi^2c^2}{l^2}+K^2}\,t \tag{6.59}$$

where the value of A_s is given by Fourier analysis, as

$$A_s = \frac{2}{l} \int_0^l f(\lambda).\ \sin \frac{S\pi\lambda}{l}\, d\lambda.$$

$$\therefore\ y = \frac{l}{2}\, e^{-Kt} \sum_{S=1}^{S=\infty} \sin \frac{S\pi x}{l} \cos \sqrt{\frac{c^2S^2\pi^2}{l^2} + K^2}.\ t. \int_0^l f(\lambda).\ \sin \frac{S\pi\lambda}{l}\, d\lambda. \tag{6.60}$$

Let us now see whether this equation satisfies the condition

$$\dot{y} = 0 \text{ at } t = 0$$

Putting

$$n_S' = \sqrt{\frac{c^2S^2\pi^2}{l^2} + K^2}$$

$$y = e^{-Kt} \sum_{S=1}^{S=\infty} \sin \frac{S\pi x}{l} \cos n_s' t.\ A_s \tag{6.61}$$

$$\dot{y} = -Ke^{-Kt} \sum_{S=1}^{S=\infty} \sin \frac{S\pi x}{l} \cos n_s' t\ A_s' - e^{-Kt} \sum_{S=1}^{S=\infty} n_s' \sin \frac{S\pi x}{l} A_s \operatorname{Sin} n_s' t$$

When $t = 0$

$$\dot{y} = -K \sum_{S=1}^{S=\infty} \sin \frac{S\pi x}{l}.\ A_s$$

which is not equal to zero.

The solution which satisfies all the boundary conditions is thus given by

$$y = e^{-Kt} \sum_{S=1}^{S=\infty} \left\{ \cos n_s' t + \frac{K}{n_s'} \sin n_s' t \right\} \sin \frac{S\pi x}{l}.\ A_s. \tag{6.62}$$

$$y = e^{-Kt}.\ \frac{l}{2}.\ \sum_{S=1}^{S=\infty} \left[\cos \left(\sqrt{\frac{S^2\pi^2c^2}{l^2} + K^2} \right) t \right.$$

$$\left. + \frac{K}{\sqrt{\frac{S^2\pi^2c^2}{l^2} + K^2}} \sin \left(\sqrt{\frac{S^2\pi^2c^2}{l^2} + K^2} \right) t \right]$$

$$\times \sin \frac{S\pi x}{l} \int_0^l f(\lambda).\ \sin \frac{S\pi\lambda}{l}\, d\lambda \tag{6.63}$$

Every constituent vibration is thus damped and the note is discordant. If $K = 0$, we have the ideal solution

$$y = \frac{l}{2} \sum_{S=1}^{S=\infty} \sin \frac{S\pi x}{l} \cos \frac{S\pi ct}{l} \int_0^l f(\lambda).\ \sin \frac{S\pi\lambda}{l}\, d\lambda \tag{6.64}$$

In the case of vibration of a string when the two end supports are not rigid, i.e. vibration of a string which is subjected to yielding, y is not equal to zero when $x = 0$. If T_1 is the tension then the vertical component of tension is T_1

$\partial y/\partial x$ and if μ is the force per unit displacement,

We have, when $x=0$

$$\mu y = T_1 \frac{\partial y}{\partial x} \tag{6.65}$$

and when $x=l$, $\mu y = -T_1 \dfrac{\partial y}{\partial x}$ (6.66)

In general, the solution acceptable for the above differential equation is

$$y = A \sin(mx - \alpha) \cos(mct - \epsilon) \tag{6.67}$$

$$\frac{\partial y}{\partial x} = Am\,[\cos(mx - \alpha)] \cos(mct - \epsilon)$$

$$= Am\,[\cos mx \cos \alpha + \sin mx \sin \alpha] \cos(mct - \epsilon)$$

When $x=0$, $\dfrac{\partial y}{\partial x} = Am \cos \alpha \cos(mct - \epsilon)$.

Hence from equation (6.65)

$$-\mu A \sin \alpha \cos(mct - \epsilon) = T_1\, Am \cos \alpha \cos(mct - \epsilon)$$

$$\therefore \quad -\sin \alpha = \frac{T_1}{\mu}\, m . \cos \alpha$$

or

$$\tan \alpha = -\frac{T_1}{\mu}\, m \tag{6.68}$$

When $x=l$,

$$A \sin(ml - \alpha) . \cos(mct - \epsilon) \tag{6.69}$$

$$= -\frac{T_1}{\mu}\, Am \cos(mct - \epsilon) \cos(ml - \alpha)$$

$$\therefore \quad \tan(ml - \alpha) = -\frac{T_1}{\mu}\, m = \tan \alpha \text{ from (6.68)}$$

Then

$$\tan(ml - \alpha) = \tan(S\pi + \alpha)$$

$$\therefore \quad ml - \alpha = S\pi + \alpha$$

$$\therefore \quad S\pi = ml + 2 \tan^{-1}\left(\frac{T_1\, m}{\mu}\right) \tag{6.70}$$

Further, we have $mc = 2\pi\nu$ where ν is the natural frequency. If the support is very stiff, μ is large and T_1/μ is very small. We can then write

$$\tan^{-1}\left(\frac{T_1\, m}{\mu}\right) = T_1 \frac{m}{\mu}$$

$$S\pi = ml + \frac{2T_1\, m}{\mu}$$

$$= m\left[l + \frac{2T_1}{\mu}\right]$$

Hence the frequency of the *S*th harmonic is given by

$$\frac{SC/2}{l + \dfrac{2T_1}{\mu}}. \tag{6.71}$$

Hence equation (6.71) shows that energy is communicated to some distance beyond the supports because the length of string becomes now $l + 2T_1/\mu$. If μ is infinitly high then l remains the same. The general solution of the equation is thus given by

$$y = \sum_{S=1}^{S=\infty} A_s \psi_s \cos(2\pi\nu_s t - \epsilon).$$

where $$\psi_s = \sin\left[\frac{2\pi\nu_s x}{c} + \tan^{-1}\left(\frac{2\pi\nu_s T_1}{c\mu}\right)\right]$$

A_s and ϵ are to be determined from the boundary conditions of the problem.

In case of rigid support, if the effective mass is M, the equations of motion are

$$M.\frac{d^2y}{dt^2} + \mu y = T_1\frac{\partial y}{\partial x} \text{ when } x = 0 \tag{6.73}$$

and $$M.\frac{d^2y}{dt^2} + \mu y = -T_1\frac{\partial y}{\partial x} \text{ when } x = l.$$

As before, if we assume $y = A \operatorname{Sin}(mx - \alpha)\cos(mct - \epsilon)$, then from equation (6.73)

$$\begin{aligned} &-MAm^2c^2 \sin(mx - \alpha)\cos(mct - \epsilon) \\ &+\mu A \sin(mx - \alpha)\cos(mct - \epsilon) \\ &= T_1 Am \cos(mx - \alpha)\cos(mct - \epsilon). \end{aligned} \tag{6.74}$$

$$\text{when } x = 0,\ Mm^2c^2 \sin\alpha - \mu\sin\alpha = T_1.m.\cos\alpha$$

$$\tan\alpha = \frac{mT_1}{[Mm^2c^2 - \mu]}$$

when $x = l$, we get

$$\tan(ml - \alpha) = \frac{mT_1}{[Mm^2c^2 - \mu]}$$

$$\therefore \quad (ml - \alpha) = S\pi + \alpha$$

or $$ml + 2\tan^{-1}\left(\frac{mT_1}{\mu - Mm^2c^2}\right) = S\pi$$

If $\mu = 1$, we see the effect will be a decrease of length by

$$\frac{1}{1 - 2T_1/McS^2\pi^2 l}$$

Further, it can be shown that if μ is $\neq m^2c^2M$ an approximation leads to the result

$$\nu_s = \frac{Sc}{2}\left[l + \frac{2T_1 l}{\mu l^2 - \pi^2 S^2 cM}\right]$$

for the lower allowed frequency and final approximation leads to the actual result, viz. $\nu_s = Sc/2l$.

6.7 ENERGY OF THE VIBRATING STRING

By calculating the kinetic energy and the potential energy of the vibrating string it is possible to find out the total energy of the string. Assuming the expression for the displacement of the vibrating string as

$$y = A_1 \sin\frac{\pi x}{l}\cos\frac{\pi ct}{l} + A_2 \sin\frac{2\pi x}{l}\cos\frac{2\pi ct}{l}$$

$$+ A_3 \sin\frac{3\pi x}{l}\cos\frac{3\pi ct}{l} + \ldots\ldots \tag{6.76}$$

we get, if $U_s = \sin\dfrac{S\pi x}{l}$ and $\phi_s = A_s \cos\dfrac{S\pi ct}{l}$,

$$y = \phi_1 U_1 + \phi_2 U_2 + \phi_3 U_3 + \ldots\ldots \tag{6.77}$$

where ϕ_1, ϕ_2 etc. are called normal coordinates and U_1, U_2 etc. are called normal functions

$\therefore$
$$y = \sum_{S=1}^{S=\infty} \phi_s U_s \tag{6.78}$$

and
$$\dot{y} = \sum_{S=\infty}^{S=\infty} \dot{\phi} U_s \tag{6.79}$$

as ϕ_s are functions of time.

Kinetic energy
$$\dot{T} = \int_0^l \frac{1}{2}\rho\,\dot{y}^2\,dx.$$

$$= \frac{1}{2}\rho.\int_0^l \left[\sum \dot{\phi}_s \sin\frac{S\pi x}{l}\right]^2 dx.$$

$$= \frac{1}{2}\rho.\int_0^l \sum_{S=1}^{S=\infty} \dot{\phi}_s^2 \sin^2\frac{S\pi x}{l}\,dx$$

$$= \frac{\rho l}{4}\sum_{S=1}^{S=\infty} \dot{\phi}_s^2 \tag{6.80}$$

Potential energy $V=\frac{T_1}{2}\int_0^l\left(\frac{\partial y}{\partial x}\right)^2 dx$

$$=\frac{T_1}{2}\int_0^l\sum_{S=1}^{S=\infty}\left[\phi_s^2\,\frac{S^2\pi^2}{l^2}\cos^2\frac{S\pi x}{l}\right]dx$$

$$=\frac{T_1 l}{4}\sum_{S=1}^{S=\infty}\phi_s^2\,\frac{S^2\pi^2}{l^2} \tag{6.81}$$

But $T_1=c^2\rho$

$$\therefore \quad V=\frac{1}{4}\,c^2\rho l\sum_{S=1}^{S=\infty}\phi_s^2\,\frac{S^2\pi^2}{l^2}$$

Hence the total energy

$$W=T+V=\frac{1}{4}\,\rho l\left\{\sum_{S=1}^{S=\infty}\dot{\phi}_s^2+c^2\phi_s^2\,\frac{S^2\pi^2}{l^2}\right\}$$

$$=\frac{M}{4}\left\{\sum_{S=1}^{S=\infty}\frac{l^2}{S^2\pi^2c^2}\,\dot{\phi}_s^2+\phi_s^2\right\}\frac{S^2\pi^2c^2}{l^2}$$

where M is the mass of the string.

But as $\phi_s=A_s\cos\frac{S\pi ct}{l}+B_s\sin\frac{S\pi ct}{l}$.

$$\dot{\phi}_s^2\,\frac{l^2}{S^2\pi^2c^2}=A_s^2\cos^2\frac{S\pi ct}{l}+B_s^2\sin^2\frac{S\pi ct}{l}-2A_sB_s\cos\frac{S\pi ct}{l}.\sin\frac{S\pi ct}{l}$$

$$\therefore \quad \left\{\dot{\phi}_s^2\,\frac{l^2}{S^2\pi^2c^2}+\phi_s^2\right\}=A_s^2+B_s^2$$

$$\therefore \quad W=\frac{M}{4}\sum_{S=1}^{S=\infty}\left[A_s^2+B_s^2\right]\frac{S^2\pi^2c^2}{l^2}$$

Since $\quad \frac{1}{T_s}=\frac{Sc}{2l}$

$$W=\pi^2M\sum_{S=1}^{S=\infty}\frac{A_s^2+B_s^2}{T_s^2}$$

7

VIBRATION OF BARS AND TUNING FORKS

Just as in the case of strings, bars are also capable of vibration either longitudinally or in a transverse fashion. We shall, however, first consider the transverse vibration of a bar because this mode of vibration is important in considering and understanding the vibration of tuning forks. In the case of string, tension is the important factor which controls the vibration but if the ratio of diameter to length of the wire be increased then the stiffness becomes of more relative importance than tension and in our following discussion we shall assume the effect of tension to be negligible.

7.1 TRANSVERSE VIBRATION OF BAR

In our treatment of the transverse vibration of a bar it will be assumed that the bar is straight and uniform in cross-section and density and is not subjected to tension or compression. Further, it is assumed that the amplitude of motion is so small that the rotatory effect can be neglected. The x-axis is taken along the length of the bar and the assumed vibrations are taking place in the y-axis so that if R denotes the radius of curvature then

$$\frac{1}{R} = \frac{d^2y/dx^2}{[1 + (dy/dx)^2]^{3/2}}$$

and if it is assumed that $\left(\dfrac{dy}{dx}\right)$ is small compared to unity then the curvature can be taken as

$$\frac{1}{R} = \frac{d^2y}{dx^2}$$

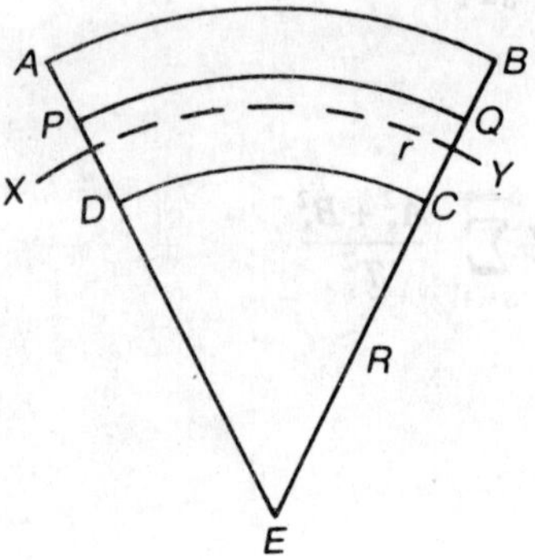

Fig. 7.1

In calculating the equation of motion we require first of all the expression for the bending moment of the bar. Let $ABCD$ represent the cross-section of a bar in its bent position and let YER, the radius of curvature and let the angle $\theta = \angle AEB$. Let XY represent the neutral filament of the bar so that the filaments above XY are extended whereas the filaments below XY are contracted. Let us take a filament PQ at a distance r from XY and let $XY = dx$ and if Δ is the extension of PQ then $PQ = dx + \Delta$ and let ω represent the area of cross-section of the filament. Then we get

$$\theta = \frac{dx}{R} = \frac{dx+\Delta}{R+r}$$

$$dx.\ r = R.\ \Delta.$$

$$\Delta = dx.\ \frac{r}{R}$$

Thus the strain $= \dfrac{\Delta}{dx} = \dfrac{r}{R} = r.\ \dfrac{d^2y}{dx^2}.$

If Y denotes the Young's modulus of the material of the wire, the stress $= Y\ r.\ \dfrac{d^2y}{dx^2}$. So the force acting on the filament $= Y.\ r.\ \dfrac{d^2y}{dx^2}.\ \omega$ and the moment of the force about the neutral axis is given by $Y.\ r^2.\ \dfrac{d^2y}{dx^2}\ \omega$. Hence the total moment M of all horizontal tensile and compressive stresses acting perpendicular to the section AC is

$$M = Y\frac{d^2y}{dx^2}\sum r^2\omega = Y.\ AK^2\ \frac{d^2y}{dx^2} \tag{7.1}$$

where A = area of the cross-section and K the radius of gyration about XY. In order to find a relation between the bending moment M, the shearing force F and the forces applied to the bar, we observe that if ρ is the density of the material of the bar and A the area of cross-section the force acting on the filament dx is

$$\rho.\ A\ dx.\ \frac{d^2y}{dt^2} = dF$$

or

$$\rho.\ A.\ \frac{d^2y}{dt^2} = \frac{dF}{dx} \tag{7.2}$$

If, further, the angular motion of the bar is considered, since a transverse slice of thickness dx is rotated through an angle θ where $\theta = \dfrac{dy}{dx}$, and I is the moment of inertia we get,

$$I\frac{d^2\theta}{dt^2} = dM + F.\ dx. \tag{7.3}$$

$$\rho.\ dx.\ AK^2\ \frac{d^2\theta}{dt^2} = dM + F.\ dx. \tag{7.3}$$

or
$$\rho.\ AK^2.\ \frac{d^2\theta}{dt^2} = \frac{dM}{dx} + F.$$

$$\rho\ AK^2.\ \frac{d^4y}{dx^2\ dt^2} = \frac{dM}{dx} + F. \tag{7.4}$$

$$\rho\ AK^2.\ \frac{d^5y}{dx^3\ dt^2} = \frac{d^2M}{dx^2} + \frac{dF}{dx}.$$

$$\rho\ AK^2.\ \frac{d^5y}{dx^3\ dt^2} = \frac{d^2M}{dx^2} + \rho\ A.\ \frac{d^2y}{dt^2} \tag{7.5}$$

and
$$\frac{d^2M}{dx^2} = Y.\ A\ K^2.\ \frac{d^4y}{dx^4}.$$

Thus equation (7.5) reduces to

$$\rho\ AK^2\ \frac{d^5y}{dx^3\ dt^2} = Y.\ AK^2\ \frac{d^4y}{dx^4} + \rho.\ A.\ \frac{d^2y}{dt^2}.$$

The term on the left hand side denotes the effect of rotatory motion of the bar and so if we neglect the effect of rotation,

$$YAK^2\ \frac{d^4y}{dx^4} + \rho.\ A.\ \frac{d^2y}{dt^2} = 0.$$

or
$$\frac{Y}{\rho}\ K^2.\ \frac{d^4y}{dx^4} + \frac{d^2y}{dt^2} = 0 \tag{7.6}$$

$$\frac{d^2y}{dt^2} + c^2.\ K^2.\ \frac{d^4y}{dx^4} = 0.$$

where $c = \sqrt{\frac{Y}{\rho}}$ is the velocity of longitudinal waves in a bar. This equation is identical with that obtained by Lord Rayleigh from the full equation and discarding the effect of ratatory intertia.

7.2 BOUNDARY CONDITIONS

The ends of the bar may be fixed, free or supported. At a fixed end it is clear that for all values of t, we have $y = 0$ and $\frac{dy}{dx} = 0$. Whereas in case of a free end, y and $\frac{dy}{dx}$ are arbitrary but as there is nothing beyond the free end to produce a couple or transmit force there cannot be any bending moment or shearing force at a free end. We then get the following conditions at a free end.

At the free end, y and dy/dx are arbitrary

$$\frac{d^2y}{dx^2} = \frac{d^3y}{dx^3} = 0$$

Further if the end is supported, there cannot be any displacement so that $y = 0$ but there can be slope so that dy/dx is not zero. In this case, the only external force added by the constraint is applied at the end and consequently has no moment there. Thus there is no curvature at the supported end and hence. $d^2y/dx^2 = 0$.

7.3 SOLUTION OF THE GENERAL EQUATION

Following Lord Rayleigh we assume that the motion in a bar is harmonic. Then y can be put as $y = a \cos nt$ (7.7)

From equation (7.6) $$\frac{d^4y}{dx^4} = \frac{\rho n^2}{Y K^2} y = m^4 y \tag{7.8}$$

If further $y = Ue^{\alpha x}$ then α is a root of m^4.
i.e. $\alpha = \pm\, m$ or $\pm\, im$. Hence the complete solution is given by

$$y = (A \cosh mx + B.\ \sinh mx + C.\ \cos mx + D \sin mx) \cos nt \tag{7.9}$$

This expression involving the constants A, B, C and D gives the amplitude at the point x and these constants as well as the value of m can be determined by the end conditions and when m is determined we obtain the value of frequency $n/2\pi$ from equation (7.8).

7.4 CONDITIONS AT ENDS

The ends of the bar may be fixed, free or supported; at a fixed end we have for all values of t,

$$y = 0 \text{ and } \frac{dy}{dx} = 0 \tag{7.10}$$

At a free end, on the contrary, y and dy/dx are arbitrary. But as there is nothing beyond to produce a couple to transmit force there can be at the end neither bending moment nor shearing force. Then from equation (7.1),

$$\frac{d^2y}{dx^2} = 0 \text{ and } \frac{d^3y}{dx^3} = 0 \tag{7.11}$$

At the supported end there can be no displacement but any slope however is allowed. In this case, only external force aided by the constraint is applied at the end and consequently there can be no moment there. Thus there can be no curvature and so the condition is

$$y=0 \text{ and } \frac{d^2y}{dx^2}=0 \tag{7.12}$$

CASE 1: Bar free at both ends – Consider a bar of length l; free at both ends taking the origin at middle point, the end conditions are

$$\frac{d^2y}{dx^2}=\frac{d^3y}{dx^3}=0 \text{ at } x=\pm l/2.$$

Then from equation (7.9) we get,

$$\tan\frac{ml}{2}= -\tan h.\ \frac{ml}{2}. \tag{7.13}$$

In the case of symmetrical vibrations, when $y=(A\cos h\, mx+C\cos mx)$ cost nt the roots of the equation (7.13) are obtained by graphical construction. If graphs are plotted with $y=\tan ml/2$ and $y=\tan h.\ ml/2$, the intersections of these curves are found to be closely represented by

$$x=\frac{ml}{2}=\left(S-\frac{1}{4}\right)\pi+\beta \tag{7.14}$$

where $S=1, 2, 3$, etc. and β a small quantity only appreciable in case of fundamental. Then

$$m=\frac{2\pi\ (S-1/4)}{l}.$$

and from equation (7.8) $m=[\rho n^2/YAK^2]^{1/4}$
Consequently the frequency of vibration is given by

$$N=\frac{n}{2\pi}=\frac{\pi\ (4S-1)^2}{8}\ \frac{K}{l^2}\sqrt{\frac{Y}{\rho}} \tag{7.15}$$

From equation (7.15) we note that

(1) Frequency N is approximately proportional to $(4S-1)^2$ i.e. the frequencies are proportional to 3^2, 7^2, 11^2 and 15^2 etc. The overtones are therefore not harmonics as in the case of vibration of strings.
(2) The frequency N is inversely proportional to square of the length of the bar, i.e. the velocity of transverse vibration is dependent on frequency.
(3) The frequency is proportional to longitudinal velocity in bar, i.e.

$$N\propto\sqrt{\frac{y}{\rho}}\propto C.$$

CASE 2: Bar fixed at both ends – By applying the conditions for fixed bar,

$y=0$ and $\frac{dy}{dx}=0$, we obtain the same condition as in the case of free-free bar.

CASE 3: Bar clamped at one end – At the clamped end, $(x= -l/2)$ we must have $y=0$ and $\frac{dy}{dx}=0$ and at the free end $(x=l/2)$, $\frac{d^2y}{dx^2}=\frac{d^3y}{dx^3}=0$

Applying these conditions we get,

$$\tan\frac{ml}{2}=\pm\cot h.\ \frac{ml}{2} \tag{7.16}$$

which can be solved graphically. The intersections of curves, $y=\tan.\ \frac{ml}{2}$ and $y=\coth.\ ml/2$ give

$$\frac{ml}{2}=\left(S\pm\frac{1}{4}\right)\pi+\beta. \tag{7.17}$$

where $S=$ 1, 2, 3, etc. and β is a small quantity.

Then $m=2\pi\left(S\pm\frac{1}{4}\right)$, for overtones neglecting β.

$$=\left[\frac{\rho n^2}{YK^2}\right]^{1/4}$$

$$N=\frac{n}{2\pi}=\frac{\pi\,(4S\pm1)^2}{8}\frac{K}{l^2}\sqrt{\frac{Y}{\rho}}. \tag{7.18}$$

Here also the frequencies of the overtones are proportional to 3^2, 5^2, 7^2 etc. having 1, 2, 3 nodes in addition to the clamped end. The frequencies are again inversely proportional to square of the length of the bar. The frequencies are proportional to longitudinal velocity in the bar.

CASE 4. Bar supported at both ends – We have the end equations at $(x=\pm l/2)$, $y=0$ and $\frac{d^2y}{dx^2}=0$ and then from equation (7.9)

$$\frac{ml}{2}=\frac{S\pi}{2}\quad (S=1, 2, 3, 4, \text{etc.})$$

$$N=\frac{\pi S^2}{2}\frac{K}{l^2}\sqrt{\frac{Y}{\rho}} \tag{7.19}$$

Hence the frequencies of the overtones are proportional to squares of natural numbers, inversely proportional to square of the length and directly proportional to velocity of sound.

7.5 ENERGY OF A VIBRATING BAR

The potential energy of the bar is equal to 1/2 (stress × strain).

$$dV = \frac{1}{2}\,(\text{stress} \times \text{strain})$$

$$\text{Strain} = \frac{r}{R} = r.\,\frac{d^2y}{dx^2}$$

$$\text{Stress} = Y.\,r.\,\frac{d^2y}{dx^2}.\,\omega$$

$$dV = \frac{1}{2}\,YAK^2\,\frac{1}{R^2}\,dx = \frac{1}{2}\,YAK^2.\left[\frac{d^2y}{dx^2}\right]^2 dx$$

The total potential energy becomes $V = \frac{1}{2}\,YAK^2 \int \left[\frac{d^2y}{dx^2}\right]^2 dx$

The kinetic energy $T = \frac{1}{2}\int \rho A \left(\frac{dy}{dt}\right)^2 dx$

$$+\frac{1}{2}\int \rho AK^2.\left[\frac{d}{dt}\left(\frac{\partial y}{\partial x}\right)^2\right] dx$$

The first term is due to strain and the second term is due to rotation; neglecting rotation we get the kinetic energy equal to

$$T = \frac{1}{2}\int \rho.\,A.\left(\frac{dy}{dt}\right)^2 dx$$

Hence the total energy becomes

$$E = T + V = \frac{1}{2}\,\rho\,A\left[\int_0^l \left\{\dot{y}^2 + \frac{YK^2}{\rho}.\left(\frac{\partial^2 y}{\partial x^2}\right)^2\right\} dx\right] \qquad (7.20)$$

From equation (7.9) the general equation of vibration of the bar is given by

$$y = \sum_{S=1}^{S=\infty} S_s\,U_s \cos\,(n_s t + \epsilon_s) \qquad (7.21)$$

where $U_s = \cos\,(mx)$

Then the kinetic energy is given by

$$T = \frac{1}{2}\,\rho\,A \int_0^l \dot{y}^2\,dx$$

$$= \frac{1}{2}\rho A \int_0^l \sum_{S=1}^{S=\infty} C_s^2\, U_s^2 \sin^2(n_s t+\epsilon_s)\, n_s^2\, dx$$

$$= \sum_{S=1}^{S=\infty} \frac{1}{2}\rho A\, C_s^2 \sin^2(n_s t+\epsilon_s)\, n_s^2 \int_0^l \cos^2 mx\, dx$$

$$= \frac{1}{2}\sum_{S=1}^{S=\infty} C_s^2\, \rho.\, A\, 4\, \pi^2\, \nu_s^2 \sin^2(n_s t+\epsilon_s) \int_0^l \left(\frac{1+\cos 2\,mx}{2}\right) dx$$

$$= \sum_{S=1}^{S=\infty} C_s^2\, \rho\, Al.\, \pi^2\, \nu_s^2 \sin^2(2\pi\, \nu_s t+\epsilon_s).$$

In the same manner, potential energy is given by

$$V = \frac{1}{2}\, YAK^2 \int_0^l \left(\frac{\delta^2 y}{\delta x^2}\right)^2 dx$$

$$= \frac{1}{2}\, YAK^2 \int_0^l \left[\sum_{S=1}^{S=\infty} C_s^2\, (m^2 \cos mx)^2\right] dx.\, \cos^2(n_s t+\epsilon_s)$$

$$= \frac{1}{2}\, YAK^2 \int_0^l C_s^2\, m^4 \sum_{S=1}^{S=\infty} \cos^2 mx\, dx.\, \cos^2(n_s t+\epsilon_s)$$

$$V = YAK^2\, C_s^2 \sum_{S=1}^{S=\infty} \cos^2(n_s t+\epsilon_s).\, l/2.$$

but $m^4 = \rho n^2/YK^2$

Then the potential energy $= V = \sum_{S=1}^{S=\infty} \pi^2\, \nu_s^2\, \rho\, \omega\, l\, C_s^2 \cos^2(n_s t+\epsilon_s).$

So the total energy becomes

$$W = \sum_{S=1}^{S=\infty} 2\, \pi^2\, \frac{\rho AL}{2}.\, \nu_s^2\, C_s^2 \tag{7.22}$$

7.6 TUNING FORKS

Though for a long time, the utility of tuning fork was recognised, the experimental development of tuning fork is due to Konig who succeeded in making tuning forks of great purity of tone and covering a wide range of frequencies. Some of the tuning forks developed by Konig had a frequency as high as 90,000 c/s. In recent times tuning forks are growing in importance as standards of frequency in acoustical determinations. In the electrically driven fork they serve to control electrical circuits so as to form standards of electrical frequency of high accuracy. Forks are now commonly used as substandards of time. The period of vibration of a fork is a constant quantity and serves as a convenient subdivision of a second when time intervals have to be measured with great accuracy.

Tuning forks have been regarded by different workers in different ways. Chladni regarded it as developed from a free-free bar by bending it in the form of an U. Rayleigh considered it as consisting of two clamped free bars mounted on a heavy stiff block of metal. Considered from the point of view of a free-free bar, it is shown in Fig. (7.2). It will be seen that when the bar is straight,

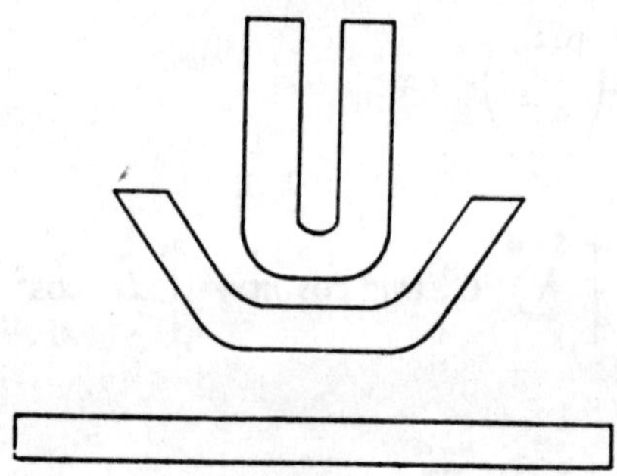

Fig. 7.2

the nodes are situated at *n, n* and when the bar is gradually bent at the middle the nodes approach each other. When the limbs are parallel the arrangement forms a tuning fork and as the nodes are very near each other the amplitude of vibration at the antinode at the middle point of the bend is small compared to the vibrations at the prong; when a stem is added at the bend between the nodes it has the effect of adding mass at the antinode and of increasing the stiffness of that portion of the fork between the two nodes. This results in the further approach of the nodes towards the stem and of reducing the vibration at the stem. When the tuning fork is used to excite vibration in the resonance box or a sounding board the stem attached to the fork is gently pressed on the board and the small vibration of the stem communicates vibration to the sounding body. Similar results may be obtained by considering a tuning fork as a made up of two clamped free bars. The frequency of the fork in case of a rectangular clamped free bar of thickness t will be given by

$$N = (1\cdot 1937)^2 \frac{\pi}{8} \frac{t}{\sqrt{12}} \frac{1}{l^2} \sqrt{\frac{Y}{\rho}}. \tag{7.20}$$

$$= 8 \cdot 24 \times 10^4 .\ t/l^2$$

where $\sqrt{\dfrac{Y}{\rho}} = 51 \times 10^4$ cm/s. in case of steel.

Thus the frequency of the fork will vary as inverse of square of length and directly as thickness of the fork and velocity of sound in the material of the fork.

7.7 TEMPERATURE EFFECT ON FREQUENCY

Change of temperature is one of the serious causes of the change of frequency. of the fork. This is due to change in the elastic property of the fork and its dimensions due to heat. Let α be the coefficient of linear expansion and β be the coefficient of decrease of Young's modulus with rise of temperature. Then from equation (7.20) we get

$$N_t = (1 \cdot 1937)^2 \frac{\pi}{8} \frac{t\,(1+\alpha\theta)}{\sqrt{12}} \frac{1}{l^2\,(1+2\alpha\theta)} \cdot \sqrt{\frac{Y\,(1-\beta\theta)}{\rho\,(1-3\,\alpha\theta)}} .$$

$$= (1 \cdot 1937)^2 \frac{\pi}{8\sqrt{12}} \frac{t}{l^2} \sqrt{\frac{Y}{\rho}} .\ (1+\alpha\theta)\,(1-2\,\alpha\theta).\left(1-\frac{\beta\theta}{2}\right)$$

$$\left(1+\frac{3\alpha\theta}{2}\right).$$

$$= (1 \cdot 1937)^2 \frac{\pi}{8\sqrt{12}} \frac{t}{l^2} \sqrt{\frac{Y}{\rho}} .\ (1+\alpha\theta-2\,\alpha\theta).\left(1-\frac{\beta\theta}{2}+\frac{3\alpha\theta}{2}\right)$$

$$= (1 \cdot 1937)^2 \frac{\pi}{8\sqrt{12}} \frac{t}{l^2} \sqrt{\frac{Y}{\rho}} \left\{(1-\alpha\theta)\,(1-\frac{\beta\theta}{2}+\frac{3\alpha\theta}{2}\right\}.$$

$$= (1 \cdot 1937)^2 \frac{\pi}{8\sqrt{12}} \frac{t}{l^2} \sqrt{\frac{Y}{\rho}} .\left[(1-\alpha\theta)+\frac{3\alpha\theta}{2}-\frac{\beta\theta}{2}\right]$$

$$= (1 \cdot 1937)^2 \frac{\pi}{8\sqrt{12}} \frac{t}{l^2} . \sqrt{\frac{Y}{\rho}} . \left\{(1-\frac{\beta-\alpha}{2}\,\theta\right\}$$

$$\text{as } N = (1 \cdot 1937)^2 \frac{\pi}{8\sqrt{12}} \frac{t}{l^2} \sqrt{\frac{Y}{\rho}}$$

$$N_t = N_0\left(1-\frac{(\beta-\alpha)}{2}.\,\theta\right) \tag{7.21}$$

Konig experimentally found that the temperature coefficient of frequency, namely $\frac{N_t - N_0}{N_0\,\theta} = -\frac{\beta - \alpha}{2}$ is approximately $1{\cdot}12 \times 10^{-4}$ per degree celsius from which the temperature coefficient of Young's modulus is given by $\beta = 0{\cdot}000236$.

7.8 ELECTRICALLY MAINTAINED TUNING FORK

A tuning fork may be maintained in a constant state of vibration with the help of an electromagnet. The tuning fork is fixed to a stand with an electromagnet M between the prongs. The battery B is connected as shown in Fig. 7.3. A steel

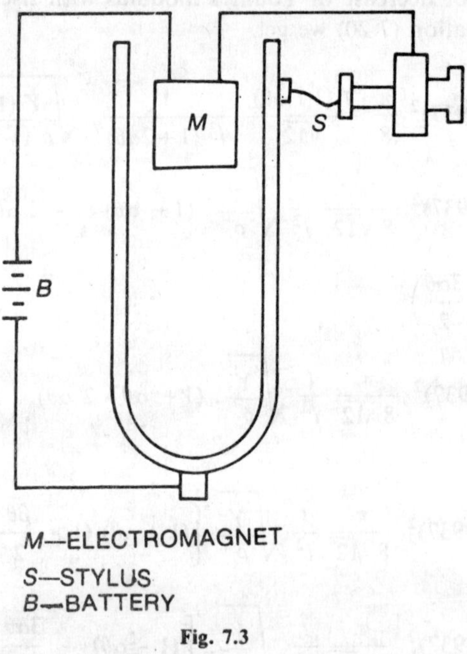

Fig. 7.3

stylus S is attached to the tuning fork which dips into a container containing mercury and the electric circuit is thereby completed. When the current passes, the electromagnet gets magnetised and the prongs are drawn towards the magnet. Due to attraction, the stylus is drawn away from the mercury cup and the electric contact is broken. Consequently the magnet becomes demagnetised and the prongs fall back to their original position. Again the contact is restored and the process is repeated.

Valve maintained tuning fork. Beyond 100 c/s, the above method of maintaining a tuning fork in constant vibration is not practicable and Eccles[1] described a method of maintaining the fork in vibration for frequencies above 1000 c/s.

In this arrangement (Fig. 7.4) a valve is taken and the tuning fork *M* is

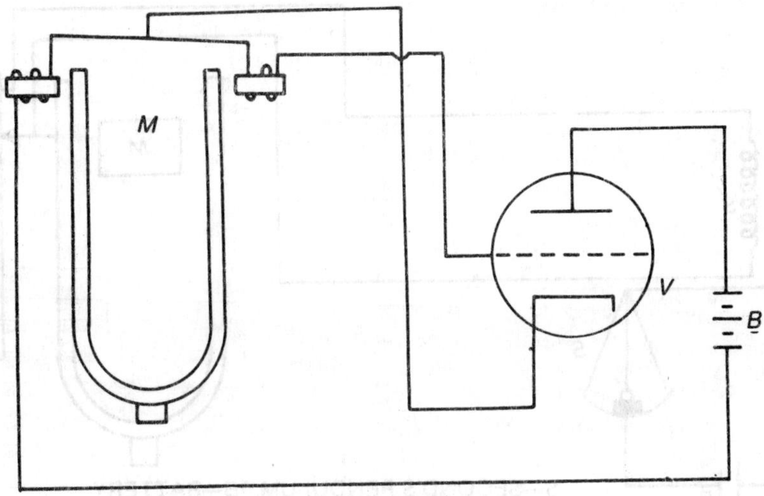

Fig. 7.4

placed between the two electromagnets which are placed in the grid and plate circuit respectively, the windings of the two being in opposite directions. As soon as the plate current flows in the plate circuit the electromagnet is energised and the tuning fork is drawn towards it. The movement of the fork induces voltage in the grid circuit which controls the plate current and causes a variation of the same. This variation causes a change in the magnetic strength of electromagnet and in its turn will cause the tuning fork to vibrate and in the same way the vibration of the fork is maintained. (Butterworth[2]).

7.9. DETERMINATION OF FREQUENCY OF TUNING FORK

The following methods may be utilised for the determination of the frequency of the tuning fork.

(1) By chronograph

An aluminium stylus is attached to the tuning fork which draws a wave curve in a smoked paper rolled round a cylinder which is made to rotate with hand, and as it rotates it goes up along the screw so that wave curves may not overlap; a coil is introduced into the tuning fork circuit and it is coupled inductively to a primary circuit completed as shown in Fig. 7.5. As soon as the second's pendulum touches the mercury cup a current flows in the primary circuit which produces a momentary current in the secondary; consequently a spark passes between the stylus and the smoked paper and the soot is removed. Since the time period is two seconds, we get a mark after each second. The number of waves between two marks gives us the number of waves per second and hence the frequency of the fork.

(2) Falling plate method

A smoked glass plate is made to fall vertically while a light stylus attached

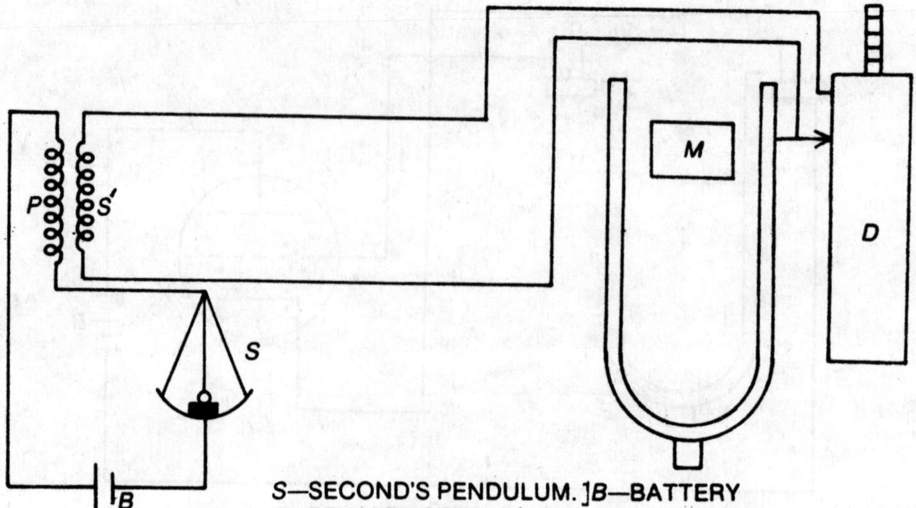

Fig. 7.5

to the fork discribes a wavy curve against it. Since the plate falls slowly first and then rapidly its velocity will increase and the traced curve will be as shown in Fig. 7.6.

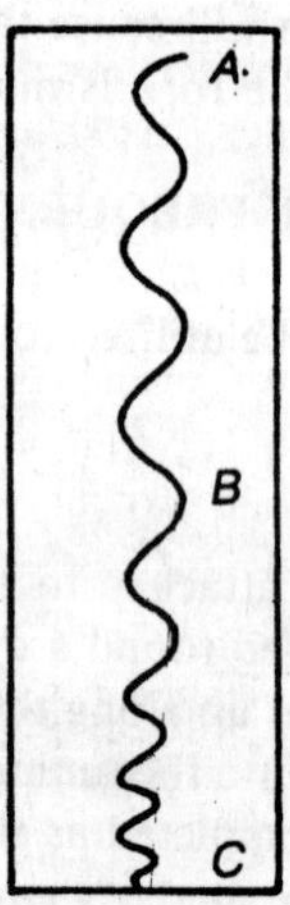

Fig. 7.6

Points *A B* and *C* are marked in the paper such that the number of waves *m* contained between *A* & *B* = number of waves contained between *B* and *C*; *n* = frequency of the fork; velocity of the paper when it crosses *A* is *U*.

$$\frac{1}{n} = \text{time for one vibration.}$$

$\therefore \frac{m}{n}$ = time for m vibrations.

$\therefore \frac{2m}{n}$ = time for 2 m vibrations.

Then if $d_1 = AB$ and $d_2 = BC$.

$$\text{there } d_1 = U.\frac{m}{n} + \frac{1}{2}g.\left(\frac{m}{n}\right)^2.$$

$$d_1 + d_2 = U.\frac{2m}{n} + \frac{1}{2}\,2\delta g.\left(\frac{2m}{n}\right)^2.$$

$$= \frac{2m\,U}{n} + 2g.\frac{m^2}{n^2}.$$

$$2d_1 = \frac{2m\,U}{n} + g.\frac{m^2}{n^2}.$$

$$d_2 - d_1 = g.\frac{m^2}{n^2}.$$

$$\text{or } n = m\sqrt{\frac{g}{(d_2 - d_1)}}.$$

(3) Phonic wheel method

It is meallic wheel and above it there is a soft iron armature with a number of slots dug longitudinally (Fig. 7.7). The wheel is placed between an elec-

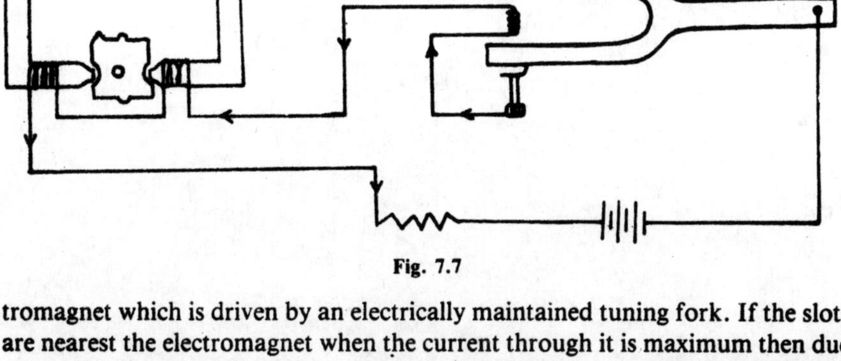

Fig. 7.7

tromagnet which is driven by an electrically maintained tuning fork. If the slots are nearest the electromagnet when the current through it is maximum then due to two equal and opposite forces the wheel will rotate with constant speed. If after P revolutions there is an arrangement to ring a bell and if the time interval is t then the time of revolution of the wheel is t/p. During one revolution the wheel is magnetised m times where m = number of slots in the armature. The interval between two successive excitations is t/Pm. This must equal the time taken by the fork to make one Oscillation, i.e.

$$\frac{1}{n} = \frac{t}{Pm}$$

$$\text{or } n = Pm/t$$

Thus n can be determined.

REFERENCES

1. Eccles, W.H. (1919), *Proc. Phys. Soc.* London, **31**, 269.
2. Butterworth (1920), *Proc. Phys. Soc.* London, **32**, 345.

8

VIBRATION OF MEMBRANES AND RINGS

8.1 CASE OF STRETCHED MEMBRANES

As stringed instruments are sources of sound so also are the membranes and as the vibrating strings are always kept under a tension so the vibrating membranes are always kept stretched; sound instruments employing membranes find extensive use in musical instruments. A theoretical membrane is defined as a thin and perfectly flexible solid sheet of uniform material and thickness. It is stretched in all directions in its plane by a tension which is great enough so as not to be altered when the membrane vibrates in its own plane. Considered from this point of view, the vibration of the membrane is very similar to that of a string but now the vibrations extend over a surface and not along a line as in the case of a string. In general, vibration of three types of membranes are of interest to us, viz. rectangular, square and circular. We shall deal with the case of rectangular membrane first.

8.2 RECTANGULAR MEMBRANE

Let *ABCD* in Fig. 8.1 represent a rectangular membrane the sides *AD* and *AB* being parallel respectively to *x* and *y*-axis and let the plane *xy* be tangential to

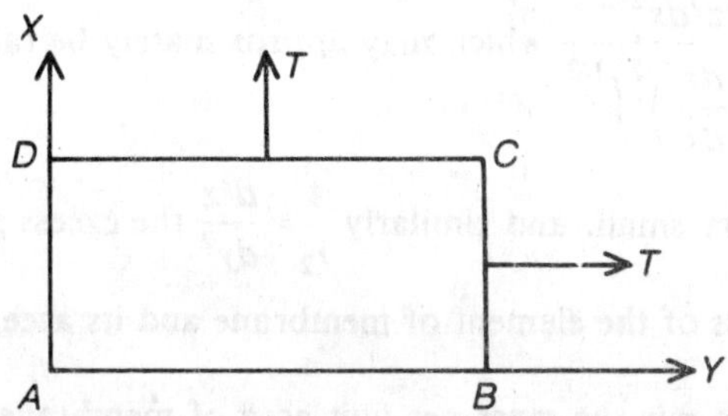

Fig. 8.1

the surface. Let the length of the two sides of the rectangle be *a* and *b* respectively. To form the differential equation of the vibration of the membrane, we need a relation between the curvature of an element of the surface and the restoring force thereby called into play. Let us imagine each point of the element in question to experience an infinitesmal normal displacement. Then the work done is the product of the excess pressure on the concave side and the increment in volume described by the element. Let the displacement be denoted by

dz and the radia of curvature of the surface be r_1 and r_2. If P denotes the excess pressure, then the work done dw is given by

$$dw = P\,ab\,dz \tag{8.1}$$

To obtain the increment of the surface area as a consequence of the displacement, we need an expression for the increase in length of each side of the rectangle. Thus

$$\frac{a}{r_1} = \frac{a+da}{r_1+dz} \tag{8.2}$$

Hence $$da = \frac{a}{r_1}\,dz \text{ and similarly } db = \frac{b}{r_2}\,dz. \tag{8.3}$$

The expression dw for the work done can be equated to the work done by tension, which is the product of tension and the increment in area. The expression for the later is $T_1\,d\,(ab)$.

Hence work done by tension is $T_1\,d\,(ab) = T_1\,bda + T_1\,adb$.

Substituting the expressions for da and db

$$\text{work done} = T_1\,b.\,\frac{a}{r_1}\,dz + T_1\,a.\,\frac{b}{r_2}\,dz$$

$$dw = T_1\,ab\left(\frac{1}{r_1} + \frac{1}{r_2}\right)dz. \tag{8.4}$$

Equating the expressions in equations (8.1) and (8.4)

$$P = T_1\left[\frac{1}{r_1} + \frac{1}{r_2}\right]. \tag{8.5}$$

If the displacement parallel to z-axis, be taken as z

then $\dfrac{1}{r_1} = \dfrac{d^2z/dx^2}{\left\{1+\left(\dfrac{dz}{dx}\right)^2\right\}^{3/2}}$ which may approximately be taken as

$\dfrac{d^2z}{dx^2}$ as $\left(\dfrac{dz}{dx}\right)$ is very small. and similarly $\dfrac{1}{r_2} = \dfrac{d^2z}{dy^2}$ the excess pressure P is the product of the mass of the element of membrane and its acceleration so that

$P = \sigma.\,ab\,\dfrac{d^2z}{dt^2}$ where σ is the mass per unit area of membrane and the restoring force is $T_1\left\{\dfrac{d^2z}{dx^2} + \dfrac{d^2z}{dy^2}.\right\}ab.$

Hence from equation (8.5) we get,

$$\sigma.\,ab.\,\frac{d^2z}{dt^2} = T_1\left\{\frac{d^2z}{dx^2} + \frac{d^2z}{dy^2}\right\}ab.$$

$$\frac{d^2z}{dt^2}=\frac{T_1}{\sigma}\left\{\frac{d^2z}{dx^2}+\frac{d^2z}{dy^2}\right\}.$$

$$=c^2\left\{\frac{d^2z}{dx^2}+\frac{d^2z}{dy^2}\right\} \tag{8.6}$$

where $c=\sqrt{\dfrac{T_1}{\sigma}}.$

If we assume a solution $z=e^{i(\alpha x+\beta y+rt)}$

then from equation (8.6) we get,

$$r^2\,e^{i(\alpha x+\beta y+rt)}=c^2\,[\alpha^2+\beta^2]\,e^{i(\alpha x+\beta y+rt)}.$$

$$r^2=c^2\,(\alpha^2+\beta^2)$$

$$r=\pm c\,(\alpha^2+\beta^2)^{1/2}$$

$$\therefore \quad z=e^{i\{\alpha x+\beta y\pm c\sqrt{\alpha^2+\beta^2}t\}}. \tag{8.7}$$

or $\quad z=\sin\,(\alpha x+\beta y\pm ct\,\sqrt{\alpha^2+\beta^2}\,)$

or $\quad =\cos\,(\alpha x+\beta y\pm ct\,\sqrt{\alpha^2+\beta^2}\,).$ (8.8)

We get these values of z as a particular solution of (8.6), the values of α and β being unrestricted. From these relations, we can get the solutions of the following types:

$$\begin{aligned}
z&=\sin\alpha x\,\sin\beta y\,\sin rt\\
&=\sin\alpha x\,\sin\beta y\,\cos rt\\
&=\sin\alpha x\,\cos\beta y\,\sin rt\\
&=\sin\alpha x\,\cos\beta y\,\cos rt\\
&=\cos\alpha x\,\sin\beta y\,\sin rt\\
&=\cos\alpha x\,\sin\beta y\,\cos rt\\
&=\cos\alpha x\,\cos\beta y\,\sin rt\\
&=\cos\alpha x\,\cos\beta y\,\cos rt.
\end{aligned} \tag{8.9}$$

each of which will satisfy equation (8.6).

In case of a membrane, we have the general condition that $z=0$ when $x=0$ for all values of t and also $z=0$ when $y=0$ for all values of t. Of the solutions given by equation (8.9) the last four are discarded as they do not make $z=0$ when $x=0$ also the next upper two are discarded as they do not make $z=0$ when $y=0$. So the first two are only retained and we get

$$\begin{aligned}
z&=\sin\alpha x\,\sin\beta y\,\sin rt\\
z&=\sin\alpha x\,\sin\beta y\,\cos rt
\end{aligned} \tag{8.10}$$

In case of rectangular membrane, $z=0$ when $x=0$ as well as when $x=a$; also $z=0$ when $y=0$ as well as when $y=b$. Then from equation (8.10)

$$0=\sin\alpha a\,\sin\beta y\,\sin rt$$

$$\therefore \quad \alpha a=m\pi.$$

where m is an integer, and similarly $\beta b=n\pi$, where n is also an integer.

$$z = \sin \frac{m\pi x}{a} \sin \frac{n\pi y}{b} \sin c\pi t \sqrt{\frac{m^2}{a^2} + \frac{n^2}{b^2}}.$$

$$z = \sin \frac{m\pi x}{a} \sin \frac{n\pi y}{b} \cos c\pi t \sqrt{\frac{m^2}{a^2} + \frac{n^2}{b^2}}. \tag{8.11}$$

The more general solution is given by

$$z = \sum_{m=1}^{m=\infty} \sum_{n=1}^{n=\infty} \sin \frac{m\pi x}{a} \sin \frac{n\pi y}{b} [A_{mn} \cos pt + B_{mn} \sin pt] \tag{8.12}$$

where $p^2 = c^2\pi^2 \left(\frac{m^2}{a^2} + \frac{n^2}{b^2}\right)$.

8.3 INITIAL CONDITIONS

Let the initial displacement and velocity be given by

$$z_0 = f_1 (x, y) \text{ when } t = 0$$

$$\dot{z}_0 = f_2 (x, y) \text{ when } t = 0 \tag{8.13}$$

Hence the constants of the equation (8.12) must be chosen so as to satisfy equation (8.13).

Then from (8.12) $z_0 = f(x, y) = \sum_{m=1}^{m=\infty} \sum_{n=1}^{n=\infty} \sin \frac{m\pi x}{a} \sin \frac{n\pi y}{b} . A_{mn}$.

Hence, from Fourier's analysis,

$$A_{mn} = \frac{4}{ab} \int_0^a \int_0^b z_0 \sin \frac{m\pi x}{a} \sin \frac{n\pi y}{b} \, dx \, dy \tag{8.14}$$

Also differentiating equation (8.12) and putting $t = 0$ and equating to the second equation in (8.13)

$$\dot{z}_0 = f_2 (x, y) = \sum_{m=1}^{m=\infty} \sum_{n=1}^{n=\infty} \sin \frac{m\pi x}{a} \sin \frac{n\pi y}{b} \, dx \, dy . p . B_{mn}$$

and consequently

$$B_{mn} = \frac{4}{ab\,p} \int_0^a \int_0^b \dot{z}_0 \sin \frac{m\pi x}{a} \sin \frac{n\pi y}{b} \, dx \, dy \tag{8.15}$$

NODAL LINES

When either m or n is equal to or greater than unity, nodal lines will occur in the membrane, i.e. for these lines $z = 0$. The positions are given by

$$x = \frac{a}{m}, \frac{2a}{m}, \frac{3a}{m} \ldots\ldots \frac{(m-1)\,a}{m} \tag{8.16}$$

$$y = \frac{b}{n}, \frac{2b}{n}, \frac{3b}{n} \ldots\ldots \frac{(n-1)\,b}{n}.$$

The nodal system therefore divides the membrane into *mn* equal parts.

8.4 DISCUSSION OF THE RESULT

(1) From equation (8.12) it is clear that as z is not a periodic function of time, a vibrating rectangular membrane will not in general give a musical note.

(2) A stretched rectangular membrane can be made to produce a musical note by starting the vibration properly. For, if the initial circumstances are such that the solution reduces to a single term as will be the case if the initial distortion in our general problem is given by

$$f(x, y) = A_{mn} \sin \frac{m\pi x}{a} \sin \frac{n\pi y}{b}$$

then the vibration will be periodic and the time period of vibration will be given by,

$$T = \frac{2}{c\,[m^2/a^2 + n^2/b^2]^{1/2}}$$

Since T is a function of m and n where m and n are any whole numbers, the same membrane is capable of giving a great variety of musical notes of different pitches. If m and n are both equal to unity, we get the lowest tone which the membrane is capable of giving and which is called its fundamental tone. Its period is given by

$$T_1 = \frac{2}{c\,[\,1/a^2 + 1/b^2]^{1/2}} = \frac{2\,ab}{c\,[a^2 + b^2]^{1/2}}.$$

If m and n are both equal to K,

$$T_k = \frac{2ab}{cK\,(a^2 + b^2)^{1/2}}.$$

so the membrane can be made to produce any harmonic of its fundamental note. Moreover, as we have

$$T_{mn} = \frac{2}{c\,[m^2/a^2 + n^2/b^2]^{1/2}}$$

is the period of any note that the membrane can give, and since m and n are replaced by mK and nK

then

$$T_{mn} = \frac{2}{cK\,[m^2/a^2 + n^2/b^2]^{1/2}}.$$

the membrane can sound all the harmonics of the fundamental note.

(3) In the case referred to above, where the solution reduces to a single term,

$$z = \sin\frac{m\pi x}{a}\sin\frac{n\pi y}{b}\left[A_{mn}\cos c\pi t\sqrt{\frac{m^2}{a^2}+\frac{n^2}{b^2}} + B_{mn}\sin c\pi t\sqrt{\frac{m^2}{a^2}+\frac{n^2}{b^2}}\right].$$

If $x = \frac{a}{m}, \frac{2a}{m}, \frac{3a}{m} \ldots\ldots \frac{(m-1)\,a}{m}$ then $z = 0$ for all values of t and the lines $x = \frac{a}{m}, \frac{2a}{m}, \frac{3a}{m} \ldots\ldots (m-1)\,a/m$ remain at rest during the whole motion and are known as nodes. The same is true for the lines $y = \frac{b}{n}, \frac{2b}{n}, \frac{3b}{n} \ldots\ldots (n-1)\,b/n$. Thus the nodal lines divide the membrane into mn equal parts.

8.5 SQUARE MEMBRANE

To treat the case of square membrane, we are simply to put $a = b$ in the preceding equations. We then find the frequencies and nodal lines by giving different values to m and n. The displacement of a square membrane can thus be written as

$$z = \frac{\sin m\pi x}{a}\sin\frac{n\pi y}{a}\cos pt. \tag{8.17}$$

The frequencies are correspondingly given by

$$N_{mn} = \frac{p}{2\pi} = \frac{c}{2a}(m^2+n^2)^{1/2} \tag{8.18}$$

Prime tone: $m = n = 1$ The lowest tone or the fundamental is given by $m = n = 1$

then $$z = \sin\frac{\pi x}{a}\sin\frac{\pi y}{a}\cos pt \tag{8.19}$$

and the frequency $$N_{11} = \frac{c}{2a}\sqrt{2}. \tag{8.20}$$

The nodal lines are found from equation (8.18) by putting $z = 0$ for all values of t. Hence we get,

$$\sin\frac{\pi x}{a}\sin\frac{\dot{\pi} y}{a}=0 \tag{8.21}$$

Hence either $\sin\frac{\pi x}{a}=0$ or $\sin\frac{\pi y}{b}=0$

So the equation (8.21) gives the lines whose equations are $x=0$, $x=a$, $y=0$, $y=$ a (a i.e. the side of the square). So for the fundamental tone there are no other nodal lines.

Second tone: The next higher tone is obtained by putting $m=1$, and $n=2$ or $m=2$ and $n=1$. In either case the frequency will be given by

$$N_{12}=N_{21}=\frac{C}{2a}\sqrt{5} \tag{8.22}$$

Thus in this case, two distinct vibrations are possible whose periodic times are the same. If these two exist simultaneously, nodal lines will be obtained provided the vibrations are in the same phase. The whole motion can now be represented by the equation

$$z=\left[C\sin\frac{2\pi x}{a}\sin\frac{\pi y}{b}+D\sin\frac{\pi x}{a}\sin\frac{2\pi y}{b}\right] \tag{8.23}$$

To get the nodal lines, putting $z=0$, we get,

$$\sin\frac{\pi x}{a}\sin\frac{\pi y}{a}\left[C\cos\frac{\pi x}{a}+D\cos\frac{\pi y}{a}\right]=0$$

which gives for nodal lines $x=0$, $x=a$, $y=0$, $y=a$ which are the sides of the square. Further, the equation $C\cos\frac{\pi x}{a}+D\cos\frac{\pi y}{a}$ gives the equation of a curve which always passes through the centre of a square. In special cases it reduces to the diagonal of the square and the conditions for this are evidently $C=0$, $C+D=0$, $D=0$.

The other higher notes can be similarly obtained.

8.6 ENERGY OF A VIBRATING MEMBRANE

The kinetic energy of the membrane is given by

$$T=\frac{\sigma}{2}\iint\left(\frac{dz}{dt}\right)^2 dx\,dy.$$

The length of one side of the membrane becomes $dx\left[1+\left(\frac{\partial z}{\partial x}\right)^2\right]^{1/2}$ and that of the other side $dy\left[1+\left(\frac{\partial z}{\partial y}\right)^2\right]^{1/2}$ and so the area becomes $dx\left[1+\left(\frac{\partial z}{\partial x}\right)^2\right]^{1/2}$ $dy\left[1+\left(\frac{\partial z}{\partial y}\right)^2\right]^{1/2}$ and hence the new area is given by

$$dx\,dy+\frac{1}{2}\left[\left(\frac{\partial z}{\partial x}\right)^2+\left(\frac{\partial z}{\partial y}\right)^2\right]dx\,dy$$

Thus increase in area is $\dfrac{dx\,dy}{2}\left[\left(\dfrac{\partial z}{\partial x}\right)^2+\left(\dfrac{\partial z}{\partial y}\right)^2\right]$

$$\text{Potential energy}=\frac{T_1}{2}\iint\left[\left(\frac{\partial z}{\partial x}\right)^2+\left(\frac{\partial z}{\partial y}\right)^2\right]dx\,dy$$

$$\text{and Total energy}=\frac{1}{2}\left[\sigma\iint\left(\frac{\partial z}{\partial t}\right)^2 dx\,dy+T_1\iint\left[\left(\frac{\partial z}{\partial x}\right)^2+\left(\frac{\partial z}{\partial y}\right)^2\right]dx\,dy\right] \tag{8.24}$$

8.7 CASE OF CIRCULAR MEMBRANE

When the fixed boundary of the membrane is circular, the first step towards the solution of the problem is to express the general differential equation in polar coordinates.

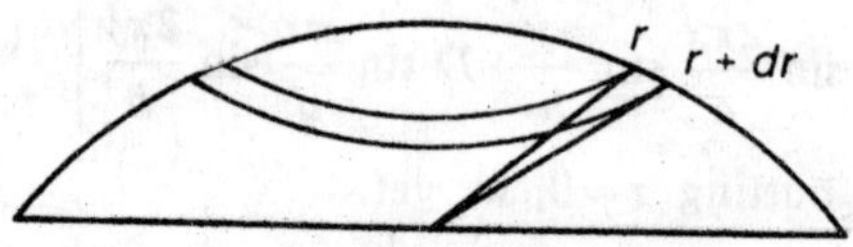

Fig. 8.2

The complete tension at r is $2\pi rT_1$ whose vertical component is

$$2\pi rT_1\frac{dz}{dr}+\frac{d}{dr}\left(2\pi rT_1\frac{dz}{dr}\right)\delta r=2\pi rT_1\frac{dz}{dr}+2\pi rT_1\frac{d^2z}{dr^2}\,\delta r.+2\pi T_1\frac{dz}{dr}\,\delta r.$$

Hence the resultant vertical component along the element bounded by r and $r+dr$ is given by

$$2\pi rT_1\left\{\frac{1}{r}\frac{dz}{dr}+\frac{d^2z}{dr^2}\right\}\delta r.$$

The force acting on the element is $2\pi r.dr.\sigma.\dfrac{d^2z}{dt^2}$ where σ is the mass of the membrane per unit area. Therefore the equation of motion of the vibrating membrane is

$$2\pi r\,\delta r.\,\sigma.\,\frac{d^2z}{dt^2}=2\pi rT_1\left[\frac{1}{r}\frac{dz}{dr}+\frac{d^2z}{dr^2}\right]\delta r.$$

$$\frac{d^2z}{dt^2}=\frac{T_1}{\sigma}\left[\frac{1}{r}.\frac{dz}{dr}+\frac{d^2z}{dr^2}\right].$$

$$=c^2\left[\frac{1}{r}.\frac{dz}{dr}+\frac{d^2z}{dr^2}\right]. \tag{8.25}$$

Assuming the vibration to be harmonic in nature, $z \propto \cos(pt+\epsilon)$.

$$\frac{d^2z}{dt^2} = -p^2Z$$

so that we get equation (8.25)

$$p^2z + c^2\left[\frac{1}{r}\cdot\frac{dz}{dr} + \frac{d^2z}{dr^2}\right] = 0$$

or assuming $K^2 = \frac{p^2}{c^2}$

$$\frac{1}{r}\frac{dz}{dr} + \frac{d^2z}{dr^2} + K^2z = 0 \tag{8.26}$$

Equation (8.26) is a Bessel type equation; the solution of these types of equations is given by

$$z = cJ_0(Kr)\cos(pt+\epsilon) \tag{8.27}$$

where $J_0(z) = 1 - \frac{z^2}{2^2} + \frac{z^4}{2^2.4^2} - \frac{z^6}{2^2.4^2.6^2} + \ldots..$

This is called the Bessel function of zero order and of first kind. The condition for evaluation of K is obtained from the condition that when $r=a$, $J_0(Ka)=0$ then $J_0(Ka) = 0 = 1 - \frac{K^2a^2}{2^2} + \frac{K^4a^4}{2^2.4^2}$ taking only the first two terms. Then it can be proved that $\frac{Ka}{\pi} = 0.7655$

$= 1.7571$

$= 2.7546$

$= 3.7534$

The series approaching $\left(m - \frac{1}{4}\right)$ where m is an integer.

The radius of the nodal ring is obtained from the relation $J_2(Kr)=0$ since vibration in a node is zero and since $J_0(Kr)=0$ we get $\frac{Kr}{\pi} = 0.7655$ and at the boundary $\frac{Ka}{\pi} = 1\cdot7571$ so that $\frac{r}{a} = 0.4536$.

The frequencies of vibration are given by ν_{01}, ν_{02} etc.

$$\nu_{01} = \frac{p_1}{2\pi} = \frac{K_1c}{2\pi} = \frac{0.7655\ c}{2a} = \frac{c}{2a}\ .\ \beta_{01}.$$

$$\nu_{02} = \frac{p_2}{2\pi} = \frac{K_2c}{2\pi} = \frac{1.7571\ c}{2a} = \frac{c}{2a}\ .\ \beta_{02}.$$

so that $\nu_{02} = 2.2955\ \nu_{01}$.

where $\beta_{01} = 0.7655$, $\beta_{02} = 1.7571$ and $\beta_{0m} = \left(m - \frac{1}{4}\right)$ approximately.

8.8 KINETIC ENERGY OF THE VIBRATING MEMBRANE

If dm represents the mass of a small area of the membrane, then T = kinetic energy

where $T=\frac{1}{2}\int \dot{z}^2\, dm$

As $\quad z=cJ_0(Kr)\cos(pt+\epsilon)$ and taking $J_0(Kr)=1-\frac{K^2r^2}{4}$

$$z=c\left[1-\frac{K^2r^2}{4}\right]\cos(pt+\epsilon)\ ;\ \dot{z}=-cp\left[1-\frac{K^2r^2}{4}\right]\sin(pt+\epsilon)$$

$$dm=2\pi r.dr.\sigma$$

where σ is the mass per unit area of the surface.

$$T=\frac{1}{2}\sigma\, c^2p^2\sin^2(pt+\epsilon)\int_0^a\left[1-\frac{K^2r^2}{4}\right]^2 2\pi r.\ dr.$$

$$=\frac{1}{2}\sigma\, c^2p^2\sin^2(pt+\epsilon)\, 2\pi\left[\int_0^a r\, dr+\int_0^a\frac{K^4r^5}{16}\, dr-\int_0^a\frac{K^2r^3}{2}\, dr\right]$$

$$=\frac{1}{2}\sigma\, c^2p^2\sin^2(pt+\epsilon)\, 2\pi\left[\frac{a^2}{2}+\frac{K^4a^6}{96}-\frac{K^2a^4}{8}\right].$$

$$=\frac{1}{2}\sigma\, c^2p^2\sin^2(pt+\epsilon).\ \frac{2\pi a^2}{2}\left[1+\frac{K^4a^4}{48}-\frac{K^2a^2}{4}\right].$$

and since $\frac{Ka}{\pi}=0.7655$, $Ka=2.1$. (approximately)

$$=\frac{1}{2}\sigma\, c^2p^2\sin^2(pt+\epsilon)\,\pi a^2\left[1+\frac{16\cdot 36}{48}-1\cdot 1\right]\left[1-\frac{K^2r^2}{4}\right]_{r=0}$$

$$=\frac{1}{2}\sigma\, c^2p^2\sin^2(pt+\epsilon).\ \pi a^2\frac{1}{3}\left(1-\frac{K^2r^2}{4}\right)_{r=a}$$

$$=\frac{1}{2}\, c^2p^2\sin^2(pt+\epsilon).\ \frac{\pi a^2\sigma}{3}\left(1-\frac{K^2r^2}{4}\right)_{r=a}$$

$$=\frac{1}{2}.\ \dot{z}^2_{r=a}\ \frac{\pi a^2\sigma}{3}.$$

Consequently the effective mass is $\frac{1}{3}$ rd the total mass.

8.9 POTENTIAL ENERGY OF THE VIBRATING MEMBRANE

The potential energy

$$V=\frac{1}{2}\int_0^a \left(\frac{\partial z}{\partial r}\right)^2 2\pi r T_1\, dr$$

$$V=\frac{1}{2}c^2\cos^2(pt+\epsilon)\int_0^a \left[\frac{\partial}{\partial r}\left(1-\frac{K^2r^2}{4}\right)\right]^2 2\pi r.T_1\, dr$$

$$=\frac{1}{2}c^2\cos^2(pt+\epsilon).\int_0^a \left[\frac{K^4r^2}{4}\,2\pi r.T_1\right] dr$$

$$=\frac{1}{2}c^2\cos^2(pt+\epsilon).\frac{2\pi T_1}{4}\int_0^a K^4r^3\, dr$$

$$=\frac{1}{2}c^2\cos^2(pt+\epsilon)\,2\pi T_1.\frac{K^4a^4}{16}.$$

Since $Ku \simeq 2\cdot 1$, $\dfrac{K^4a^4}{4} \approx 1$.

$$V=\frac{1}{2}c^2\cos^2(pt+\epsilon).\left(1-\frac{K^2r^2}{4}\right)_{r=0} 2\pi T_1 = \frac{1}{2}.\,2\pi T_1\, z^2_{r=0}$$

Hence the effective tension is 2π times the actual tension.

8.10 THE KETTLEDRUM

The kettledrum is a circular membrane stretched over one end of a vessel tha is airtight. Here the tension is not the only restoring force, for the vibration of the membrane alternately compresses and expands the air in the vessel which reacts back on the membrane changing its natural frequency and its general behaviour. If the velocity of transverse wave in the membrane is considerably less than the velocity of sound then the compression or expansion of air in the vessel is more or less the same over the whole extent of the membrane and will depend upon the average displacement of the membrane; when the membrane is displaced from equilibrium, the volume of the vessel is diminished by the amount

$$dv=\int_0^a\int_0^{2\pi} zr.\, dr.\, d\phi \tag{8.28}$$

Let v_0 be the equilibrium volume and ρ_0 the equilibrium density and P_0 be the equilibrium pressure inside the vessel. Then if the compressions and rerefactions inside the vessel are rapid enough then the change can be taken as adiabatic and if P denotes the final pressure and v the final volume, we get

$$P_0 v_0^r = P v^r$$

$$\left(\frac{P}{P_0}\right) = \left(\frac{v_0}{v}\right)^r.$$

But from equation (8.28) $v = v_0 - \int_0^a \int_0^{2\pi} zr.\ dr.\ d\phi$ and $P = P_0 + \delta P$ where P is the excess pressure, then

$$1 + \frac{\delta P}{P_0} = \left[\frac{v_0}{v_0 - \int_0^a \int_0^{2\pi} zr\ dr\ d\phi}\right]^r$$

$$= 1 + \frac{r}{v_0}.\int_0^a \int_0^{2\pi} z.\ r.\ dr.\ d\phi \text{ (approximately).}$$

If C_a represents the velocity of sound in air at equilibrium pressure P and temperature in the vessel, then

$$C_a^2 = \frac{rP_0}{\rho_0}$$

or the excess pressure

$$\delta P = -\frac{\rho_0 C_a^2}{v_0} \int_0^a \int_0^{2\pi} z.\ r.\ dr.\ d\phi. \tag{8.29}$$

The negative sign indicates that the pressure is always acting in the direction opposite to displacement; consequently the equation of vibration of the ketledrum can be obtained from equation (8.25).

$$\sigma.\frac{d^2 z}{dt^2} = T_1\ \nabla^2 z - \frac{\rho_0 C_a^2}{v_0} \int_0^a \int_0^{2\pi} z.\ r.\ dr.\ d\phi$$

$$\frac{\sigma}{T_1}.\frac{d^2 z}{dt^2} = \nabla^2 z - \frac{\rho_0 C_a^2}{v_0 T_1} \int_0^a \int_0^{2\pi} z.\ r.\ dr.\ d\phi$$

$$\frac{1}{C^2}.\frac{d^2 z}{dt^2} = \nabla^2 z - \frac{\rho_0 C_a^2}{v_0 T_1} \int_0^a \int_0^{2\pi} z.\ r.\ dr.\ d\phi \tag{8.30}$$

where C is the velocity of sound through the membrane.
Let us assume

$$z = Y(r, \phi).\, e^{-2\pi i \nu t}$$

where ν is the frequency of vibration

$$\nabla^2 Y + \frac{4\pi^2\nu^2}{C^2}.Y = \frac{\rho_0 C_a^2}{\nu_0 T_1}.\int_0^a \int_0^{2\pi} Y.r.\, dr.\, d\phi \tag{8.31}$$

If, as before, it is assumed that $Y = {}^{\cos}_{\sin}\,(m\phi)\, J_m\,(2\pi\nu r/C)$, then for values of $m > 0$, the integral on the right hand side of equation (8.31) will be zero (owing to integration over ϕ) and the solution will be of the same type as equation (8.27) with the corresponding frequencies. The presence of the airtight vessel has therefore no effect on the normal modes of vibration when m is not equal to zero. When $m = 0$, the integral on the R.H.S. is not zero and since the solution of the equation without the integral is $J_0\,(2\pi\nu r/c)$, let us assume in this case,

$$Y = J_0\left(\frac{2\pi\nu r}{C}\right) - J_0\left(\frac{2\pi\nu a}{C}\right) \tag{8.32}$$

which satisfies the boundary condition $Y = 0$ when $r = a$.

The integral then reduces to

$$a^2 \frac{\rho_0 C_a^2}{\nu_0 T_1}\int_0^a \int_0^{2\pi} Y.r.\, dr.\, d\phi = \frac{A}{a^2}\left[2\left(\frac{C}{2\pi\nu a}\right) J_1\left(\frac{2\pi\nu a}{C}\right) - J_0\left(\frac{2\pi\nu a}{C}\right)\right].$$

where

$$A = \pi\rho_0 C_a^2\, a^4/\nu_0 T_1$$

Consequently equation (8.31) reduces to

$$\nabla^2 Y + \frac{4\pi^2\nu^2}{C^2}\, Y = \frac{A}{a^2}\left[2\left(\frac{C}{2\pi\nu a}\right) J_1\left(\frac{2\pi\nu a}{C}\right) - J_0\left(\frac{2\pi\nu a}{C}\right)\right].$$

The L.H.S. $= -J_0\,(\omega)\,\dfrac{4\pi^2\nu^2}{C^2}$ where $\omega = \dfrac{2\pi\nu a}{C}$.

so that we get $J_0\,(\omega) = \dfrac{A}{\omega^2}\left[J_0\,(\omega) - \dfrac{2}{\omega}\, J_1\,(\omega)\right]$

$$= -\frac{A}{\omega^2}\, J_2.\,(\omega) \tag{8.32}$$

which determines the allowed values of frequency for those normal modes that are independent of ϕ. The constant A is a measure of the relative importance of the air confined in the vessel with respect to tension as a restoring force on the membrane. It is small if the tension is large or if the volume of the vessel is large.

Allowed frequencies: The allowed frequencies and corresponding characteristic functions for the membrane plus the vessel are given by

$$\psi_{eon} = J_0\left(\frac{\pi r_{on}\gamma}{a}\right) - J_0\,(\pi r_{on}).$$

$$\psi_{emn} = \cos\,(m\phi)\; J_m\left(\frac{\pi\beta_{mn}\,r}{a}\right)$$

$$\psi_{omn} = \sin\,(m\phi)\; J_m\left(\frac{\pi\beta_{mn}\,r}{a}\right)$$

$$\nu_{on} = \left(\frac{r_{on}}{2a}\right)\sqrt{\frac{T_1}{\sigma}}.$$

$$\nu_{mn} = \frac{\beta_{mn}}{2a}\sqrt{\frac{T_1}{\sigma}}\quad m>0.$$

where ν_{on} are allowed frequencies, $r_{on} = 2a\nu_{on}/C\ \psi_{eon}$ is the characteristic functions for the membrane plus vessel, $\nu_{mn} = c\beta_{mn}/a$.

8.11 VIBRATION OF RINGS

A complete ring of elastic material may be made to exhibit either longitudinal or flextural vibration. The first experimental observation of vibration of a ring was made by Chladni in 1787. The ring may be placed horizontally resting on three supports of cork or other soft material at the nodes. If the vibrating segment projects beyond the table then the ring can be excited to vibration by means of a violin bow, the ring being placed in position by holding at the nodes by the tips of the finger. In this case the vibrations are mainly flextural, taking place in a direction perpendicular to the plane of the ring. In order to analyse the motion of the ring we shall suppose the section to be uniform and symmetrical with respect to a plane and perpendicular to the axis of the ring and we consider the vibrations to be parallel to this plane or perpendicular to it. The problem of vibration of rings can be divided into three parts.

(a) The displacement of any section is radial and transverse, i.e. the ring remains in its own plane being alternately stretched and contracted.

(b) The ring vibrates tangentially, i.e. there is no contraction or extension of circumference.

(c) The vibrations are normal to the plane.

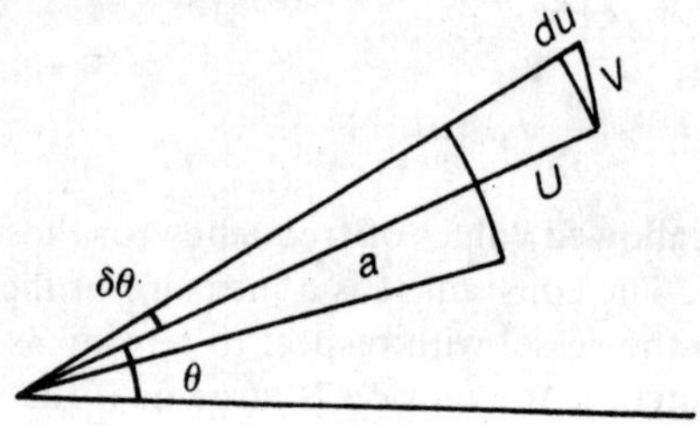

Fig. 8.3

Here we shall consider the first two cases simultaneously. Let the radial displacement of the element A of the ring be U and let v be the displacement perpendicular to the original radius vector where v is the tangential displacement of the element A. The polar coordinates of A are a and θ, and so after displacement it becomes $a + U$ and $\theta + d\theta$, but as $d\theta = v/a$ the coordinates become $a + U$ and $\theta + v/a$. To consider the expressions for extension and change of curvature, we may consider in view of the smallness of displacements, the instalments of these quantities which are due to U and v separately and add the results.

Radial displacement changes the length of the element from $a\delta\theta$ to $(a + U)\,\delta\theta$.

$$\therefore \text{ extension} = \frac{a\delta\theta + U\delta\theta - a\delta\theta}{a\delta\theta}$$

$$= U/a$$

Due to transverse vibration, θ becomes $\theta + v/a$ so $\delta\theta$ becomes $\delta\theta + \frac{1}{a}\frac{\partial v}{\partial\theta}\,\delta\theta$

so $\delta\theta$ becomes $\delta\theta + \frac{1}{a}\frac{\partial v}{\partial\theta}\,\delta\theta$

$$\therefore\ a\delta\theta \text{ becomes } a\left[\delta\theta + \frac{1}{a}\frac{\partial v}{\partial\theta}\,\delta\theta\right]$$

$$= a\delta\theta + \frac{\partial v}{\delta\theta}\,\delta\theta$$

The extension due to this becomes $\dfrac{a\delta\theta + \frac{\partial v}{\partial\theta}\,\delta\theta - a\delta\theta}{a\delta\theta} = \dfrac{1}{a}\dfrac{\partial v}{\partial\theta}$

Thus the total extension becomes $\dfrac{U}{a} + \dfrac{1}{a}.\dfrac{\partial v}{\partial\theta}$ **(8.34)**

Change of Curvature

In consequence of radial displacement alone, the normal to the curve is rotated backwards; at θ, it is rotated through

$$\frac{\partial U}{a\partial\theta} = \frac{1}{a}.\frac{\partial U}{\partial\theta}.$$

and at $\theta + d\theta$, it is rotated through $\dfrac{1}{a}\dfrac{\partial U}{\partial\theta} + \dfrac{1}{a}.\dfrac{\partial^2 U}{\partial\theta^2}\,\delta\theta$

So the angle between the normals at the extremities of the element becomes

$$\delta\theta - \frac{1}{a}.\frac{\partial^2 U}{\partial\theta^2}.\,\delta\theta$$

Therefore the altered curvature is

$$\frac{\delta\theta - \frac{1}{a}.\frac{\partial^2 U}{\partial\theta^2}.\,\delta\theta}{(a + U)\,\delta\theta}$$

$$= \left[1 - \frac{1}{a} \cdot \frac{\partial^2 U}{\partial \theta^2}\right] [a+U]^{-1} = \frac{1}{a} - \frac{1}{a^2}\left[\frac{\partial^2 U}{\partial \theta^2} + U\right].$$

$$\text{Change of curvature} = -\frac{1}{a^2}\left[\frac{\partial^2 U}{\partial \theta^2} + U\right] \tag{8.35}$$

The resultant stress across any section may be resolved into a radial shearing force P, a tangential tension Q and a bending moment M. Hence if q be the Young's modulus of the material of the ring and ω the area of its cross-section.

then $Q = q \times \omega$ and extension $= \dfrac{q\omega\left(U + \dfrac{\partial U}{\partial \theta}\right)}{a}$.

Moment $M = q\omega K^2 \times$ change in curvature. $= q\omega k^2 \left[-\dfrac{1}{a^2}\left\{\dfrac{\partial^2 U}{\partial \theta^2} + U\right\}\right]$.

where K is the radius of gyration as the bending moment becomes equal to change of curvature. Resolving along and perpendicular to the radius vector

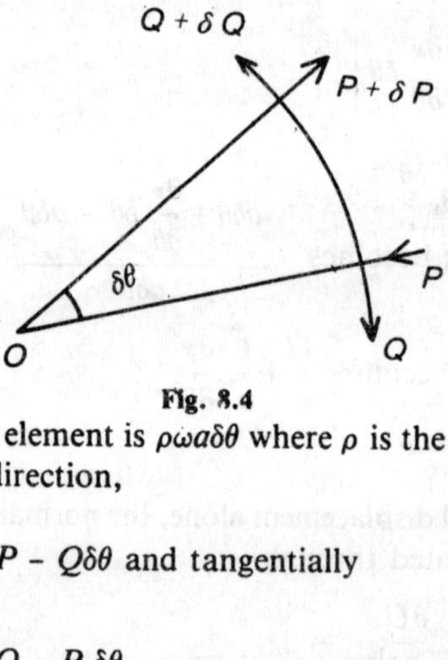

Fig. 8.4

the forces on a mass element is $\rho\omega a\delta\theta$ where ρ is the mass per unit volume, we have, in the radial direction,

(a) $\rho\omega a\delta\theta \dfrac{\partial^2 U}{\partial t^2} = \delta P - Q\delta\theta$ and tangentially

(b) $\rho\omega a\delta\theta \dfrac{\partial^2 V}{\partial t^2} = \delta Q - P.\delta\theta$

and taking moments about a normal to the plane of the ring (c) $dM - Pa\delta\theta = 0$ the rotational inertia being neglected.

Thus, we get, the equation of vibration of ring as

$$\rho\omega a \frac{\partial^2 U}{\partial t^2} = \frac{\partial P}{\partial \theta} - Q$$

$$\rho\omega a \frac{\partial^2 v}{\partial t^2} = \frac{\partial Q}{\partial \theta} - P$$

$$\frac{\partial M}{\partial \theta} = P.a \tag{8.36}$$

These equations are the equations of the problem. It is easily seen that they cannot be satisfied on the assumption that tension Q vanishes and accordingly some degree of extension is involved in any mode of vibration. This is readily accounted for, a stress of this kind being necessarily called into play by the inertia of the different portions swinging in the opposite direction. It may be shown however that in the flextural modes to be referred to presently, the corresponding strains are small compared with those involved in the change of curvature. Eleminating P, Q and M between the equations given by (8.36)

$$\frac{\partial^2 U}{\partial t^2}+\frac{q}{\rho a^2}\left[U+\frac{\partial v}{\partial \theta}+\frac{K^2}{a^2}\left\{\frac{\partial^2 U}{\partial \theta^2}+\frac{\partial^4 U}{\partial \theta^4}\right\}\right]=0$$

$$\frac{\partial^2 v}{\partial t^2}-\frac{q}{\rho a^2}\left[\frac{\partial U}{\partial \theta}+\frac{\partial^2 v}{\partial \theta^2}-\frac{K^2}{a^2}\left\{\frac{\partial U}{\partial \theta}+\frac{\partial^3 U}{\partial \theta^3}\right\}\right]=0$$

To ascertain the normal modes, we assume that U and V vary as $\cos(nt+\epsilon)$. The ring being complete, U and v are necessarily periodic functions of θ, the period being $2\pi/T$. and can then be accordingly expressed in the form of Fourier series of sines and cosines of the multiples of θ. Moreover, it is easily proved that the terms of any given rank in the expansion must satisfy the equations separately. We see that a sufficient assumption for the purpose is

$$U=A_s \cos S\theta \cos(nt+\epsilon)$$

$$V=B_s \sin S\theta \cos(nt+\epsilon) \tag{8.37}$$

where S may be any integer or zero.

Putting these values of U and v in the above equation we get after reduction,

$$\left[\beta-1-S^2(S^2-1)\frac{K^2}{a^2}\right]A_s-SB_s=0$$

$$-\left[S+S(S^2-1)\frac{K^2}{a^2}\right]A_s+(\beta-S^2)B_s=0 \tag{8.38}$$

where $$\beta=\frac{n^2a^2\rho}{q}$$

Eliminating A_s and B_s from the above equations

$$\beta^2-\left[S^2+1+S^2\{S^2-1\}\frac{K^2}{a^2}\right]\beta+S^2(S^2-1)^2\frac{K^2}{a^2}=0.$$

The sum of the two roots of the above equation is

$$S^2+1+S^2(S^2-1)\frac{K^2}{a^2}$$

and since K/a is small, we get the sum as approximately S^2+1 and product of the two roots

$$S^2(S^2-1)^2\frac{K^2}{a^2}.$$

Hence, approximately the roots are,

$$S^2+1 \text{ and } \frac{S^2\,(S^2-1)^2}{(S^2+1)}.\frac{K^2}{a^2}$$

On reference to equation (8.36), we note that the former of the above two roots makes $B_s = SA_s$ nearly. The corresponding modes are closely analogous to the longitudinal modes of a straight bar, the potential energies being mainly due to extension and the frequencies in the first case are given by,

$$n^2 = (S^2+1)\,\frac{q}{\rho a^2}.$$

If $S=0$, $n^2 = \frac{q}{\rho a^2}$ which refers to purely radial vibration. The vibrations corresponding to second part are more important. We have then from equation (8.36), $A_s + SB_s = 0$

Thus $\quad U_s = A_s \cos S\theta \cos(nt+\epsilon)$

$\quad V_s = B_s \sin S\theta \cos(nt+\epsilon)$

$$n^2 = \frac{S^2\,(S^2-1)^2}{(S^2+1)}\,\frac{qK^2}{\rho a^4}$$

It follows from equation (8.34) the expression for total extension $(U/a + 1/a\ \partial v/\partial\theta)$, that the extension is negligible and the energy is mainly flextural. The frequencies are however comparable with those of the transverse vibration of a bar. In the mode of order S there are $2S$ nodes or places of vanishing radial motion but these are not points of rest, the tangential motion there being a maximum. In the case $S=1$ the circle is merely displaced as a whole without deformation and the period is accordingly infinite. The most important case is that of $S=2$ where the ring oscillates between two slightly elliptical extreme forms and has four nodes distant from each other by 90°.

9

VIBRATION OF AIR COLUMNS

We have previously discussed the vibration in an extended medium of air and it is of interest to note and analyse the vibration of air columns contained in a cavity of any type because the analysis of such a column of air provides us with some data in understanding the vibration and production of sound in some of the musical instruments.

9.1 VIBRATION OF AIR COLUMNS IN CYLINDRICAL PIPE

The simplest case of air vibration in such a cavity is that of air column contained in a cylinderical cavity. To deduce mathematical theory the following assumptions will be made:

(a) The diameter of the cylinder is large enough so that the effects of viscosity on vibration can be neglected to a first order.

(b) The diameter of the pipe is small enough in comparison to its length and wave length of sound.

(c) The walls of the enclosure are perfectly rigid.

In general the two ends of the cylindrical pipe may be open or the two ends may be closed or one end may be open and the other closed. We shall deal with these cases one by one. It will further be assumed that the sound wave in such an enclosure is a plane wave of sound. When a plane wave of sound travels within the pipe it gets reflected from the open end and a change of phase occurs but at every reflection some sound energy is radiated outside and a damping of the amplitude of the sound wave occurs within the pipe. Thus the open end produces the end effect, the effect of which is to increase the effective length of pipe and consequently a lowering of frequency; when a cylindrical column of air is set into resonant vibration by means of an external agency, stationary waves will be set up in the pipe due to superimposition of direct wave and reflected wave just as in the case of strings. Thus the vibration can be represented by

$$\frac{d^2y}{dt^2} = c^2 . \frac{d^2y}{dx^2} \qquad (9.1)$$

[Refer to equation (5.9)]

where c = velocity of sound = $\sqrt{\frac{E}{\rho}}$

E = bulk modulus and ρ = density of air.

If it is assumed that $y = a \cos \omega t$
then from equation (9.1),

$$\frac{d^2y}{dx^2} + \frac{\omega^2}{c^2} y = 0 \tag{9.2}$$

The solution of this equation can be written as,

$$y = \left[A \cos \frac{\omega x}{c} + B \sin \frac{\omega x}{c} \right] \cos \omega t \tag{9.3}$$

where A and B are arbitrary constants which are to be determined from the boundary conditions.

CASE 1: Pipe open at both ends

In this case if the pipe is open at $x = 0$ and also at $x = l$ where l is the length of the pipe then $dy/dx = 0$ both at $x = 0$ and $x = l$ where (dy/dx) denotes a compression.

Then as $dy/dx = 0$ at $x = 0$, we get from equation (9.3) that B must be zero.

Also $\left(\frac{dy}{dx}\right)_{x=l} = 0 = -A. \frac{\omega}{c} \sin \frac{\omega l}{c} \cos \omega t$

$\therefore \quad \sin \frac{\omega l}{c} = 0 = \sin S\pi$

or $\quad \omega = 2\pi N = \frac{S\pi c}{l}$, S being an integer.

$\therefore \quad N = \frac{Sc}{2l} = \frac{S}{2l}\sqrt{\frac{E}{\rho}}$

The frequency of the fundamental $N_1 = \frac{1}{2l}\sqrt{\frac{E}{\rho}}$

CASE 2: Pipe closed at both ends

In this case $y = 0$ at $x = 0$ and $x = l$

Then from equation (9.3) $A = 0$

and

$$y = 0 = B \sin \frac{\omega l}{c} \cos \omega t$$

i.e. $\quad \frac{\omega l}{c} = S\pi$, where S is an integer.

$$\therefore \quad N = \frac{Sc}{2l} = \frac{S}{2l}\sqrt{\frac{E}{\rho}}.$$

It is the same frequency as in the case 1.

CASE 3: Pipe open at $x = 0$ and closed at $x = l$

Hence at $x=0$, $\frac{dy}{dx}=0$ and at $x=l$, $y=0$. From the condition $\left(\frac{dy}{dx}\right)_{x=0}$ $=0$ we get $B=0$. Hence, from equation (9.3)

$$y=A\cos\frac{\omega x}{c}\cos\omega t$$

$$0=A\cos\frac{\omega l}{c}\cos\omega t$$

$$\frac{\omega l}{c}=\frac{S\pi}{2}$$

where $S=1, 3, 5$ etc. (any odd number)

Thus
$$N_s=\frac{Sc}{4l}=\frac{S}{4l}\sqrt{\frac{E}{\rho}}$$

The above equations represent different modes of vibration in an open pipe, closed pipe and in a pipe which is open at one end and closed at the other. It will be seen that the effective length of the open pipe is twice that of the closed pipe of corresponding frequency.

9.2 END CORRECTION

It has been assumed in the previous deduction that the open end of the pipe is an antinode and consequently the plane sound waves are perfectly reflected at the open end. This assumption is not strictly correct for some amount of sound energy escapes in the medium outside at each reflection and the air beyond the open end of the pipe is therefore set into vibration and thus the effective length of the pipe is increased. The correct theory of this effect was first given by Helmholtz.

Lord Rayleigh has also given a theory which is in agreement with the result obtained by Helmholtz. These theories are based on two assumptions:

(a) The diameter of the open end of the pipe is small compared with the wavelength of sound.

(b) The pipe is fitted to an infinite flange to which the axix of the pipe is perpendicular.

Under the above conditions, Helmholtz gave the correction factor as $R\pi/4$ whereas Lord Rayleigh gave the correction as $0\cdot82\ R$ to be added to the length of the tube where R is the radius of the tube. The experimentally determined corrections for an unflanged end was $0\cdot6$ where the diameter is small in comparison with wavelength. Helmholtz maintains that the correction to be added is a function of the wavelength and tends to vanish for small wavelength. The end correction is found experimentally by means of a pipe closed at one end by means of an adjustable piston or a column of water, the different lengths l_1, l_2 etc. being determined which resonate with frequency of a tuning fork. Hence if ϵ denotes the end correction then from equation (9.4)

$$N = \frac{c}{2l_1} \text{ when } S = 1 \therefore l_1 = \frac{c}{2N}$$

If end correction made, $l_1 + \epsilon = \frac{c}{2N}$. (9.5)

and if the length of the air column is changed so that a new length l_2 is now in resonance with the same fequency of the tuning fork,

$$l_2 + \epsilon = \frac{2c}{2N} \tag{9.6}$$

then from equations (9.5) and (9.6)

$$(l_2 - l_1) = \frac{c}{2N}$$

or

$$c = 2N(l_2 - l_1) \tag{9.7}$$

Thus the end effect always lowers the frequency of an open ended pipe.

9.3 EXAMPLES OF VIBRATING AIR COLUMN: ORGAN PIPES

The air vibrations which we have discussed in the previous section take place in some musical instruments, one of the familiar examples being an organ pipe. It is constructed in the form of a cylindrical metal tube or a wooden pipe of square cross-section. In order to form resonant vibrations in the air column, one end of the pipe is specially constructed. In the flue organ pipe the blast of air impinges on a thin lip which forms the upper end of the slit opening into the tube. At a certain minimum blast pressure impulses are set up, within the tube, of such a frequency that resonance is set up in the air column and the pipe begins to emit sound with its fundamental frequency. When the pressure within the tube is increased by increasing the power of the blast, higher harmonics are generated. In the organ pipe the jet is adjusted that it is very sensitive to flow of air into and out of the tube so that a small change in its direction makes a change in pressure at the open end. Since the organ pipe is open at one end and closed at the other the frequency is given by

$$\frac{\omega l}{c} = \frac{S\pi}{2} \quad \text{where } S = 1, 3, 5, \text{ etc.}$$

or

$$\frac{2\pi Nl}{c} = \frac{S\pi}{2}$$

$$N = \frac{Sc}{4l}.$$

If now the closed organ pipe is blown at just the right air speed, the frequency of the transverse vibration of the jet will equal the fundamental frequency of the tube $N = \frac{c}{4l}$ and the sound will consist entirely of the fundamental.

The overtones will be present to some extent because the jet oscillations are not purely sinusoidal even when aided by tube resonance.

Reed Pipe

In another form of organ pipe, known as reed pipe, the blast of air impinges on a reed of metal which controls the amount of air entering into the pipe. The reed and pipe are tuned to the same fundamental frequency and consequently the inharmonic overtones of the reed do not coincide with the harmonic overtones of the pipe. The reed is set into vibration by the air blast and puffs of air are emitted to the pipe, which is thereby set into resonance.

Conical Pipe

In case of conical pipes, the travelling wave is spherical and either divergent or convergent and consequently the equation of wave propagation is given by

$$\frac{d^2}{dt^2}(rs) = c^2 . \frac{d^2}{dr^2}(rs) \tag{9.8}$$

where r is the radius vector from the centre of disturbance, s the condensation and assuming

$$rs = a \cos(\omega t)$$

$$\frac{d^2}{dr^2}(rs) + \frac{\omega^2}{c^2}(rs) = 0$$

and the solution of the equation is given by

$$rs = \left[A \cos\frac{\omega r}{c} + B \sin\frac{\omega r}{c}\right] \cos \omega t \tag{9.9}$$

and, as before, the constants A and B are to be determined from boundary conditions. We shall discuss three special cases.

(1) **Open Cone:** At the open end $r = l$, where l is called the slant length, we get, $s = 0$ and at the vertex $r = 0$ and the condensation s must be finite whether the end is closed or open, so that $rs = 0$. Hence putting the conditions, $A = 0$ and

$$B \sin\frac{\omega l}{c} = 0$$

$$\frac{\omega}{2\pi} = N = \frac{mc}{2l} \quad \text{where } m = 1, 2, 3 \text{ etc.}$$

(2) **Closed Cone:** At the close ends where $r = 0$ and $r = l$, the condition to be fulfilled is the equation, as before, given by

$$\frac{d^2}{dr^2}(rs) + \frac{\omega^2}{c^2}(rs) = 0$$

and consequently the solution of the equation is given by

$$rs = \left[A \cos \frac{\omega r}{c} + B \sin \frac{\omega r}{c}\right] \cos \omega t$$

Applying the above equation we obtain the relation

$$\tan \frac{\omega l}{c} = \frac{\omega l}{c}$$

and the solution of the equation can be obtained by drawing curves $y = \omega l/c$ and $y = \tan \omega l/c$ and the intersections of the straight line with the tangent curve give the roots of the equation. It is found that for the solution we have $\omega l/c = 0$, 1·43, 2·46, 3·47, 4·47, 5·48, etc. and the frequency N is given by $N = mc/2l$, where $m\pi =$ 0, 1·43, 2·46, etc. which shows that overtones are not harmonics of the fundamental.

(3) Truncated Cone: Let $r = l_1$ and $r = l_2$ at the ends. It can be shown that if the truncated cone is open at both ends then it has the fundamental frequency and harmonic overtones like those of an open parallel pipe of length equal to slant length $(l_2 - l_1)$ of the conical pipe. If the cone is closed at both ends, then it can be shown that

$$\tan^{-1}\left(\frac{\omega l_2}{c}\right) - \tan^{-1}\left(\frac{\omega l_1}{c}\right) = \frac{\omega}{c}(l_2 - l_1)$$

If $l_1 = 0$ then $\tan\left(\frac{\omega l_2}{c}\right) = \frac{\omega l_2}{c}$ and the solution is of the same type as in the case of a closed cone dealt before. When l_1 and l_2 are very large then $\tan^{-1}\frac{\omega l_2}{c} = \tan^{-1}\frac{\omega l_1}{c} \approx \frac{\pi}{2}$ so that $(l_2 - l_1)$ is a multiple of $\lambda/2$, in accordance with the theory of parallel pipes.

9.4 HIGH FREQUENCY PIPES: GALTON'S WHISTLE

Galton's whistle is a certain form of organ pipe. By means of a piston which is moveable across the length of the pipe the frequency emitted from the pipe can be varied, and by adjusting the length of the tube very high frequency can be generated. The instrument can be utilised for generation of low frequency ultrasonic waves and we shall discuss it in greater detail in the chapter on Ultrasonics.

Hartman and Trolle's air jet generator: still higher frequencies can be generated by means of Hartman and Trolle's air jet generator. The air jet they have employed has a velocity greater than that of sound and the air jet breaks up into regular pulses as it leaves the jet. When these pulses fall on the open end of the cylinder, resonance is set up for a certain length of the pipe depending upon the frequency of these pulses and the pipe begins to emit a powerful supersonic vibration the frequency of which may be as large as 10^5 c/s. If a jet of hydrogen is employed still higher frequencies can be generated and this powerful source of sound can be employed either for experimental purposes or for sound signalling.

9.5 VIBRATIONS IN AIR CAVITY: HELMHOLTZ RESONATOR

Another form of device in which the vibration of air can be maintained is called Helmholtz resonator, after the name of the discoverer. The resonator consists either of a spherical (Fig. 9.1) or a cylindrical cavity (Fig. 9.2) with a small neck which communicates with the air outside. In case of spherical cavity the volume of the cavity is fixed whereas in case of the cylindrical cavity

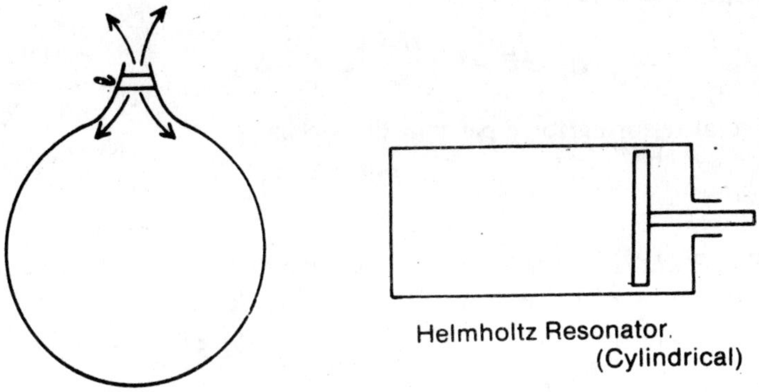

Helmholtz Resonator.
(Cylindrical)

Fig. 9.1

the volume inside is variable. In this type of cavity the air is completely enclosed so that only a very small portion of energy is radiated outside the medium. Since there is no loss of energy from the cavity, the damping is very small and the tuning is very sharp. Consequently the resonator can be a detector of sound of a definite frequency and since there is practically little communication with the outside air, the resonator cannot be utilized as a transmitter of sound since the loss of energy due to damping is extremely small; a vibration once started persists for quite a long time and it has been noted by Helmhotz that vibration at the neck of the resonator is many times larger than the vibration inside the cavity. In whatever shape the cavity may be constructed the dimension of the neck should be small compared with the dimension of the cavity.

Theory of the Resonator: Rayleigh maintained that the air contained at the neck of the resonator acts like a piston alternately compressing and rarefying the air within the cavity of the resonator and it was further assumed that the wavelength λ of the vibration in free air is large compared with the dimension of the cavity. If l is the length of the neck and S is the area of cross-section, ρ the density of the gas in the neck, then the mass of the piston of air is $M=\rho lS$. If further it is assumed that the change of pressure and volume is adiabatic, then

$$Pv^r = \text{constant}$$

$$\frac{dP}{dv} v^r + rv^{r-1} P = 0$$

$$\frac{dP}{dv} = -rPv$$

$$\delta P = -\frac{rP}{v}\,\delta v$$

Thus the total force acting on the piston is $\delta P.\,S$ and the change of volume for unit displacement of piston is S. Then for unit displacement of the piston, the force per unit area is

$$\delta P = -\frac{rPS}{v} \text{ as } \delta v = S$$

and the total restoring force per unit displacement

$$\delta P.\,S = -\frac{rPS^2}{v} = \frac{ES^2}{v}$$

where $E = rP$ and E is the adiabatic elasticity of the gas. The equation of undamped motion of the piston is then

$$M.\frac{d^2y}{dt^2} + fy = 0 \qquad \text{where } f = \frac{rPS^2}{v}$$

$$N = \frac{1}{2\pi}\sqrt{\frac{f}{M}} = \frac{1}{2\pi}\sqrt{\frac{rPS^2}{vM}} = \frac{1}{2\pi}\sqrt{\frac{rPS^2}{v\rho lS}}$$

$$= \frac{1}{2\pi}\sqrt{\frac{rP}{\rho}.\frac{S}{lv}} = \frac{c}{2\pi}\sqrt{\frac{S}{lv}} \qquad (9.11)$$

The above theoretical expression has been verified experimentally by Sandhauss and Helmholtz who obtained experimental values of frequency which were always slightly lower than the theoretical values given above. The difference has been ascribed to end effect as in the case of pipes and the value of l should be modified from l to $(l+0{\cdot}6R)$, where R is the radius of the neck. The above theory gives only the frequency of the fundamental tone but higher harmonics are also generated which are not predicted by the theory.

Use of resonator in sound analysis: As deduced above, the natural frequency of the resonator is a function of the dimensions of the resonator and has a fixed value for a particular resonator. Consequently when a sound wave of frequency resonant with the natural frequency of the resonator is incident on it, the resonator will give greater response. In general, it is practicable to select a large number of resonators with a wide range of natural frequencies or to take a resonator whose inside volume can be changed regularly. The detector may be the ear or a hot wire microphone.

10
TRANSMISSION OF SOUND

As we know, the sound waves are longitudinal in character and while considering the case of vibration in an extended medium in chapter 5 we have deduced an expression for the velocity of propagation of the longitudinal waves which is given by $v=\sqrt{K/\rho}$ where K is the bulk modulus of elasticity of the medium and ρ its density. The experimental determination of the velocity of sound in a medium and its exact agreement with the theoretical value lends further support to the idea that sound waves in a medium are longitudinal in character. The amplitude of a soundwave, however, decreases as we move away from the source of sound due to viscosity and heat conduction of the medium.

10.1 VELOCITY OF SOUND IN A GAS

Newton assumed that during the propagation of longitudinal waves compressions and rarefactions take place so slowly that heat developed as a result of compression was fully dissipated away in to the medium and coolness produced during rarefaction was made up by absorbing heat from the surrounding medium. He thus maintained that the changes are isothermal. According to Boyl's law

$$Pv=\text{constant}$$

where P is the pressure and v the volume.

then
$$Pdv+vdP=0$$

or
$$Pdv=-vdP$$

$$-\frac{dv}{v}=\frac{dP}{P}$$

$$K=\text{bulk modulus}=\frac{dP}{-\frac{dv}{v}}=P$$

Hence,
$$V=\text{velocity of sound}$$

$$V=\sqrt{\frac{K}{\rho}}=\sqrt{\frac{P}{\rho}} \qquad (10.1)$$

If $P=76$ cm of Hg, and $\rho=0\cdot001293$ g/cc for dry air at 0°C,

$$V=278 \text{ m/s}$$

The earlier experimental determination of velocity had shown that the velocity of propagation is 330 m/s and thus the theoretical value was 16 percent lower than the experimental value.

This discrepancy was explained by Laplace in 1817. He maintained that compressions and rarefactions in sound wave take place so rapidly that the heat developed during compression or the cooling produced during rarefaction has no time to dissipate itself in to the surrounding medium i.e. the changes are adiabatic and not isothermal.

Hence, in this case we have $Pv^\gamma = \text{const.}$, where γ is the ratio of specific heats. Thus

$$Pv^\gamma = \text{constant}$$

$$\frac{dP}{dv} v^\gamma + \gamma v^{\gamma-1} P = 0$$

or

$$\frac{dP}{dv} v + \gamma P = 0$$

$$-\frac{dP}{\frac{dv}{v}} = \gamma P$$

$$K = \gamma P$$

$$V = \sqrt{\frac{\gamma P}{\rho}} \tag{10.2}$$

The value of γ for air $= 1{\cdot}41$ and consequently $V = 330$ m/s from equation (10.2) which is in very good agreement with experimental observation and justifies the assumption made by Laplace.

10.2 EFFECT OF PRESSURE, TEMPERATURE AND HUMIDITY ON THE SOUND VELOCITY IN A GAS

(a) Effect of pressure

If the temperature of the gas is kept constant then a change of pressure does not change the velocity of sound in a gas; from equation (10.2)

$$V = \sqrt{\frac{\gamma P}{\rho}}$$

If the pressure is changed to P' then the density of the gas is changed to ρ' so that V' the new velocity is given by

$$V' = \sqrt{\frac{\gamma P'}{\rho'}}$$

$$\frac{V'}{V} = \sqrt{\frac{P'\rho}{P\rho'}} \quad \text{from Boyle's law } \frac{P}{\rho} = \frac{P'}{\rho'}$$

and so

$$V = V'$$

Thus a change of pressure does not change the velocity of sound in a gas.

(b) Effect of temperature

A change of temperature changes the density of a gas and hence causes a change of the velocity of sound through it. Let V_0 and V_t denote the velocities of sound in a gas at temperature 0°C and t°C respectively. If it is assumed that pressure remains constant,

$$\frac{V_t}{V_0} = \sqrt{\frac{\rho_0}{\rho_t}}$$

where ρ_0 and ρ_t are densities of the gas at temperatures 0°C and t°C respectively. Then if α denotes the coefficient of expansion,

$$\rho_0 = \rho_t\,(1 + \alpha t)$$

$$\therefore \quad \frac{V_t}{V_0} = \sqrt{1 + \alpha t} \text{ as } \alpha = \frac{1}{273}$$

$$\therefore \quad \frac{V_t}{V_0} = \sqrt{\frac{273 + t}{273}} = \sqrt{\frac{T_t}{T_0}}$$

Hence, the velocity of sound in a gas is directly proportional to square root of the abosolute temperature of the gas.

(c) Effect of humidity

The presence of moisture in air lowers its density and hence increases the velocity of sound through it. The higher the degree of saturation, the greater will be the velocity of sound through it. Let V_D represent the velocity of sound in dry air at a temperature t and let V_M denote the velocity at the same temperature but in moist air. Then P_M is the density of moist air and P_D that of dry air

$$V_D = \sqrt{\frac{\gamma P}{\rho_D}} \text{ and } V_M = \sqrt{\frac{\gamma P}{\rho_M}}$$

$$\frac{V_D}{V_M} = \sqrt{\frac{\rho_M}{\rho_D}} \qquad V_D = V_M \sqrt{\frac{\rho_M}{\rho_D}}$$

Let H be the height of the mercury barometer in cm of mercury and P be the equivalent pressure in dyn/cm^2 and let f be the pressure of aqueous vapour present in it in cm of mercury. Then the partial pressure of dry air is $(H - f)$ cm of mercury and f is the aqueous tension. Then

ρ_M = density of moist air at pressure H and temperature t

= mass of 1 cc of dry air at pressure $(H - f)$

+ mass of 1 cc of water vapour at temp t and pressure f

= mass of $\left(\frac{H - f}{H}\right)$ cc of dry air at pressure H

+ mass of f/H cc of water vapour at pressure H and temperature t

$$= \frac{(H - f)}{H}\rho_D + \frac{f}{H} \times 0{\cdot}622\ \rho_D = \frac{\rho_D}{H}[H - f + 0{\cdot}622\ f] = \frac{\rho_D}{H}[H - 0{\cdot}378\ f]$$

Because the specific gravity of water vapour with regard to air at the same temperature and pressure is 0·662,

$$\rho_M = \frac{\rho_D}{H}[H - 0{\cdot}378f]$$

$$\frac{\rho_M}{\rho_D} = \frac{H - 0{\cdot}378f}{H}$$

substituting this value in equation $\frac{V_D}{V_M} = \sqrt{\frac{\rho_M}{\rho_D}}$,

$$\frac{V_{D'}}{V_M} = \sqrt{\frac{H - 0{\cdot}378f}{H}} \qquad (10.3$$

d) Effect of wind

The velocity of sound is affected by wind. If wind blows with a velocity W in the direction of sound then the resultant velocity of sound will be $(V + W)$ whereas if it blows against it the velocity of sound will be $(V - W)$ and further if the direction of velocity of wind makes an angle θ with the direction of sound propagation then the resultant velocity will be given by

$$(V + W \cos\theta) \text{ or } (V - W \cos\theta).$$

10.3 VELOCITY OF SOUND IN OPEN AIR

The velocity of sound in open air has been determined by a large number of workers from time to time. The members of the Paris Academy of Sciences experimentally determined the velocity of sound in 1738 by a method known as the method of reciprocal observation. This method eliminated the correction for the wind. Cannons were fired at half hour intervals alternately at the two ends of a baseline 18 miles long and intervals between the flash and the report were noted by each observer at each end of a base. The value obtained by them was 332 m/s at 0°C.

During the First World War, a series of observations on the velocity of sound were made by Esclangon. His experiments were made under various conditions of temperature (between 0°C and 20°C) and humidity. The source of sound in these experiments was a set of guns of different calibres and the sound was received by means of hot wire microphone which were placed at distances of 1400 m and 14000 m along the same line. The instants of arrival at the receiver were recorded by means of an Einthovan string galvanometer. The final result of the velocity of sound was found to be 339·7 m/s at 15°C.

There has been some inconsistency in the velocity of sound determination between the results obtained by different workers. It is very natural to suppose that in the long base line taken in the open-air determination of the velocity of sound, the temperature, pressure and humidity may change from time to time and this combined with the personal equation of the observer and the different intensities of the sources of sound are sufficient to explain the discrepancy among the observations. In order to eliminate these difficulties, T.C. Hebb at the suggestion of A.A. Michelson devised a method of determining the velocity of sound by accurately measuring the wavelength of sound in air from a source of known frequency. In this method, two parabolic reflectors M_1 and M_2 (made of plaster of Paris 5 ft in diameter and 15″ in focal length) are placed at a certain distance apart and coaxially so that sound waves sent out from the focus of one were received at the focus of the other. A telephone transmitter, i.e. a carbon granular microphone is placed at the focus of each parabolic mirror and the transmitters are connected to the primary winding of a telephone transformer (Fig 10.1).

Fig. 10.1

The transformer has two primary coils and to each of telephone transmitters is connected one primary coil and there is a common secondary which in turn is connected to a pair of telephones. A source of sound, a high pitched whistle of frequency 2376 PPS was placed at the focus of M_1; one sound is directly transmitted to the transformer and the other one gets reflected from M_1 and then proceeding in a parallel beam to M_2 comes to focus at M_2 and then transmitted to the telephone transmitter. It is thus clear that the sound received by the telephones connected to the secondary of the transformer is the vector sum of the effects at T_1 and T_2. If now the mirror M_2 is moved parallel to itself then at certain points the sounds will annual each other and at other points they will reinforce each other. Let d_1 be the distance apart of the two mirrors when a maximum sound is heard; then $d_1 = n\lambda$, where n is an integer and λ is the wavelength of the sound wave. If the second maximum is now heard at a distance d_2 of the mirror, $d_2 = (n+1)\ \lambda$ so that

$$\lambda = (d_2 - d_1)$$

As the frequency of the source of sound is known very accurately the sound velocity can be calculated from the relation

$$V = n\lambda = n\ [d_2 - d_1]$$

From a series of observations, Hebb obtained the mean value for V as $331{\cdot}29 \pm {\cdot}04$ m/s. The theoretical value for the velocity of sound comes as $331{\cdot}80$ m/s. assuming $r = 1{\cdot}45$.

10.4 VELOCITY OF SOUND CONTAINED IN TUBES

The open air determination of the velocity of sound is liable to various sources of error such as the variation of temperature, pressure, humidity along the long path length that is usually taken. These sources of error can be eliminated to a considerable extent when measurement of velocity of sound is made with the experimental gas contained in a tube. This method is also useful in the sense that the velocity of sound can be measured in different gases and also when the gas is available in small quantities. The previous theoretical deductions regarding the effect of pressure, temperature and humidity can also be tested by this method. The velocity of sound is also affected by the viscosity and heat conduction when the gas is contained in a tube. The expression for velocity of sound has been deduced by Helmholtz and Kirchoff taking into consideration the effect of viscosity and heat conduction, and is given by

$$V' = V\left[1 - \left(\frac{\nu'}{4\pi N}\right)^{1/2}\frac{1}{a}\right] \tag{10.4}$$

where V' is the actual velocity; V is the measured velocity; ν' is a constant $= 2{\cdot}5\ \mu/\rho$ and (μ is the viscosity coefficient and ρ is the density of the gas) and N, is the frequency of the sound wave a is the radius of the tube.

The method that is widely used for the measurement of velocity of sound is the Kundt's tube method (Fig. 10.2). In the simplest arrangement, the gas

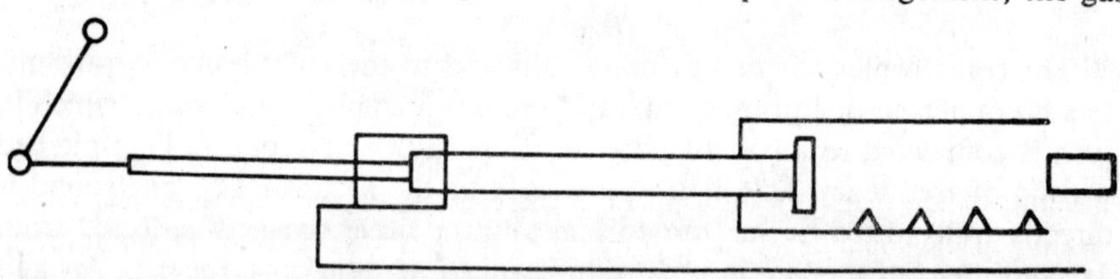

Fig. 10.2

is contained in a cylindrical glass tube (5 cm in diameter and 1m in length) containing some fine powder such as lycopodium powder or fine corkdust or quartz dust. Both the ends of the tube are sealed by perfectly sound reflecting walls. The vibrations are excited by means of a metallic rod clamped at the middle, one end of which is inserted into the tube or by means of a suitable piezoelectric vibrator mounted at one end of a tube. The sound waves travel down the length of the tube and get reflected from the opposite end and combining with the incoming waves form a system of stationary waves. At resonance, the dust is thrown into vigorous vibration and will collect at the nodes, the nodes and antinodes being formed due to stationary waves. The tube should preferably be connected with a vacuum pump which can produce various pressures and the velocity can be determined at various pressures or alternatively, the tube can be exhausted of air and various gases can be introduced and the velocity can be determined.

The lycopodium powder will collect at the nodes as shown in Fig. 10.2. This distance can be very accurately measured with the help of a travelling microscope; as the distance between the successive nodes and antinodes is $\lambda/2$ where λ is the wavelength of sound, the distance d between the successive heaps is equal to $\lambda/2$ and consequently

$$V = N\lambda = 2d \cdot N.$$

where N is the frequency of the sound wave.

If the vibrations are excited by clamping the rod at its middle point, then

$$N = \frac{S}{2l}\sqrt{\frac{E}{\rho}}$$

where for fundamental vibration $S = 1$ and l is the length of the rod, E is the Young's modulus of elasticity of the material of the rod and ρ the density.

Hence the velocity V is given by

$$V = \frac{2d}{2l}\sqrt{\frac{E}{\rho}} = \frac{d}{l}\sqrt{\frac{E}{\rho}} \tag{10.5}$$

In performing the experiment with Kundt's tube, the following points should be carefully noted.

(1) The vibrator used for the excitation of sound should be placed in such a way that it is not damped by touching the sides of the tube, as in that case a damped sound wave will be propagated through the column of air instead of a plane sound wave.
(2) The length of the tube should be adjusted accurately for resonance.
(3) The interior of the tube and the dust should be carefully dried so that the dust may not stick to the side of the tube.

Besides determining the velocity of sound in a gas at a particular pressure temperature and density, comparison of the velocity of sound in a gas and solid available in the form of a bar can be carried out with the help of Kundt's tube. The rod is clamped at the middle and vibrations are excited by scratching the rod. The frequency of vibration in the solid is given by

$$N_s = \frac{S}{2l} V_{\text{Solid}}$$

In the gas we have $\lambda_{\text{air}} = 2d$ and hence velocity in air

$$V_{\text{air}} = \frac{2d\ V_{\text{Solid}}}{2l} \qquad S = 1$$

$$V_{\text{Solid}}/V_{\text{air}} = (l/d)$$

where l is the length of the rod.

Comparison of velocity of sound can be carried on with the double tube method in which the same rod is used to excite vibrations in both the tubes and the distances d_1 and d_2 between the successive heaps of lycopodium powder are measured. Then

$$\frac{V_1}{V_2} = \frac{d_1}{d_2}$$

Determination of *r*

Kundt's dust tube method can also be utilized for determining r, the ratio of the specific heats of a gas and this is the only experimental method of determining r when the gas is available in small quantity. We note that

$$V=2\,Nd=\sqrt{\frac{rP}{\rho}}$$

or

$$r=\frac{4N^2d^2\rho}{P} \tag{10.6}$$

where the symbols have their usual significance. Kundt and Warburg determined the value of r for mercury vapour by this method and obtained the value of 1.66. Ralyeigh and Ramsay determined the value of r for argon and helium by the same method, also obtaining the value of 1.66 for these gases. The determination of r can give us some idea regarding the molecular structure of the gas. From thermodynamics it can be shown

$$r=1+\frac{2}{n} \tag{10.7}$$

where n denotes the degrees of freedom of the molecules of a gas. If the gas is monatomic and if, as a first approximation, we assume the atoms to be structureless points, then each molecule can move along the three axes of reference and hence a monatomic gas will have three degrees of freedom; consequently the value of r will be

$$r=1+\frac{2}{3}=1.66$$

in case of a monatomic gas. Thus the experimental determination of r in case of mercury vapour, helium and argon indicates that the gas will be monatomic in character.

In case of diatomic gases, the molecules can be pictured as made up to two similar atoms joined together. Thus the system will have three degrees of translation and two of rotation about the two axes perpendicular to the line joining them. Consequently, a diatomic molecule will have five degrees of freedom, three of translation and two of rotation. Hence, r in case of diatomic gases will be given by

$$r=1+\frac{2}{5}=1\cdot4.$$

This is true in case of diatomic gases like hydrogen, nitrogen, oxygen, etc. consequently if the value of r determined experimentally equals $1\cdot4$ or a very near value, the gas under examination will be a diatomic one.

In case of triatomic gases, the number of degrees of freedom will be six, three of translation and three of rotation and hence r will be

$$r=1+\frac{2}{6}=1\cdot33$$

In case of polyatomic molecules, it is not possible to calculate in a simple way the degrees of freedom of a molecule, because the vibrations are not fully developed but are considerably restricted and restrained; r will diminish with greater complexity of the molecule but will always be greater than unity. Hence the determination of r enables us to get some idea regarding the structure of molecules, i.e. whether they are monatomic, diatomic or polyatomic.

The above treatment regards the atom as a simple rigid body but actually the modern theory of atomic structure shows that atoms are complex systems composed of positively charged nucleus and shells of electrons. Such a system possesses rotational motion as well as internal vibrations. The component electrons by their vibrations give rise to spectral lines but such type of vibration giving rise to spectral lines can only be excited at extremely high temperatures and so this factor can be neglected at ordinary temperature. The rotational motion of the electrons can also be neglected because electrons have negligible mass in comparison with the mass of the nucleus and the whole mass is concentrated at the nucleus which has an extremely small radius of the order of 10^{-13} cm. The moment of inertia is, therefore, extremely small of the order of 10^{-40}g cm^2 and the energy of rotation is extremely small; hence it can be assumed that at ordinary temperature such motions do not exist; with the above assumption it can be seen from the theory given above that determination of r of a gas enables us to get some idea regarding the structure of atom.

Correction to be applied to Kundt's tube measurement

In considering the propagation of sound through a tube, it is noted that the velocity of sound is considerably modified due to the effects of viscosity and heat conduction. Helmholtz and Kirchoff calculated the change of velocity due to these factors. The velocity V' in a tube of radius a is given by

$$V' = V\left[1 - \left(\frac{\nu'}{4\pi N'}\right)^{1/2}\frac{1}{a}\right]$$

where ν' is a constant depending upon viscosity and heat conduction coefficient. The correction factor can be eliminated by taking two tubes radii a_1 and a_2 and determining the velocity V_1 and V_2. Putting

$$\left(\frac{\nu'}{4\pi N'}\right)^{1/2} = \alpha,\quad V_1 = V\left[1 - \frac{\alpha}{a_1}\right] \text{ and } V_2 = V\left[1 - \frac{\alpha}{a_2}\right].$$

$$V = \frac{a_2 V_2 - a_1 V_1}{(a_2 - a_1)}$$

10.5 VELOCITY OF SAND BY RESONANCE AIR COLUMN

This method is generally used in the laboratory for determining the velocity of sound in air. In considering the vibration of air enclosed in a tube of length l and closed at one end, it was shown that the fundamental frequency N is given by

$$N = \frac{V}{4l}$$

The actual experimental apparatus consists of a long cylindrical glass tube fixed in a calibrated stand and the bottom end being connected by means of a long rubber tubing to a container of water which can slide along the wooden stand and consequently the other end of the glass tube is closed by means of water surface. A tuning fork of known frequency is used to excite vibrations and the height of the water column is adjusted to get resonance. In this way the effective length of air column can be changed. The end correction δ at the open end can be eliminated by finding two successive lengths l_2 and l_1 of the tube which will resonate with the frequency N of the tuning fork; the difference $(l_2 - l_1)$ must be equal to half a wavelength of the sound wave in the tube. Thus we get,

$$\frac{\lambda}{2} = (l_2 - l_1)$$

$$V = N\lambda = 2N(l_2 - l_1)$$

10.6 VELOCITY OF SOUND IN DIFFERENT GASES AND VAPOURS AT DIFFERENT TEMPERATURES

The velocity of sound in different gases and vapours at different temperatures has been determined by various workers employing either a resonance column or more conveniently a Kundt's tube. Stevens determined the velocity of sound in air and in different organic vapours at temperatures between 0°C and 185°C. Dixon, Campbell and Parker determined the velocity in argon, carbondioxide, nitrogen and methane between 0°C and 1000°C and Cook measured the velocity in oxygen and air at various temperatures down to – 180°C. The values of velocity of sound in different gases at specific temperatures are given in Table 10.1.

10.7 VELOCITY OF SOUND IN A LIQUID

Just as in the case of gas, the velocity of sound in a liquid is given by

$$V = \sqrt{\frac{rK_\theta}{\rho}}$$

where K_θ is the isothermal bulk modulus of the liquid. In some liquids such as water K_θ and K_ϕ, i.e. isothermal and adiabatic bulk modulii differ by a small amount, but in most liquids such as benzene, acetone ethyl alcohol, K_θ is greater than K_ϕ by a significant amount. The value of r can also be evaluated from the relation,

$$r = \frac{1}{1 - \dfrac{\alpha^2 K_\theta\, v T'}{C_P}}$$

where, α = coefficient of critical expansion, K_θ = coefficient of isothermal elasticity, v = volume of unit mass, T = absolute temperature, and r = specific heat at constant pressure.

TABLE 10.1
Velocity of Sound in Different Gases

Gas	Velocity in m/s	
	18°C	0°C
Hydrogen	1301	1286
Carbon dioxide	265·8	258
Sulphur dioxide	216.2	
Ammonia	428·2	415
Ethyl chloride	203·8	
Nitrogen		336·79
Water vapour	405 (at 100°C)	
Heavy water vapour	451 (at 100°C)	
Dry air (CO_2 free)*		331·78
	344·00 (at 20°C)	
	386·00 (at 100°C)	
	553·00 (at 500°C)	
	700·00 (at 1000°C)	
Carbon monoxide		337·1
Carbon disulphide		189·0
Chlorine		205·3
Ethylene		314·0
Methane		432·0
Nitric oxide		325·0
Nitrous oxide		261·8
Oxygen		317·2

*The results show the validity of the equation:

$$\frac{V_t}{V_0} = \sqrt{\frac{T_t}{T_0}}$$

Liquids in bulk

The determination of velocity of sound in a liquid in bulk, such as sea-water, has been carried out by the same method as in the case of the determination of velocity of sound in open air. The significance of determination of velocity in a large volume of liquid can be seen by noting that this quantity is of fundamental importantance in determining the depth of ocean and for sound signaling.

The general principle can be illustrated by the experiments carried out by Marti in 1919 who determined the velocity in sea-water at a depth of 113 m near Cherburg in France. The sound was produced by an explosion of a charge of gun cotton and was received by three hydrophones laid on a straight line at intervals of 900 m approximately. The sound was made first on one side of the hydrophone and then on the otherside at a distance of 1200 m. The passage of the explosion wave over the microphones was recorded automatically on a smoked drum chronograph, a tuning fork of frequency 500 c/s traced a time-mark along the explosion records. The mean value of velocity reduced to a temperature of 15°C in sea-water of density 1.026 at a pressure of 1 atm. was found to be 1504.15 m/s. In recent times and specially during the last war, a large number of determinations of the velocity of sound were carried out with improved techniques.

A question of importance which naturally arises in these cases is the effect of pressure at great depths, say, in some places where the depth of the ocean is about 7,000 m or less. The pressure of water there is extremely high and the effect of pressure is to change both the elasticity and density of the liquid but the rate of increase of elasticity is greater than that of the density and D.J. Mathews found that at a depth of 9,000 m below the sea level, the velocity increased by amount 160 m/s than that at the surface.

Liquids in tubes

As Kundt's tube can be utilised for the determination of velocity of sound in a gas, the same apparatus can be utilised also for the determination of sound velocity in a liquid contained in a tube. But if stationary waves are produced in a liquid, the pressure variations at the nodes become so great that the tube yields at those points causing the pressure to drop. If K is the bulk modulus of elasticity of the liquid contained in the tube of mean radius a, of wall thickness r and Young's modulus E, then the apparent bulk modulus of the liquidK' is given by

$$K' = \frac{K}{1 + 2\,aK/hE}$$

and hence

$$V_0 = V_t \left[1 + \frac{2\,aK}{E\,h}\right]^{1/2}$$

This method of measurement has been utilised by Wood for measuring the velocity of sound in different liquids. A vertical steel tube is closed at its lower end by a thin rubber membrane; a small quartz crystal is placed under the membrane and the tuoe is filled with the liquid under test and sound waves generated by the crystal travel through the liquid. A small piezoelectric pickup is attached by soft wax near the lower end of the tube. A glass rod carrying at its lower end a sound-reflecting disc of cork or rubber can slide up or down the tube. The vibrations picked up by the piezoelectric receiver are amplified and recorded by a cathode ray oscillograph. The amplitude and phase of the recorded signal are the resultant of the direct sound transmitted by the crystal and that reflected from the piston. As the piston is removed from the bottom to the top of the tube, the received signal passes through a succession of maxima and minima which give a measure of the wavelength of sound.

The velocities of sound in a number of liquids in the temperature range 15-31°C are presented in Table 10.2.

10.8 VELOCITY OF SOUND IN A SOLID

Depending upon the state in which the solid is presented, there are different expressions for the velocity of sound in a solid. If the solid is in the form of

TABLE 10.2
Velocity of Sound in Liquids

Liquid	*Velocity in m/s*	*Temp. in °C*
Benzene	1166	17
Toluene	1297	
Carbon tetrachloride	926	
Xylene	1345	
Alcohol	1213	20·5
Ammonia (conc)	1663	16
Carbon disulphide	1161	15
Chloroform	983	15
Ether	1032	15
NaCl (10%sol.)	1470	15
NaCl (20% sol.)	1650	15
Water	1441	13
	1505	31

a thin long wire, the modulus of elasticity is evidently the Young's modulus, and the velocity

$$V=\sqrt{\frac{Y}{\rho}}$$

where Y is the Young's modulus.

On the other hand, the velocity of transverse waves in a string is given by

$$V=\sqrt{\frac{T}{m}}$$

where T is the tension and m = mass/unit length.

If the solid is in the form of a bar, the velocity of transverse waves in a bar is given by

$$V\propto\frac{1}{\lambda}\sqrt{\frac{E}{\rho}}$$

which shows that velocity is a function of λ.

If the solid is in the form of a solid bulk such as earth's crust,

$$V=\sqrt{\frac{K+4/3\ n}{\rho}}$$ for a longitudinal waves and for transverse waves

$$V=\sqrt{\frac{\mu}{\rho}}$$

here K is the bulk modulus of elasticity and μ denotes the rigidity modulus.

The velocities of sound in a few metals in the form of wise and some dielectrics, are summarized in Table 10.3.

Measurement of velocity when the solid is in the form of bars or pipes

A direct determination of the velocity of sound in a long rod or pipe was

TABLE 10.3
Velocity of Sound in Some Metals (in the form of wire)

Solid	*Velocity in m/s*
Metals	
Iron	5074
Nickel	4937
Nichrome	4981
Stainless steel	5430
Aluminium	5104
Brass	3500
Cadmium	2307
Cobalt	4724
Copper	3560
Gold (soft)	1743
Gold (hard)	2100
Lead	1227
Magnesium	4602
Nickel	4973
Palladium	3150
Platinum	2690
Silver	2610
Tin	2500
Zinc	3700
Dielectrics	
Marble	3810
Paraffin	1304
Slate	4510
Glass	5000–6000
Vulcanised rubber	3013
Was	880

obtained by Biot in which a source of sound was mounted at the end of the long pipe or cylinder; when the source begins to emit sound two sounds were heard, one travelling through the solid and the other through air. The time interval between the reception of these two sounds was noted carefully. If t is the time interval then

$$l = V_a\, t_1 = V_s\, t_2$$

$$V_s = \frac{V_a\, t_1}{t_2}$$

$$(V_s - 1) = \frac{V_a\,(t_1 - t_2)}{t_2} = \frac{V_a\, t}{t_2} = \frac{V_a\, t}{l/V_s}$$

from which V_s can be obtained as V_a is known.

When the solid is in the form of a thin rod, Kundt's tube method is generally utilised for the determination of the velocity of sound. The principle of the method has already been described in connection with the determination of the velocity of sound in a gas.

11
REFLECTION, REFRACTION, INTERFERENCE AND DIFFRACTION OF SOUND

As sound waves are wavelike disturbances in air they suffer reflection, refraction, interference and diffraction just like light waves. When a sound wave is incident on the surface of separation between two media they are reflected, the requisite condition being that the wavelength of the sound wave should be small compared with the dimension of the reflecting surface. Sound waves are also reflected when, travelling in dry air, they come into contact with moist air which has a density different from dry air and plays the function of a medium different from the dry air. The geometrical laws of reflection and refraction of sound waves are the same as those of light i.e. the angle of reflection is equal to the angle of incidence and the incidence and reflected waves are in the same plane.

11.1 REFLECTION AT THE BOUNDARY OF TWO MEDIA

The laws of reflection of sound follow directly from the wave theory. These laws follow from the fact that the velocity of sound in each medium is independent of the direction of wavefront and wavefronts on the plane of separation have equal velocities. In Fig. 11.1, *AB* represents the incident

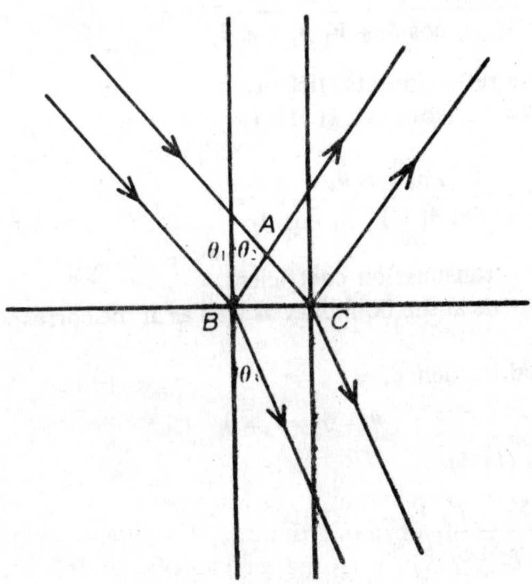

Fig. 11.1

wavefront, AC the reflected wavefront and BC the refracted wavefront; θ_1, θ_2 and θ_3 are the angles of incidence, reflection and refraction. Consequently, if V_1 and V_2 are the velocities in the two media, we get from the wave theory

$$\frac{\sin\theta_1}{V_1} = \frac{\sin\theta_2}{V_1} = \frac{\sin\theta_3}{V_2} \tag{11.1}$$

from which we get $\theta_1 = \theta_2$, i.e. the angles of incidence and reflection are equal.

Boundary Conditions

The boundary conditions which must be satisfied are:

(a) The component of particle velocity normal to the boundary must be continuous.

(b) The pressure variation δP must be continuous

From the first condition, as C_i is the particle velocity in the incident beam and C_r the velocity in the reflected beam and C_t the velocity in the transmitted beam, we get,

$$C_i \cos\theta_i + C_r \cos\theta_r = C_t \cos\theta_t \tag{11.2}$$

and from the second condition,

$$\delta P_i + \delta P_r = \delta P_t \tag{11.3}$$

but as $\delta P = \pm V\rho\dot{y}$ where ρ is the density of the medium

$$V_1\,\rho_1\,C_i - V_1\,\rho_1\,C_r = V_2\,\rho_2\,C_1 \tag{11.4}$$

The - sign in the second term of the equation (11.4) is used because the reflected wave is in the opposite direction of the incident wave.

Eliminating C_t from (11.2) and (11.4)

$$\frac{C_r}{C_i} = -\frac{V_2\,\rho_2\cos\theta_i - V_1\,\rho_1\cos\theta_2}{V_2\,\rho_2\cos\theta_1 + V_1\,\rho_1\cos\theta_2} = r \tag{11.5}$$

where r is called the reflection coefficient.

Similary, eliminating C_r from (11.2) (11.4)

$$\frac{C_t}{C_i} = \frac{2V_1\,\rho_1\cos\theta_1}{V_2\,\rho_2\cos\theta_1 + V_1\,\rho_1\cos\theta_2} = t \tag{11.6}$$

where t is called the transmission coefficient.

These equations are true at the boundary as well as at the corresponding points in the wave surface.

In case of normal incidence,

$$\theta_1 = \theta_2 = \theta_3 = 0$$

then form equation (11.5)

$$\frac{C_r}{C_i} = \frac{\rho_1\,V_1 - V_2\,V_2}{V_2\,\rho_2 + \rho_1\,V_1}$$

If $R_1 = \rho_1 V_1$ and $R_2 = \rho_2 V_2$ where R_1 and R_2 are the radiation resistances,

$$\frac{C_r}{C_i}=\frac{R_1-R_2}{R_1+R_2}=r \tag{11.7}$$

where r is called the reflection coefficient.
Similarly, from equation (13.6)

$$\frac{C_t}{C_i}=\frac{2R_1}{R_1+R_2}=t \tag{11.8}$$

using equation (11.5) percentage reflection can be calculated as shown in Table (11.1).

TABLE 11.1
Percentage reflection of sound wave when the sound enters the medium from air and vice versa

Medium	*Velocity, m/s*	*Density*	*Percentage reflection*
Water	1457	1	99·940
Rubber (soft)	70	0·98	98·000
Steel	5100	7·8	99·997

11.2 PHASE CHANGE ON REFLECTION

In this case we shall consider two cases: (a) reflection from a rigid surface and (b) reflection from a yielding surface. A rigid surface will not yield to alternate compressions and rarefactions present in a longitudinal wave. The side of a wall or the closed end of an organ pipe approximate to a rigid wall. If a pulse of a compressed air reaches such a surface, the motion of the air particles is checked, and consequently a pulse of compression will be reflected from the wall as another pulse of compression and similarly a pulse of rarefaction will be reflected from the wall as a pulse of rarefaction. Consequently, when sound waves are incident on a rigid wall there will not be any change in phase.

In the second case, when the sound wave is incident on a yielding boundary, there is greater freedom for the wave to expand outwards. It can expand not only outwards but it also expands sideways; consequently when a compressed wave reaches such a surface, a wave of rarefaction will travel outwards and consequently a wave of rarefaction also travels inwards. Hence when the sound wave is incident on a reflecting surface which yields to the compression present in the longitudinal wave, a phase change occurs and the phase of the reflected wave is opposite to that of the incident wave.

11.3 REFLECTION OF SOUND WAVE FROM A PLATE OF FINITE THICKNESS

We have earlier considered reflection of sound wave from a medium which is extended infinitely but it is interesting and also of practical importance to consider the case when the second medium is of finite thickness. We come across such familiar cases in optics and in this case also the boundary conditions regarding the pressure and particle velocity hold good as in the case just considered. Rayleigh, in his theory of sound, considered the case when the waves are incident normally, and derived the expression

$$\frac{C_r}{C_i}=r=\frac{\left[\frac{R_1}{R_2}-\frac{R_2}{R_1}\right]}{\left\{4\cot^2\frac{2\pi l}{\lambda}+\left[\frac{R_1}{R_2}+\frac{R_2}{R_1}\right]^2\right\}^{1/2}} \tag{11.9}$$

where the symbols have their usual significance and l is the thickness of the medium and λ denotes the wavelength of incident wave. From equation (11.9) we observe that when $l=0$ or a multiple of $\lambda/2$, $\cot^2 2\pi l/\lambda 1=\infty$ and hence the ratio $C_r/C_i=0$ which means that there will not be any reflected wave. Hence a half-wave plate will reflect none and transmit all the energy that is incident on it.

If on the other hand, l is a multiple of $\lambda/4$ then cot $2\pi l/\lambda$ is zero, r the reflection coefficient becomes a maximum, and in this case

$$r=\frac{R_1^2-R_2^2}{R_1^2+R_2^2} \tag{11.10}$$

These theoretical deductions of Rayleigh were experimentally verified by Boyle and Lehman. In their experiment they used a quartz oscillator as the source of sound under water at a frequency of 135000 c/s. The reflecting surfaces were mode of different thicknesses of lead and the reflected energy was measured by a torsion pendulum. It was found that the reflected energy increased gradually as the thickness of lead plates was increased and practically remained constant for $l=0\cdot1\ \lambda$ to $l=0\cdot4\ \lambda$ at which almost all the energy incident on the plate was reflected back and then gradually decreased and become practically equal to zero when $l=\lambda/2$. The critical angle for total reflection was also determined and the experimental results were found to be in general agreement with theory.

11.4 FORMATION OF ECHOES

The repeatition of sound produced by reflection at an obstacle such as the wall of a building or a cliff is called an echo. In order that the echo of a sound may be appreciated by the ear, the reflected sound must reach the observer at least one tenth of a second later than the direct sound, because this is the minimum time necessary for the ear to distinguish between two sounds as distinct from one another. In these cases, the best echoes are produced when the dimensions of the reflector are large compared with the wavelength of the sound wave. Thus a sharp crack or a sound of impulsive nature gives a clear and loud echo whereas with a low-pitched sound of long wavelength the echo may be scarcely perceptible. The formation of echoes is conveniently utilised in determining the depth of ocean or in determining the height of an aeroplane, by a process which is known as echo depth sounding. Reverberation in an auditorium is due to multiple reflections of the speaker's voice from the surrounding wall. We shall consider these cases in chapter 14.

Harmonic Echoes

The intensity of a reflected wave of sound depends upon the dimension of the reflector with respect to its wavelength and as the length of sound diminishes the effectiveness with regard to reflection of a small reflector improves. Hence if a composite sound wave consisting of low and high frequencies is incident on a surface the reflected wave will be rich in amplitude with respect to sound waves of high frequencies; when the wavelength of sound becomes comparable with the dimension of the reflector, the phenomenon can be regarded as scattering and Rayleigh in his Theory of Sound dealt with the phenomenon in an analogous manner as the scattering of light. He showed that just as in the case of light scattering the amplitude of scattered sound varies* directly as the volume of the scatterer and inversely as the square of the wavelength and, as such, the intensity varies inversely as the fourth power of the wavelength. If I_s and I_v are the intensities of the scattered and incident sound waves, then

$$\frac{I_s}{I_v} \propto \frac{\nu}{\lambda^4 r^2}$$

where ν is the volume of the scatterer.

This formula shows that if we have a composite note consisting of fundamental and its overtones, then the higher harmonics of the note will be reflected in a much greater proportion than the fundamental note. Thus, the reflected sound will be much richer in proportion in higher harmonics than the fundamental note and echoes of such character are known as harmonic echoes.

Musical echoes

If the reflector consists of a large number of obstacles placed at regular intervals such as a row of regularly placed pailing just as in the case of an echelon grating then the echo consists of a large number of reflections of the original sound reaching the ear at regular intervals of time. The successive elements or strips reflect the impulse or its harmonics and it reaches the observer at a regular interval of time and if the reflection is sufficiently rapid they blend into a musical note. The frequency of the note depends upon d where "d" is the spacing of the steps and the angle θ the direction in which the reflection proceeds from the step. The frequency of the note will be $v/2d \cos \theta$ where v is the velocity of sound. The sound wave striking the pailing and being reflected there has to travel a little further and consequently reaches the listener's ear a little later than the wave which struck the preceding pailing in the row. R.W. Wood has demonstrated the existance of such a musical echo by means of an echelon reflector by the spark method of shadow photography.

Whispering gallery

An interesting case of reflection of sound occurs in the well known whispering gallery of St. Paul's Cathedral in London. The gallery has a hemispherical dome and a circular form running round its base. A person whispering along the wall can be heard distinctly by a listner close to the wall at any other part of the gallery but the whisper remains in audible at any point far from the wall. According to Airy, the effect is to be observed at the point of the gallery diametrically opposite to the source of sound. A complete explanation of the phenomenon is still to be found but Rayleigh gave a theory which explains some of the observed facts. He pointed out that sound tends to creep around inside of a curved wall without ever getting far from it. The abnormal loudness with which the whisper is heard is not confined to the position diametrically opposite to that of the source of sound and therefore does not depend upon the symmetry of the dome. Further, whisper which contains a greater proportion of high-pitched sounds is heard more distinctly than ordinary sound. Raman and Sutherland verified some of the consequences of Rayleigh's theory with the help of a high pitched source and a sensitive flame.

11.5 REFRACTION OF SOUND

In case of sound waves travelling from a medium of rarer density to a medium of greater density or vice versa, refraction of sound takes place. We have earlier shown that familiar laws of refraction applied to light can also be applied to sound. Sandhauss demonstrated the refraction of sound through prisms containing various gases and determined the acoustic refractive indices of the gases relative to air. If n is the refractive index of a gas

$$n = \frac{\text{Velocity of sound through air}}{\text{Velocity of sound through the gas}}$$

Propagation of sound through upper atmosphere

The phenomenon of refraction of sound has a very useful application when sound travels through the upper atmosphere, which can mainly be divided into two regions, Troposphere and Stratosphere. Troposphere extends to a height of 12 km from the surface of the earth and there is a fall of temperature of approximately 6°C per kilometre of ascent. Temperature remains constant for a few kilometres above this height and then it begins to increase. It is assumed that ozone formed due to ultraviolet radiation from the Sun absorbs this radiation and the layers are heated. This increase of temperature continues up to a height of 50 km beyond which there is again a fall of temperature as one goes up. The change of temperature can be represented by the equation

$$T = T_0 (1 - \alpha H)$$

where $\alpha = 6°\text{C/km}$ and H is the height in km.

Then $$\frac{V_T}{V_0} = \sqrt{\frac{T}{T_0}} = (1 - \alpha H)^{1/2} = \left[1 - \frac{\alpha H}{2}\right]$$

Hence with the increase of height, the velocity of sound diminishes and a sound ray travelling upwards obliquely from the earth through the successive layers of the troposphere will bend towards the normal; that is, it will tend to become vertical as the temperature diminishes. This bending will continue upto the height of 12 km that is up to the end of troposphere and then will remain constant as the temperature is constant for a few kilometres in this region. As the ray enters the stratosphere, the temperature increases which causes the velocity of the sound to increase and the ray begins to bend towards the horizontal surface. As the ray proceeds through the different layers of the stratosphere this horizontal inclination increases till, at a certain height, the ray becomes perfectly horizontal. It then begins its return journey and again crossing the different layers of the atmosphere reaches the earth. It is evident that the greater the inclination of the ray to the horizontal when it leaves the earth the greater will be the distance at which it will be received at the earth from the point of origin.

Anomalous audibility and zone of silence

From the above analysis it is clear that if sound of high intensity, such as produced by an explosion, is produced then there will be a region surrounding the site of explosion where the sound will be heard directly. Further away there will be another region where the sound reaches after reflection from the upper regions of the atmosphere. In between these two zones there will be a zone of silence. Systematic study of this phenomenon was undertaken after the first world war and distinct regions of audibility and silence were established by a group of workers at La Courtine in central France. The regions known as regions of anomalous audibility were also observed by another group of workers in Germany.

Total internal reflection

Just as in the case of light, sound waves are reflected totally when they are incident on a medium of rarer density from a medium of greater density, provided that the angle of incidence is greater than the critical angle. The critical angle is as usual defined as the angle of incidence for which the refracted ray just grazes the surface of separation. The velocity of sound in air is 340 m/s and that in water is 1440 m/s. When sound waves will enter water from air the angle of refraction will be greater and so the ray will deviate away from normal. Hence if θ is the critical angle, then

$$\frac{\sin\theta}{\sin\frac{\pi}{2}} = \frac{340}{1440} \quad \text{or} \quad \theta = 13\cdot5^\circ \text{ (nearly)}$$

Refraction of sound takes place when the wave of sound reaches a point where the wave velocity changes. Besides the change of medium, there may be other factors which may cause a change in the wave velocity of sound. Thus if there is flow of wind or there is a temperature gradient, the velocity of sound will be modified.

Effect of wind

It is observed that the velocity of wind increases from the earth's surface upwards. In still air, the wavefront of the travelling sound is perpendicular to the ground. If, however, a wind is blowing with a steady velocity in the same direction as the direction of propagation of sound then the wavefront will travel faster where the wind velocity is greater and consequently the wavefront will bend downwards towards the ground. An observer therefore hears the sound by a ray which leaves the source with a slightly upward inclination. In the same way, when wind is travelling opposite the direction of propagation of sound, the wave front bends backwards and at a moderate distance from the source passes high over the head of the observer.

Effect of temperature

In the daytime there is a fall of temperature from ground upwards and consequently the velocity of sound is greater near the ground than at higher levels. In absence of temperature variation, the wave fronts of the sound waves are all vertical and consequently during the day time the wavefronts bend upwards and the effect is thus similar to the propagation of sound against the wind and the waves are thinned near the ground so that distant voices are not heard well.

At dusk, the air near the ground falls in temperature more rapidly than air above because of its contact with the ground which loses heat more rapidly and consequently the velocity of sound wave is greater at the higher altitude and the wavefronts thus turn downwards and the effect is thus similar as the propagation of sound with the wind so that distant voices are heard clearly.

11.6. INTERFERENCE OF SOUND

As in the familiar case of light, two sound waves combine together to produce interference and Huygen's principle of superposition holds in this case also. On this principle, the resultant displacement of a particle due to the simultaneous propagation of two or more waves is the vector sum of the resultant displacements due to each wave train independently. In chapter 1, we have treated examples of combination of simple harmonic vibrations of different amplitudes and phases. Such superposition of vibrations is called interference. The familiar example of beats which has been treated in chapter 1, is an example of interference of sound. When two vibrating sources of sound of nearly equal amplitude and phase and of slightly different frequencies are sounded together, the intensity of the resultant tone increases and decreases with time, the frequency of this intensity variation is equal to the difference of the frequencies of the two. This phenomenon of beats is due to the fact that at certain equal time intervals the wave trains agree in phase and reinforce each other while at intermediate times they are opposite in phase and cancel each other and consequently the phenomenon of beats can be regarded as an example of interference.

11.7 COMBINATION TONES

It was discovered independently by Sorge, a German organist, in 1745 and later by Tartini in 1754 that when two tones of frequencies n_1 and n_2 are sounded together, a third tone of frequency $(n_1 \sim n_2)$ i.e. their difference is produced.

Soon after Tartini's discovery it was suggested by Lagrange in 1759 and later by Young in 1800 that the third tone is identical with beats and as such they were designed as difference tone due to the fact that the frequency of the tone is equal to the difference of frequency between the two.

Helmholtz later on carried an extensive experimental and theoretical work on the subject and found that when two intense tones of different frequencies are sounded together then besides the difference tone mentioned above another tone was produced whose frequency is the sum of frequencies of the combining tones, i.e. (n_1+n_2) and he called this tone as the summation tone. Besides this, he found in the resultant tones, tones having frequencies $2n_1$ and $2n_2$. All these were termed by him as combination tones. He also observed that these tones are only produced when the intensities of the primary tones are large, and feeble primaries failed to produce them. He was thus led to the 'intensity theory' which successfully explained their formation.

Intensity theory of Helmholtz

As in the case of small displacements the equation of motion of a particle is given by

$$f=ax$$

where f the external force. But in the case of large displacements, as is necessary in the formation of combination tones, the equation of motion can be written in the form

$$f=ax+bx^2+cx^3+\ldots\ldots \qquad (11.11)$$

where a, b and c are constants of motion.

If the system is subjected to two forces f_1 and f_2, the forces being sufficiently large to cause large displacements, then

$$f_1=ax_1+bx_1^2+cx_1^3+\ldots\ldots \qquad (11.12)$$

and if the displacement due to other force f_2 be x_2

$$f_2=ax_2+bx_2^2+cx_2^3+\ldots \qquad (11.13)$$

and if the resultant displacement under the simultaneous action of the two forces be (f_1+f_2), then

$$f_1+f_2=ax+bx^2+cx^3+\ldots. \qquad (11.14)$$

and from (11.12) and (11.13)

$$f_1+f_2=a\,(x_1+x_2)+b\,(x_1^2+x_2^2)+c\,(x_1^3+x_2^3)+\ldots. \qquad (11.15)$$

from (11.14) and (11.15) it can be seen that

$$x\neq(x_1+x_2)$$

Thus it is clear that if the system is subjected simultaneously to two intense forces, the resultant displacement is not equal to the sum of individual displacements, i.e. the principle of super position does not hold, and such a system is known as 'asymmetric system'. Helmholtz worked out the effect of subjecting an asymmetric system simultaneously under the action of two forces and explained satisfactorily the occurrence of combination tones.

Asymmetrical system under two forces

Let us now discuss the consequences of subjecting an asymmetrical system to two impressed harmonic forces. Then we get the equation of motion for larger displacements and remembering equation (11.11)

$$m\frac{d^2x}{dt^2}+\omega^2 mx+amx^2=mf\cos pt+mg\cos(qt+\epsilon) \tag{11.16}$$

where m is the mass of the system, ω is the natural frequency of the system, f and g are the amplitudes of the applied forces and p and q their frequencies. Then from (11.16) we get,

$$\frac{d^2x}{dt^2}+\omega^2x+ax^2=f\cos pt+g\cos(qt+\epsilon) \tag{11.17}$$

Neglecting ax^2 as a first approximation, we have

$$\frac{d^2x}{dt^2}+\omega^2x=f\cos pt+g\cos(qt+\epsilon) \tag{11.18}$$

Let $$x=A\cos pt+B\cos(qt+\epsilon) \tag{11.19}$$

then $$-Ap^2\cdot\cos pt-Bq^2\cos(qt+\epsilon)+\omega^2A\cos pt$$
$$+\omega^2 B\cos(qt+\epsilon)=f\cos pt+g\cos(qt+\epsilon)$$

Equating the coefficients of $\cos pt$ and $\cos(qt+\epsilon)$.

$$A=\frac{f}{\omega^2-p^2} \qquad B=\frac{g}{\omega^2-q^2} \tag{11.20}$$

Substituting the values of A and B, we get from equation (11.19)

$$x=\frac{f}{\omega^2-P^2}\cos pt+\frac{g}{\omega^2-q^2}\cos(qt+\epsilon).$$

Then from equation (11.17) we get,

$$\begin{aligned}\frac{d^2x}{dt^2}+\omega^2x&=f\cos pt+g\cos(qt+\epsilon)\\ &\quad -a\,[A^2\cos^2 pt+B^2\cos^2(qt+\epsilon)\\ &\quad +2AB.\cos pt\cos(qt+\epsilon)].\\ &=f\cos pt+g\cos(qt+\epsilon)\\ &\quad -\frac{a}{2}[A^2+B^2+A^2\cos 2\cdot pt+B^2\cos 2(qt+\epsilon)\\ &\quad +2AB\cos\{(p+q)t+\epsilon\}+2AB\cos\{(p-q)t+\epsilon\}].\end{aligned}$$

This form of equation suggests that the solution must contain terms involving frequencies which are double the original ones and their sum and difference also. Hence to the present approximation, the resultant vibration forced upon the system consists of primary tones and others whose frequencies are respectively double those primary frequencies and their sum and difference respectively. This explains the occurrence of various frequencies in the combination tones. It should be noticed that all these four derived tones have amplitudes proportional to the second power of amplitudes of primary tones and hence the intensity of these tones increases in relative importance with the intensity of the primary tones, being negligible in case of feeble primaries and paramount in case of large primaries which is also consistent with experimental observation.

11.8 OBJECTIVE AND SUBJECTIVE EXISTENCE OF COMBINATION TONES

There has been a great deal of discussion regarding the subjective and objective existence of combination tones. The beat tone theory of combination tones suggests that the formation of combination tones is merely a physiological effect than a real physical phenomenon. It is the ear that recognises the quick succession of beats as a distinct tone which was formed within the ear and thus only has a subjective existence. At that time only differential tones were known and they were connected with the phenomenon of beats. But this, in the first instance, leaves the summation tones entirely unexplained. Helmholtz, however, later proved the objective existence of combination tones and the requisite condition for the generation of the tones is that the same mass of air should be violently agitated by two simple tones simultaneously. He realised this condition with his double siren when the tones are produced by two series of holes blown upon simultaneously from the same wind chest. In this case, he finds that combination tones are as powerful as those from the generators. He realised the objective existence of combination tone by means of sympathetic resonance of a membrane tuned in unison with the combination tone. He also used his air resonator which is more sensitive than membrane.

In 1895, an experiment was performed by Rucker and Edser with the Michelson interferometer which conclusively proved the existence of combination tones. One of the reflecting mirrors was mounted on one end of a tuning fork of frequency 64 which acted as a resonator to one of the combination tones and the generation tones were produced by means of a Helmholtz double siren. The system was so sensitive that movement of 1/80,000th of an inch would alter the length of the path of one of the interfering beams by one wavelength. Adequate precautions were taken to eliminate all errors and when the double siren was sounded so that a new tone of frequency 64 was produced the bands in the field of view were shifted which showed that the tuning fork has responded to the new tone of frequency 64. This proves that combination tones have got an objective reality.

11.9 DIFFRACTION OF SOUND

As sound is wave-like in nature, so just like light waves the phenomenon of diffraction is also exibited by sound waves. During the propagation, whenever the wavefront is unobstructed each element of the wave front travels along a straight line, but when it is obstructed by an obstacle or a perforated screen, the waves bend round the obstacle and the phenomena of diffraction occurs.

In case of diffraction of light or X-rays by a grating having the grating space $2d$, the diffraction maxima will occur according to the equation as derived in textbooks on optics, viz.

$$2d \sin \phi = n\lambda$$

Consequently ϕ will be large when λ is large. Hence diffraction phenomena is more marked in case of sound waves than in the case of light waves; further the dimension of the obstacle should be comparable with the wavelength of sound. Hence it is easier to observe the diffraction phenomena with ultrasonic waves than with sounds of sonic frequencies.

As in the case of optics, the diffraction phenomenon is governed by Huyghen's principle. According to this principle, every point in a wave surface is the source of spherical waves and the resultant effect at any point is the vector sum of the displacements due to these spherical waves and the new wavefront will be the envelope of all such spherical waves. Just as in the case of light waves we can consider some typical cases.

11.10 DIFFRACTION THROUGH A SLIT

Let us consider a single slit AB (Fig. 11.2) on which a plane wave of sound is incident. Let C be the middle point of the slit. Then AD may be regarded

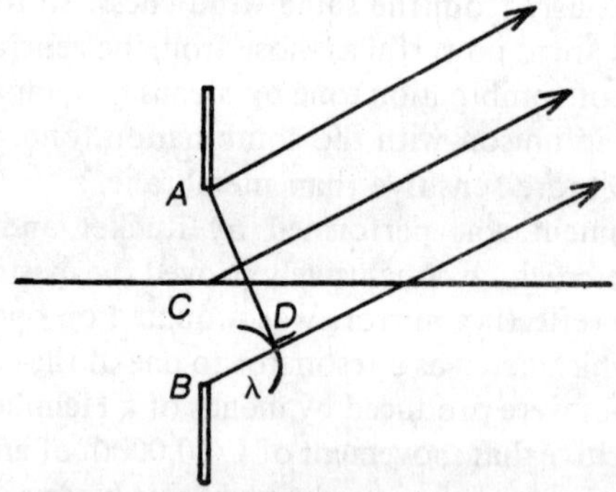

Fig. 11.2

as the instantanceous position of the wavefront and each point in it may be regarded as the source of a set of secondary waves. With centre B and radius equal to λ, the wavelength of the sound wave, let an arc of a circle be described and from A a line AD be drawn to touch this circle; then in the direction BD, the waves from B start a wavelength behind those starting from A and waves from C start half a wavelength behind those from A. This causes a progressive phase change for waves starting from different points of the wavefront. The incident wavefront can thus be divided into a series of equal elementary strips parallel to the length of the slit. The contributions of these strips at a point P will be approximately equal but will differ progressively in phase. The resultant displacement at P is given by the result obtained earlier: (Chapter 2, section 2.3 case 3).

$$\sum a \sin \theta = \frac{a \sin n\theta/2}{\sin \theta/2} \sin \frac{n-1}{2} \theta.$$

$$\sum a \cos \theta = \frac{a \sin n\theta/2}{\sin \theta/2} \cos \frac{n-1}{2} \theta.$$

where a is the amplitude of a component vibration and θ is the phase difference between the successive disturbances. Then A the resultant amplitude at P where the point P is such that the lines proceeding to it, from A and B may be considered parallel.

i.e. $A = [\{\Sigma\ a \sin \theta\}^2 + \{\Sigma\ a \cos \theta\}^2]^{1/2}$

$$= \frac{a \sin n\theta/2}{\sin \theta/2}.$$

If now n becomes very large and θ very small and if the phase difference between the first and last vibration be 2α then

$$A = \frac{a \sin \alpha}{\sin \alpha/n} = \frac{na \sin \alpha}{\alpha} \text{ since } \alpha/n \text{ is very small.}$$

In this case $2\alpha = \dfrac{2\pi\, d \sin \phi}{\lambda}$

where d is the slit width and ϕ is the angle between normal to the slit and direction of P. For the direction normal to the slit,

$\phi = 0.\ \alpha = 0,\ \dfrac{\sin \alpha}{\alpha} = 1$ and $A = na$. Let this value of A be denoted by A_0.

Then $$A = A_0 \sin \alpha/\alpha$$

Further $A = A_0$ for $\alpha = m\pi$ where $m = 1, 2, 3$, etc.

$$d \sin \phi = m\lambda, \quad \text{or} \quad \sin \phi = m\lambda/d$$

For A to be maximum, we must have $\dfrac{dA}{d\alpha} = 0$

$$\frac{\cos \alpha}{\alpha} - \frac{\sin \alpha}{\alpha^2} = 0$$

$$\text{or } \tan \alpha = \alpha$$

The values of α which satisfy this equation are obtained by plotting the values of tan α against α and are given by $\alpha = 0, \dfrac{3\pi}{2}, \dfrac{5\pi}{2}, \dfrac{7\pi}{2}$ and so on.

For the second maximum,

$$A = A_0 \frac{\sin \alpha}{\alpha} = \frac{A_0 \sin 3\pi/2}{3\pi/2} = \frac{2A_0}{3\pi}$$

The corresponding values of A/A_0 against different values of π are plotted in Fig. 11.3 dotted curve and the continuous curve represents A^2/A_0^2 against π which is proportional to intensity.

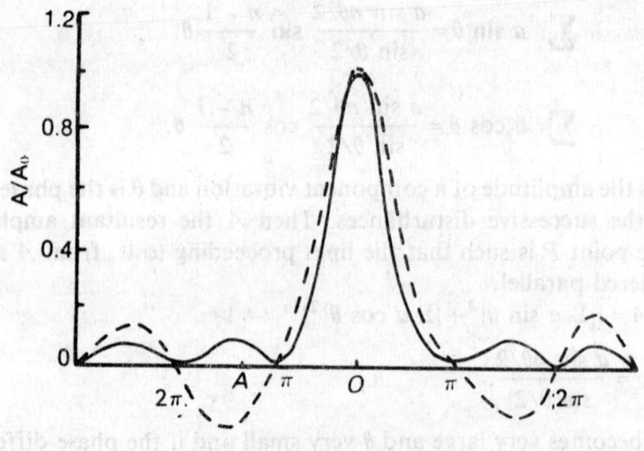

Fig. 11.3

11.11 THE CASE OF CIRCULAR APERTURE

When a sound wave is incident on a circular aperture the problem of diffraction can be treated with the help of Huyghen's principle as in the case of a rectangular slit. The circular aperture can be divided into a number of circular zones and the resultant effect on the axis is the same as the sum of the vibrations sent out by the individual circular zones. If the radius of the aperture is such that an even number of zones is included the amplitude at a point P on the axis is zero while an odd number of zones gives an amplitude double that of the unobstructed wave. Referring to Fig. 11.4, we note that if δ is the path

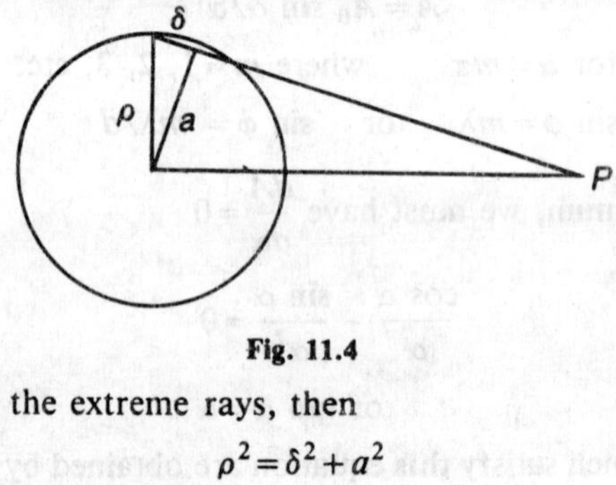

Fig. 11.4

difference between the extreme rays, then

$$\rho^2 = \delta^2 + a^2$$

where ρ is the radius of the circular aperture.
Then if r is the distance between the centre of the circular aperture and the point P at which we are to compute the resultant effect

$$r^2 = a^2 + (r - \delta)^2$$

or
$$a^2 = 2r\delta - \delta^2$$

$\therefore$
$$\rho^2 = 2r\delta \quad \text{or} \quad \delta = \rho^2/2r$$

and if the path difference equals $m\lambda/2$ where m is an integer, then the intensity will be a maximum or minimum according as m is odd or even. As in the case of rectangular slit just considered the amplitude is given by $A \sin \alpha/\alpha$.

11.12 THE DIFFRACTION GRATING

The diffraction grating is a familiar equipment in optics and is used mainly for the determination of the wavelength of light and production of spectra besides demonstrating the phenomenon of diffraction. It is not necessary to use the grating in acoustics for the production of spectra but the apparatus can be utilized for the measurement of the wavelength of sound. When sound waves are reflected from a periodic structure the waves reinforce each other or destroy themselves by destructive interference in certain directions depending on the wavelength of sound and the spacing of the reflectors. Similar effects are also observed when the sound waves are transmitted through a structure containing equidistant apertures. Thus as in optics we have both reflection and transmission gratings.

In such cases as in the case of optical diffraction grating the well known relation

$$2d \sin \phi = \pm m\lambda$$

holds where m is the order of the spectrum having the values 1, 2, 3, etc. and $2d$ is the grating constant; when d becomes smaller than λ there are no lateral maxima and the sound beam is reflected normally. However, when the wavelength becomes small as in the case of ultrasonics the sound is diffracted into spectra of various orders.

11.13 EXPERIMENTAL ARRANGEMENT

The theoretical calculations carried out so far regarding the diffraction of sound can be experimentally verified in the laboratory but, as has been noted in the above discussion, the dimension of the obstacle should be comparable with the wavelength of sound and hence it is convenient to perform these experiments with ultrasonic waves. For sound waves in air measurements were made by Pohl. The source of sound was a high frequency-generating whistle and the sound was detected by a radiometer (Fig. 11.5).

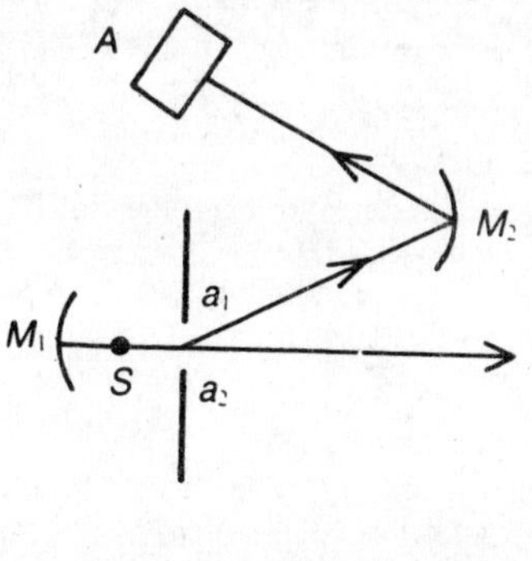

Fig. 11.5

The whistle is mounted at S at the focus of the concave mirror M_1. The sound waves are made parallel by reflection from the mirror M_1 and enter the slit a_1 a_2 which is 11.5 cm wide. The receiving mirror M_2 and the sound radiometer A are connected by a shaft which can revolve over a graduated circular scale. The intensity of the diffracted beam can be plotted against the corresponding position in the circular scale and the result obtained has been plotted in Fig. 11.6. The results are not only in qualitative agreement but also agree

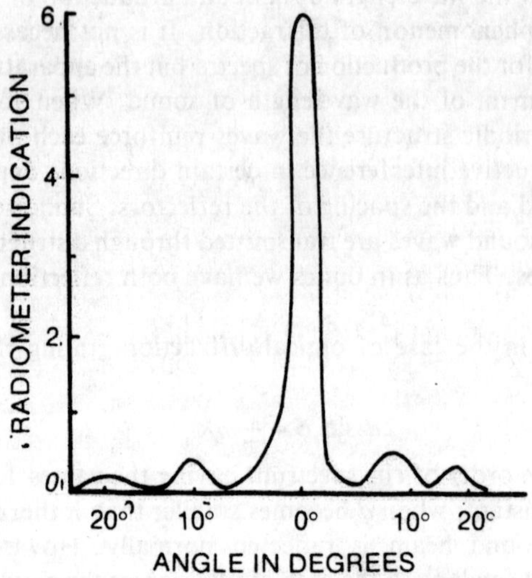

Fig. 11.6

quantitatively Experiments of the same kind were made by Boyle and Reid (1926) and a fair quantitative agreement was obtained.

12

RECEPTION AND TRANSFORMATION OF SOUND

In this chapter it is proposed to examine and analyse the receivers of sound and we shall in the first part concentrate only on those means which are capable of receiving sound as mechanical vibration and then shall treat the various devices which receive the sound but convert them to other forms of energy. The choice of receiver of sound energy will depend upon

(a) the character and property of sound wave, i.e. its amplitude, frequency and wavefront. It is natural that the frequency response of a receiver may be limited and hence different forms of receivers are necessary for different ranges of frequency.

(b) the nature of the medium which transmits the wave, i.e. the radiation resistance of a medium and the velocity of propagation may be involved.

Considered from another point of view it may be sometimes necessary just as in the case of long distance signalling, that the receiver should be sensitive enough to pick up extremely weak signals, which means that the receiver be in resonance with a particular frequency of the emitted signal. Such type of sound receiver is called the resonant receiver. It may also be sometimes necessary that a faithful record or reprodution is necessary. In such cases a nonresonant receiver which sacrifices energy and sensitiveness to faithfulness is necessary.

12.1 THE HUMAN EAR

The human ear is one of the most common examples of the receiver of sound energy. The range within which the human ear is capable of receiving sound energy usually lies between 20 and 20,000 c/s and can distinguish a change of intensity between 10^{12} to 1. The ear is also capable of resolving a complex note into its associated Fourier components and can also discriminate between different sounds at the same time.

A complete accurate structure and the functions of the different organs of hearing is beyond the scope of the present work but it is proposed to give a bare outline of the disposition and action of the more essential parts. Starting from the outside we have the external ear (Pinna) from which extends the ear passage (external auditory meatus). This terminates at the drum skin (membrane tumpani) and beyond this lies the cavity which is called the drum (tympanium). The drum is bridged across by a train of three little bones called ossicles. These are called the hammer, the anvil and the stirrup; one part of the hammer is in contact with the drum skin while another part articulates the anvil which is attached to the apex of the stirrup. The base of the stirrup is attached to a membrane which closes an oval opening which is called fenestra vestibuli in wall which forms the inner limit of the drum. There is also a round opening in the bony wall which is closed by a thin membrane. Beyond this lies the innermost part of the organ called labyrinth. The labyrinth consists of three parts called (a) the vestibule, (b) the three semicircular canals, and (c) the cochlea. The vestibule is the middle portion of labyrinth and contains the oval window that receives the foot of the strirrup; upward and backward from the vestibule proceed the three semicircular canals. Forward and downward from the vestibule there is cochlea which is a spiral canal and it faces the round window at its entrance.

12.2 THEORIES OF HEARING

Though a complete agreement has not yet been reached regarding the theory of hearing, Helmholtz's theory of audition can explain many of the observed facts and we shall discuss the theory in some detail. The vibrations of the air caused by a source of sound are collected by the pinna and they travel through the air in the external auditory meatus. The vibrations then force the tympanic membrane into corresponding vibrations and the tympanic membrane is of such a size and tension that it can readily respond to any vibrations between certain wide limits. These vibrations are then communicated through the three ossicles (which vibrate as if they were one) to the membrane closing the fenestra ovalis. The vibrations of the fenestra ovalis are transmitted through the basilar membrane and set the endolymph of the canal of cochlea into vibrations which are ultimately transmitted to the divisions of the auditory nerves. The stimuli are conveyed by the auditory nerves to the brain and produce the perception of sound. The basilar membrane contains about 24,000 fibres and they increase in length from the base to the apex of the cochlea. Helmholtz maintains that the sound wave advancing along the cochlea excites into resonance that particular radial strip of basilar membrane which is in tune with it. The actual mechanism by which the sound energy is converted to nerve energy is not easy to follow and some theories have been advanced to explain it.

12.3 SENSATION OF LOUDNESS; WEBER-FECHNER LAW

A method of measuring the sensation of loudness is given by Weber's law which states that "The increase of stimulus to produce the minimum perceptible increase of sensation is proportional to the pre-existing stimulus" i.e. starting with a certain sound intensity, the increase of intensity which produces a noticeable change of sensation may be measured. From Weber's law, Fechner derived the relation

$$\delta S = K.\ \frac{\partial E}{E}$$

or $$S = K \log E \qquad (12.1)$$

where S is the magnitude of sensation, E the intensity of stimulus and K a constant and the above relation is known as Weber-Fachner law. This relation has been somewhat verified experimentally by Knudsen.

12.4 ANALYSIS OF NOTE: OHM'S LAW

The ear is capable of receiving a simple tone and can also analyse a complex tone and the law regarding the analysis of sound has been enunciated by G.S. Ohm which states

"The ear only experiences the sensation of a simple tone when it is excited by a simple harmonic vibration. It analyses every other periodic vibration into a series of simple harmonic vibrations each of which corresponds to the sensation of a simple tone".

12.5 INTENSITY AND LOUDNESS LEVEL: THE BEL

The usual range of frequencies within which the ear can respond is very large, a region which extends from 20 to 20,000 c/s. Within this range the ear can distinguish a large gradation of intensity namely from 1 to 10^{12} or 10^{13}. This intensity range is indeed enormous and to deal with such a wide range in establishing a scale of loudness it is obviously most convenient to use a logarithmic scale. The usual unit is called a bel which is usually defined thus. If P_2 and P_1 are the output powers of two sources of sound, then the gain is defined as

$$\text{gain} = \log_{10}\left(\frac{P_2}{P_1}\right) \text{ bels} \qquad (12.2)$$

As bel is a large unit, a smaller unit called the decibel (abbreviated as db) which is 1/10th of the bel is usually used.

Thus $$\text{gain} = 10 \log_{10}\left(\frac{P_2}{P_1}\right) \text{ db} \qquad (12.3)$$

As the output power is proportional to the square of amplitude, if E_2 and E_1 represent the corresponding amplitudes, then

$$\text{gain} = 20 \log\left(\frac{E_2}{E_1}\right) \text{ db} \qquad (12.4)$$

If we have a system whose gain is 1 db

$$\log_{10}\left(\frac{P_2}{P_1}\right) = \cdot 1$$

$$P_2/P_1 = 1 \cdot 26$$

$$E_2/E_1 = 1 \cdot 12$$

Hence gain of 1 db is equivalent to amplitude amplification of 1.12.

12.6 SENSITIVE FLAMES AND JETS

In this chapter we shall also consider the sensitive flames and jets which can sometimes act also as a receiver of sound energy. They were studied extensively by Tyndall who found that flames, under certain condition, can become extremely sensitive to high pitched sound. By adjusting the gas pressure emerging from a pin-hole orifice the flame was brought to a very sensitive condition and it was observed that a flame 60 cm high falls to a height of 18 cm in response to a slight tap on a distant anvil.

Besides the flames, jets are also sensitive to sound waves; Rideout finds that fish tail flames formed by the union, at a small angle, of two similar jets exhibited directional properties with respect to a high frequency sound. The response was zero when the direction of the sound was at right angles to the line of the jets. The behaviour of flames and jets to sound waves is very imperfectly understood and it is supposed that the sensitiveness is due to instability accompanying vortex motion at the jet. Sensitive flames may be used as indicators of sound in air at practically all frequencies up to and possibly beyond 100,000 c/s.

12.7 TRANSFORMATION OF SOUND

Now a days most of the sound receivers are electrical in nature. There are some inherent difficulties in the receivers of sound that are based on mechanical principle. In order to transmit sound from one place to another, mechanical method is inadequate but if the received sound energy is converted to electrical energy then it is possible to receive sound in one place and record or reproduce it in another place without any loss in initial energy. In the second place if the sound received is converted to electrical energy, then it is possible to receive more than one sound at a time, and the total effect may be added up vectorially. The third and important point is that it is almost impossible to amplify a sound received in mechanical fashion but it is easy to amplify a sound which has been converted to electrical energy with the help of audio frequency voltage amplifiers. These are the prime reasons which are responsible for the development of the electrical receivers of sound.

The physical principle which can convert mechanical vibrations to electrical vibrations is also utilized to reconvert the electrical oscillation to original mechanical vibration. There are various forms of such devices and we shall discuss them one by one.

12.8 ELECTROMAGNETIC RECEIVER (MOVING IRON TYPE)

This type of electromagnetic receiver was invented by Alexander Graham Bell in 1876 and is commonly employed in telephones. In its most common form, a thin diaphragm of magnetic material usually steel of about 5 cm in diameter and thickness between 0·015 cm and 0·03 cm is clamped rigidly at the edges and the central portion of the diaphragm faces the end of a permanent bar magnet of steel. In front of the diaphragm, there is a saucer-shaped mouthpiece. Round the end of the magnet which faces the diaphram a coil of insulating wire is wound and the ends of the wire are connected to the outside terminals. Two such similar devices are placed, one at the transmitting and the other at the receiving station, and the terminals of the two are connected together. The magnetic field acting on the diaphragm is proportional to the square of the magnetic flux. When some one speaks before the mouthpiece the sound waves falling upon it are concentrated on the diaphragm and set it in vibration. A change in the position of the diaphragm changes the magnetic flux and thereby a transient electromotive force is developed across the coil and a current flows through it. An approach of the diaphragm strengthens the field and sends a current in one way whereas the recession of the diaphragm weakens the magnetic field and sends the current the opposite direction. Consequently an oscillatory current flows through the terminals the magnitude of which is proportional to the magnitude of the motion of the diaphragm which is proportional to the intensity of the sound wave.

These undulatory currents to various magnitudes are propagated along the line and in passing through the coil in the receiving instrument serve, according to their direction, to increase or decrease the magnetisation of the magnet of the receiving instrument. The resultant force on the diaphragm thus changes and it is set to similar vibrations as those of the diaphragm of the sending station, thereby producing similar vibrations as received by the instrument of the receiving station.

Some modifications in the design of telephone receivers were made by S.G. Brown who used a strip of soft iron or mild steel clamped firmly at one end with the free-end across the gap in the magnetic field and the pole pieces of the magnet are adjusted to approach the strip until a critical position is reached beyond which the stiffness of the strip is overcome by the attractive force of the magnet. In some other forms, an electromagnet is used to provide the field, independent windings on the pole tip being used to carry the alternating current.

The diaphragm receivers show marked resonance effect at certain frequencies and consequently, as is usually the case, they are used for a faithful reproduction of the sound for a long range of frequencies; it is advisable that the natural frequency of the diaphragm should be much higher or much lower than the range of frequency which it is expected to receive. This consequently hampers the sensitivity of the receiver but if a resistance capacity coupled audio amplifier is used in conjunction much of the sensitiveness can be restored back.

The sensitivity is also decreased due to eddy current and hysteresis loss and consequently it is essential to use laminar iron sections in those parts which have to carry alternating flux. Hysterisis loss is proportional to frequency and eddy current loss to the square of the frequency and, if the frequency of the received signal exceeds 15,000 c/s, these losses assume significant proportion.

12.9 ELECTRODYNAMIC RECEIVER

If a conducting wire or a metal strip carrying a current i is placed in a magnetic field of strength H, the mechanical force experienced by it is Hil where l is the length of the strip or wire. The reverse process is also true; if the wire is displaced in the magnetic field by the same force then a current of strength i will be generated in it. This principle is used in electrodynamic generators and receivers. In Fig. 12.1 a diagrammatic sketch of the same apparatus is given.

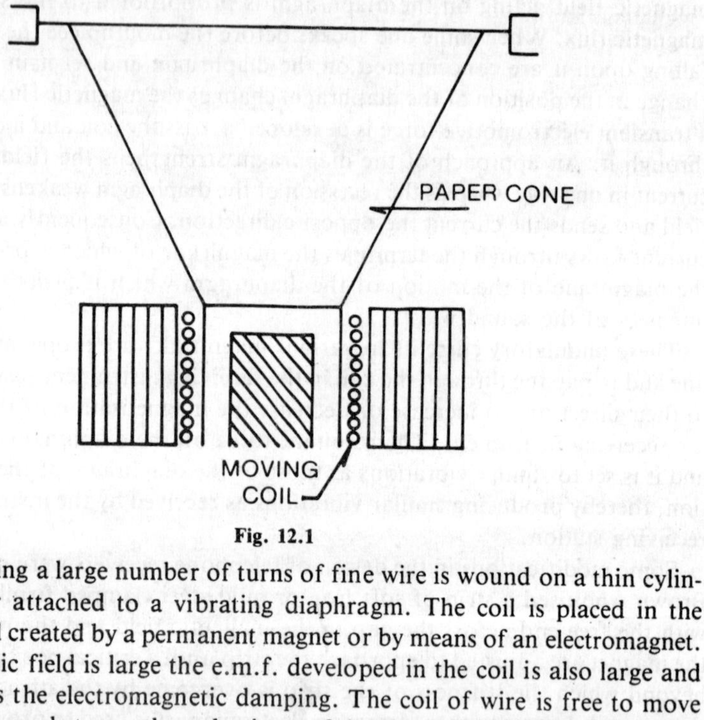

Fig. 12.1

A coil having a large number of turns of fine wire is wound on a thin cylindrical former attached to a vibrating diaphragm. The coil is placed in the magnetic field created by a permanent magnet or by means of an electromagnet. If the magnetic field is large the e.m.f. developed in the coil is also large and also greater is the electromagnetic damping. The coil of wire is free to move in the narrow gap between the pole pieces of the electromagnet and is attached to a large, light, nonmagnetic diaphragm which is either made of stiff-paper or a light disc of wood or of aluminium in the form of hollow cone. When the speaker speaks before the diaphragm, the paper diaphragm vibrates which makes the coil attached to also vibrate and consequently an electromotive force is developed across the coil and this alternating e.m.f. is proportional to intensity and frequency of the original sound. This e.m.f. can be amplified. At the receiving station this e.m.f. induces a current in the receiving coil and consequently the diaphragm vibrates and the original sound is again reproduced.

12.10 PIEZOELECTRIC PHENOMENA

It was observed by Curie brothers in 1880 that in certain crystals when a mechanical pressure or tension is applied to the two faces of a crystal, an electric charge is developed on the other two perpendicular faces of the crystal.

Their experiment showed that there was a certain relation between the mechanical pressure applied and the sign of the charge developed; the sign of the charge changed when the pressure is changed to tension. This phenomenon occurs in many crystals but is prominent in quartz and Rochelle salt. The converse effect was also shown to be true; that voltage applied to the faces of the crystal produced corresponding changes in dimensions. This phenomena is known as 'piezoelectricity'. Among the piezoelectric crystals which exhibit this property, the effect is most pronounced in Rochelle salt, but due to inferior mechanical properties, namely its brittleness, quartz or tourmaline is preferred.

Referring to Fig. 12.2, it is seen that A_1A_1, A_2A_2, A_3A_3 are particular direc-

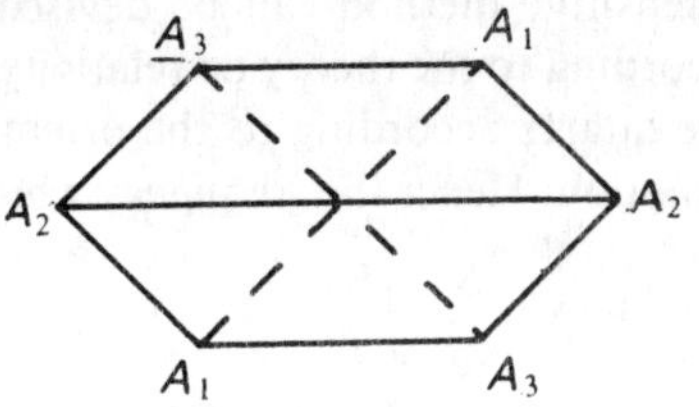

Fig. 12.2

tions in the crystal. There is also a certain direction in the crystal along which if a beam of light is sent through, the beam proceeds through the crystal in a single beam. In other directions of the crystal, for a single incident beam there are two directions for the refracted ray, one for ordinary and the other for extraordinary ray, and these are known as double refracting crystals. The axes A_1A_1, A_2A_2, A_3A_3 are the three electric axes parallel to the bounding face of the crystal. Plates are cut from this crystal having a length l perpendicular to one of the axes and a thickness t parallel to one of these axes. If now this crystal plate is placed in an electric field so that the thickness t is parallel to electric field then there will be a change in the length l of the crystal.

Resonant vibration

The above discussion mainly applies to the case of an applied *dc* field. If, however, an alternating electric field be applied to the two faces of the crystal then the crystal will be thrown into forced vibration due to applied electromotive force and when the frequency of the applied field coincides with the natural frequency of the applied field coincides with the natural frequency of the crystal, the crystal will be set into resonant vibration and the amplitude of oscillation will be large. The natural frequency of a crystal can be obtained from the relation

$$N = \frac{SC}{2l} = \frac{S}{2l}\sqrt{\frac{E}{\rho}} \tag{12.5}$$

where E is the modulus of elasticity in the particular direction within the crystal and ρ is the density and S is an integer.

12.11 USE OF PIEZOELECTRIC PROPERTY OF THE CRYSTAL

The most exhaustive use of piezoelectric property of the crystal is in the generation of ultrasonics and their detection. We shall consider in greater detail how ultrasonics are generated by piezoelectric crystals in the chapter on ultrasonics (chapter 16).

Piezoelectric crystals as standard of frequency

The extreme accuracy of the quartz crystal as the standard of frequency has been demonstrated in an experiment performed by Wood, Tomlinsoñ and Essen. According to the theory of relativity there should be a change in the length of the quartz crystal when it is roatated in the horizontal plane (Lorentz Fitzgerald contraction) and a consequent change of frequency. This change of frequency could be measured if a sensitive method can be devised.

On the other hand, according to the theory of relativity the velocity of sound should also change in the quartz according to the orientation of the bar with respect to its direction of motion. Hence the frequency which is given by equation

$$N = \frac{S}{2l}\sqrt{\frac{E}{\rho}}$$

should remain unchanged. The experiment was made with two similar longitudinal quartz oscillators, one rotating and the other stationary, the difference frequency being measured. The experiment showed no change of frequency exceedings $\pm$ 4 parts in 10^{11} or less than 1% of the estimated Lorentz Fitzer-old contraction, due to earth's orbital motion.

Quartz crystal as frequency stabilizer. Quartz crystal finds extensive use as a frequency stabilizer in valve-maintained oscillation. A very convenient circuit was devised by Pierce (Fig. 12.3). The crystal is placed between the plate

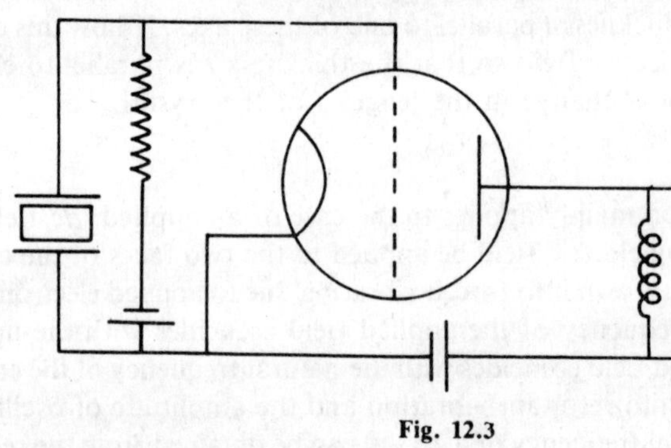

Fig. 12.3

and the grid circuit and the crystal when vibrating is similar in its effects to a parallel resonant circuit having one end connected to the anode and the other to the grid. The oscillatory voltages applied to anode and grid are therefore opposite in phase and conditions are correct for the maintenance of oscillations. Switching on the cricuit will be sufficient to shock the crystal into oscillation and this will then be maintained with energy from the anode battery supplied in the correct phase through the valve.

It is evidently essential that the anode circuit should provide high impedance in order that anode should not be short circuited to filament, specially for high frequency currents. This is usually provided by a parallel tuned circuit. As the circuit condenser is gradually reduced from a very large value, oscillations build up until a maximum is reached. Further reduction of condenser value produces a sudden fall in the output voltage until the oscillations just cease before the circuit comes into tune with the crystal frequency. It is clear therefore that the resonant frequency of the anode circuit should be below that of the crystal.

It is to be noted that care must be taken to see that the natural frequency of the LC circuit is not too near that of the crystal, in which case electrical self-oscillations may ensue. Although the effect of this is to increase the high frequency output, the LC circuit tends to pull the crystal in such a way that the crystal is not allowed to perform its work as a driver.

There are many methods for the mounting of the crystal. A pair of flat brass electrodes can be mounted with the crystal on edge between them in which case an air gap between the electrode and the crystal, will be left. Nowadays the crystal surfaces are either silvered or sputtered with gold so that very good electrical contact can be established.

Factors affecting the frequency. Due to changes of temperature, there are changes in the value of elastic constants of the crystal as well as change of length and hence the frequency of the crystal changes. In a crystal, the value of the elastic constants is different in different directions with temperature and hence the change of frequency with temperature depends upon the direction in which it has been cut. Generally speaking, crystals cut along the y-axis have a negative temperature coefficient, that is to say an increase of temperature produces a decrease in frequency. This change is of the order of 1 part in 20,000 per degree centigrade. Crystals cut along the x-axis may have either a positive or a negative temperature coefficient usually of the order of 1 part in 14,000 per degree celsius.

The change of thickness of air gap between the crystal surface and the electrode may have a marked effect in determining the frequency. If the electrodes touch or are open wide, the crystal will cease to vibrate. A change of gap will produce, on the average, a total frequency variation of 1 part in 2000.

No appreciable change of frequency is brought about either by change of anode voltage or filament volts of the maintaining valve even for a change of 20 or 30%.

12.12 PIEZOELECTRIC RECEIVERS

From the above discussion it is evident that if a mechanical force is applied to the two opposite faces of a crystal, such as quartz or rochelle salt then an electric voltage is developed across the other two faces and the phenomenon is reversible, i.e. an application of electric voltage on the two opposite faces will produce the corresponding mechanical stresses along the other faces. Piezoelectric methods have been extensively used in generating and detecting ultrasonic vibrations and the discussion of the actual methods will be taken up in chapter on ultrasonics. The principle of reception is based upon the fact that sound waves falling upon the crystal will produce the corresponding electromotive force and then it can be amplified and detected by means of a radio receiver, or alternatively the electrical voltage after amplification may be again applied to a piezoelectric receiver when the corresponding mechanical vibrations which are faithful replica of the original will be reproduced.

12.13 MAGNETOSTRICTION RECEIVER

The phenomenon of magnetostriction, which is extensively used for generation and detection of ultrasonic waves, will be dealt with in a detailed manner in the chapter on ultrasonics (Chapter 16). The phenomena may be described by the fact that a ferromagnetic rod such as that of iron, cobalt or nickel increases in linear dimension when placed in a magnetic field and as the reverse phenomenon is also true, a mechanical pull will also increase the permeability beyond that of the unstretched rod when placed in the magnetic field. G.W. Pierce who did extensive work on the phenomenon of magnetostriction used ferromagnetic elements to receive sounds covering a wide range of frequency. He used a piston diaphragm (a disc having uniform density all over its surface) which is attached rigidly to a nickel rod placed in a magnetic field. When sound vibrations fall on this diaphragm it causes the rod to alternately compress and stretch. A magnetising coil surrounding each nickel rod serves to detect the variation of magnetisation due to alternate stresses, the induced currents being detected after amplification by means of a telephone receiver or a measuring instrument.

12.14 MICROPHONES

Microphones are devices which are used for the amplification of sound. As it is very convenient to amplify an electrical voltage with the conventional use of amplifiers the mechanical vibrations are first converted to corresponding electrical voltages. There are, in general, two kinds of devices by which this conversion can be achieved: (a) the condenser microphone and (b) the carbon granular microphone.

Condenser microphone

The condenser microphone (Fig. 12.4) in its present form was invented by

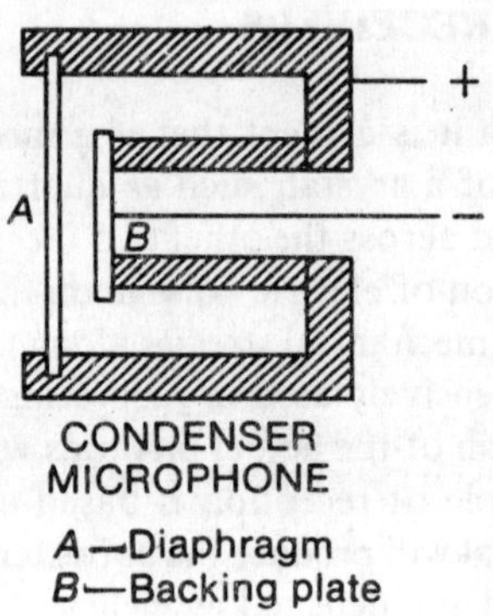

Fig. 12.4

Wente in 1917. Its principle is based upon the fact that, if a charged condenser connected to an external circuit be subjected to a vibratory mechanical stress producing variations in the separation of its plates, an alternating e.m.f. will be set up in the circuit due to the changing capacity of the charged condenser. Wente studied the sensitiveness of this microphone over a frequency range up 0 to 10^5 c/s over which range the sensitiveness is almost uniform. It can be used both as a transmitter as well as a receiver of sound waves; its great merit is its freedom from distortion. It consists essentially of a steel ring. This diaphragm forms one plate of an electrical condenser, the other plate being an insulated steel disc, parallel to the diaphragm, the distance of separation between them being 0·0025 cm. This condenser of capacity C_0 is connected in series with a battery E and a resistance R (Fig. 12.5). If the area of the plates is A and d

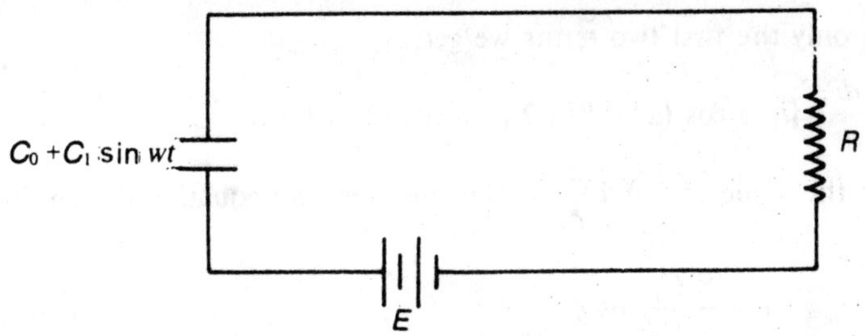

Fig. 12.5

is the equilibrium distance where no sound waves are incident, the capacity.

$$C_0 = \frac{KA}{4\pi d} \tag{12.6}$$

where K is the dielectric constant of the medium. If we assume that the motion of the condenser plate is simple harmonic when a sound wave is incident and, as a result, the additional displacement is "$a \sin \omega t$", where a is the amplitude of displacement which is proportional to the amplitude of sound wave and ω is the frequency of the note, the new capacity of the condenser becomes

$$C = \frac{KA}{4\pi (d - a \sin \omega t)} \tag{12.7}$$

$$C = C_0 \Big/ \left(1 - \frac{a}{d} \sin \omega t\right)$$

As a is small compared with d,

$$C = C_0 \left[1 + \frac{a}{d} \sin \omega t\right]$$

$$= C_0 + C_1 \sin \omega t \text{ taking the + sign}$$

where C_1 is proportional to the amplitude of the sound wave.

Considering now the circuit when the capacity of the condenser is C

$$E = Ri + \frac{\int i \, dt}{C}$$

$$E=Ri+\frac{\int i\,dt}{C_0+C_1\sin\omega t}$$

Differentiating with respect to t

$$EC_1\,\omega\cos\omega t=RC_0\frac{di}{dt}+R.\frac{di}{dt}C_1\sin\omega t+Ri\,C_1\,\omega\cos\omega t+i$$

$$(C_0+C_1\sin\omega t)\,R.\frac{di}{dt}+[1+R\omega\,C_1\cos\omega t]\,i-EC_1\,\omega\cos\omega t=0$$

Let $\qquad i=\Sigma\,i_n\sin(n\,\omega t+\phi_n)$

then $\qquad \dfrac{di}{dt}=\Sigma\,i_n\,n\omega\cos(n\,\omega t+\phi_n).$

Taking only the first two terms we get,

$$\frac{di}{dt}=[i_1\,\omega\cos(\omega t+\theta_1)+2\,i_2\,\omega\cos(2\,\omega t+\theta_2)]$$

Putting the value of i and $\dfrac{di}{dt}$ in the equation and equating the coefficients we get

$$i_1=\frac{E}{R}\frac{C_1}{C_0}\cos\phi_1$$

$$i_2=-\frac{1}{2}.\frac{E}{R}\left(\frac{C_1}{C_0}\right)^2\cos\phi_1\sin(\phi_1-\phi_2)$$

so that

$$i=\frac{E}{R}.\frac{C_1}{C_0}\cos\phi_1\sin(\omega t+\phi_1)-\frac{1}{2}\frac{E}{R}\left(\frac{C_1}{C_0}\right)^2\cos\phi_1\sin(\phi_1-\phi_2)\sin(2\omega t+\phi_2) \tag{12.8}$$

In this expression $\cot\phi_1=C_0\,R\,\omega$ and $\tan(\phi_1-\phi_2)=2\,C_0\,R\,\omega$ and hence to get good efficiency $\phi_1\approx 0$ which means that phase difference should be small; then $\dfrac{\cos\theta_1}{\sin\theta_1}=C_1\,R_0\,\omega$, and hence R_0 should be large in comparison with $\dfrac{1}{C_0\,\omega}$.

then
$$E=Ri=\frac{EC_1}{C_0}\sin(\omega t+\phi_1)-\frac{EC_1^2}{2C_0^2}\sin(2\,\omega t+\phi_2). \tag{12.9}$$

In order that the output may be a faithful representation of the input voltage, the output voltage should be a pure sine wave which means that C_1 should be limited in value.

The frequency characteristics of the condenser microphone have been studied over a wide range of frequencies between a few cycles to 10,000 c/s and the gain is almost uniform from 70-6,000 c/s.

Carbon microphone

The carbon microphone (Fig. 12.6) was invented by Hughes in 1878. It was

CARBON MICROPHONE

A—Diaphragm
B.B—Carbon electrodes
C—Carbon granules
D—Battery
P—Primary *S*—Secondary

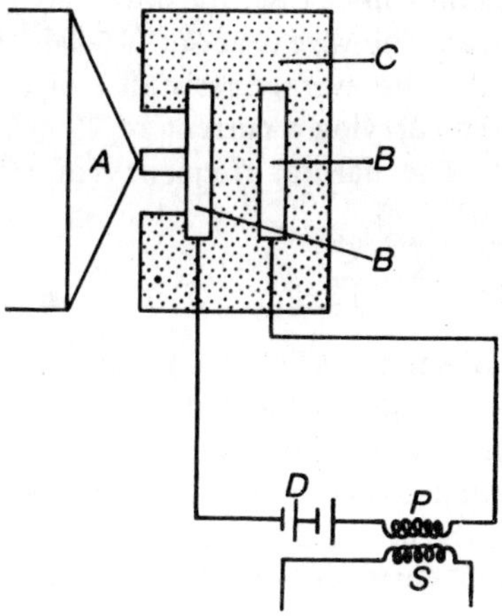

Fig. 12.6

observed that if loosely packed carbon particles are contained in a cavity and their relative positions are changed by the application of an external pressure then the electrical resistance of the carbon particles is changed and it can be shown that the change of resistance is proportional to the appplied pressure. Based upon this principle, the carbon granular microphone has been invented. It generally consists of a carbon or metal diaphragm about 5 cm in diameter and a similar diaphragm at a small distance from it. In between the cylindrical cavity thus formed carbon granules are loosely packed. Sound waves impinging on the diaphragm cause it to vibrate with a motion similar in form to the acoustic wave and this in turn produces compression and refraction of the carbon granules. A variation in resistance between the two diaphragms thus results and if this resistance is connected to a circuit containing a direct current electromotive force, the current flowing will vary with a waveform resembling the sound wave. This output can be amplified and then fed to the loudspeaker. The diaphragm is suitably damped by means of flannel or cotton wool to avoid pronounced resonance effects which tend to distort the voice of the speaker.

One disadvantage with carbon microphone is that due to accumulation of moisture, the carbon granules cling or adhere together with the result that the resistance falls to a low value and the microphone becomes insensitive.

12.15 THERMAL RECEIVER: HOT WIRE MICROPHONE

This method of transformation of sound to electrical energy is based upon the principle that if an alternating current of air is incident on an electrically heated wire or a strip a cooling effect is observed. This causes a change of resistance of the wire which is partly oscillatory and partly steady. This change of resistance can be detected by a suitable electrical device.

W.S. Tucker devised his hot wire microphone based on this principle. The instrument consists of an electrically heated grid of fine platinum wire mounted in the neck of a Helmholtz resonator. The platinum grid is held in a small rod of glass enamel mounted on a mica disc, the latter having a pair of silver electrodes attached to its faces. The wire is about 0·0006 cm in diameter and can carry a current of 30 mA. The average resistance of the grid is 140 ohms at 10°C and 350 ohms when carrying a current of 25 mA which heats the grid to just below red heat. The natural frequency of Helmholtz resonator is

$$N = \frac{C}{2\pi}\sqrt{\frac{K}{v}}$$

where C is the velocity of sound, K is the bulk modulus of the contained gas and v is the volume of the resonator including the neck. When the air in the neck is set into vibration by a sound of suitable frequency, the hot grid is cooled and a change in resistance takes place. This change of resistance causes a change of voltage across the grid and it can be applied to a low-frequency tuned amplifier and the output current passed through a telephone receiver or a tured vibration galvanometer, the magnitude of the current through which is an indication of the amplitude of the incident sound wave.

Alternatively, this change of resistance can be detected by means of a Wheatstone bridge, the hot grid forming one arm of the Wheatstone's net. The deflection in the galvanometer is generally taken as a measure of the intensity of sound.

12.16 UNDERWATER RECEIVER: HYDROPHONE

Hydrophones are receivers of sound waves which are placed under water. The modern form of hydrophone consists of a metal disc which is rigidly clamped to a metal diaphragm with a carbon microphone screwed on a small base at the centre. A cable which passes through a watertight compartment connects the microphone to a battery, transformer and telephone receiver to the listening point above water. For underwater signalling purposes the diaphragm and microphone may both be tuned to the frequency of the signal, whereas for detection of sound the receiver may be made nonresonant.

12.17 LOUDSPEAKERS

The reconversion of electrical impulses from the microphone is carried out by loudspeakers. The principle of working is just the reverse of that used in a microphone. Loudspeakers may be broadly divided into two classes, those which are provided with horn and those without horn: (a) moving coil type and (b) moving iron type.

The moving coil type of loudspeaker consists of a moving coil which is free to move between a permanent or an electromagnet. The magnet is designed to produce a strong magnetic flux across the annular gap in which the coil is placed. The coil to which the amplified current from the microphone is fed is attached to the conical diaphragm. For efficient performance, the diaphragm should be set in a baffle board in order to prevent circulation of air between its front and back. As a variable current is fed to the moving coil it experiences a mechanical force due to the presence of the magnet; this force sets the diaphragm into vibration. The relation between the current and the driving force is linear and the force is dependent on the position of the coil in the gap for considerable movement. The diaphragm is usually made of stiff paper of radius 10 to 15 cm supported round the periphery by a flexible annular strip of leather or rubber. The vibrations of the diaphragm are linearly proportional to force experienced by the diaphragm which is itself proportional to the current from the amplifier and thus the original sound is reproduced.

In the moving coil loudspeaker the efficiency is low, but it is possible to get a uniform frequency response and to radiate large power without appreciable asymmetric distortion.

Theory of moving coil loudspeaker

If it is assumed that under the combined action of the magnetic field and the variable electric current the coil experiences a mechanical force F, the equation of motion of the coil assumes a simple harmonic forced vibration, i.e.

$$m\frac{d^2x}{dt^2}+2\,km.\frac{dx}{dt}+Sx=F$$

Let $\quad x=e^{J\omega t}$

then $$\left(mJ\omega+2\,Km+\frac{S}{J\omega}\right)\frac{dx}{dt}=F$$

$$\frac{F}{(dx/dt)}=2\,Km+J\left(m\omega-\frac{S}{\omega}\right)=Z_m.$$

The quantity $F/(dx/dt)$ is known as the mechanical impedance of the system and denoted by Z_m. If a current of strength I amperes is flowing through the coil placed in a magnetic field of strength H then the mechanical force experienced by unit length of the coil is $IH/10$ and will be at right angles to the plane of the coil and the magnetic field and hence along the axis of the coil. If there are n turns in the coil of radius a, the total force F on the coil is $\frac{2\pi\, an\, IH}{10}$ dyne.

As the current is alternating,

$$F=\frac{2\pi\, an\, I_0\, He^{J\omega t}}{10}$$

and $$\frac{dx}{dt}=\frac{F}{Z_m}=\frac{2\pi\, an\, I_0\, He^{J\omega t}}{10\, Z_m}.$$

Thus the rate of displacement of the diaphragm is proportional to the current which is of the same period as that of the original sound.

Fixed coil type

In the fixed-coil type, at the throat of a large horn a diaphragm is fixed in front of a bipolar magnetic field produced by a horse shoe magnet. At both ends of this magnet two soft iron polepieces are attached and over these two pole pieces field coils are wound. Through these coils the fluctuating audio frequency current is passed which caused the steel diaphragm to vibrate. The vibration frequency of this diaphragm is the same as that of the original sound.

Horn loudspeakers

A small diaphragm is used as a radiating source in a loudspeaker and its small radiating efficiency acts as a detriment to the performance of the loudspeaker. In order to radiate sound efficiently, two modifications in the design of the loudspeakers have been incorporated. In dynamic speakers the vibrating diaphragm is made large so that it gives larger radiation output. The other method is to use a small diaphragm and to magnify its effective size by the use of a horn. It has been observed that the attachment of a horn increases the acoustical output of the loudspeaker to a great extent specially at low frequencies. The physical principle on which the horn works is that it spreads the concentrated waves coming from the diaphragm over a large area with practically no reflection back to the diaphragm. If a directional type of horn is used then the horn concentrates the sound in a particular direction.

The practical utility of the horn lies in the fact that a horn acts as an acoustic transformer. The low frequency acoustic impedance at the throat of the horn is greater than that which would act on a piston of equal area and the output of the Horn-loaded source is consequently higher. It has been found that the throat impedance of a horn is an important parameter in determining its acoustical performance and mathematical analysis shows that the throat impedance is a function of the throat area, of the mouth area and the 'flare', that is the rate of increase of the cross-sectional area of the horn. The horn must not flare too rapidly for the sound waves should cling to the inner surface of the horn, and in order that the mouth of the horn should be large in comparison to its throat the horn must be long.

Three types of horns have been in use, namely conical horn, exponential horn and catenoidal horn. The mathematics derivation in case of exponential horn is however simplified and for its utility in case of loudspeaker we can consider an exponential horn. It is assumed that acoustic energy is propagated through the horn in the form of plane waves moving parallel to the axis. The walls of the horn are perfectly rigid so that no transverse motions at the walls need be considered.

For an exponential type of horn it is assumed that

$$S_x = S_0 \, e^{mx}$$

where S_0 is the cross-sectional area of the throat of the horn and m is called the flare constant. The detailed mathematical analysis shows that if Z_0 denotes the acoustic impedance at the throat then

$$Z_0 = \frac{\rho_0 C}{S_0}\left[\sqrt{1 - \frac{m^2}{4K^2}} + J\frac{m}{2K}\right]$$

where ρ_0 is the density of air, C is the velocity of sound, $K = \omega/C$ where ω is the angular frequency of the sound wave.

From this expression for acoustic impedance it has been possible to compute the acoustic resistance and reactance of the horn. For some specific values of S_0 and m, curves have been plotted showing the variation of acoustic resistance and reactance of the horn over a range of frequencies from 100 to 4000 c/s. Comparing the values of the parameters without horn it is found that acoustic resistance with horn is much larger and remains practically constant over a wide range of frequencies investigated. Consequently the attachment of horn to the speaker will greatly enhance the acoustic output of low frequencies. It should be noted, however, that at high frequencies the effect of the use of the horn is almost negligible for these frequencies are radiated as a narrow beam and hence the confining effect of the walls of the horn is of limited significance.

12.18 MAINTENANCE OF SOUND BY HEAT

We have discussed the phenomenon of resonance previously and have seen that resonance to occur, the period of the external force must be equal to the natural period of the vibrating body. In general, if the driven and the driver vibrations are of the acoustical form then the phenomenon is termed resonance. Maintenance, however, is referred to the case when the driver system is other than that of sound. In case of resonance the action is most noticeable when the period of the force is equal to period of the vibrating body where as in case of maintenance, it is not necessary that the driver should have a definite period, yet by the reaction of the driven, the driver's action becomes periodic and of suitable frequency, but in this case also the theory of forced vibration is applicable and affords a valuable clue to the solution of the problem. Though this phenomena is not a case of transformation of sound, yet for convenience this has been included in this chapter and we shall discuss some cases where the sound is maintained by the application of heat.

12.19 TRAVELYAN'S ROCKER

In general the maintenance of vibration is obtained by the periodic communication of heat. The experiment is due to Travelyan and is referred to as Travelyan's rocker. It consists of a prism of brass or copper almost triangular in cross-section, with one edge grooved to form two adjacent parallel ridges. The prism rests with this grooved edge on a block of lead with a rounded top. The end of the prism terminates in a metal ball which rests on a smooth surface. When the prism is heated and placed on the block of lead it begins to vibrate in a continuous fashion. The cause of this rocking motion has been ascribed to the expansion of lead when it comes in contact with the hot body. Due to expansion of lead under one of the edges of rocker a hump is produced and the rocker is thrown to the other edge where the process is repeated. If both surfaces are quite clean, rapid communication of heat is possible. In order that the motion be continuous, a time lag between contact and expansion is postulated; otherwise the motion becomes checked. If there is a slight lag between contact and expansion then it will decrease the discouraging effect and increase the encouraging effect of expansion and thus there is an outstanding excess of encouragement which accounts for the maintenance of vibration. As the heat is gradually dissipated the motion ultimately stops.

12.20 SINGING FLAMES

It was observed by Huggins (1772) and later on by Chladni (1802) that a small gas flame introduced into a resonant air column of air or any other gas emits a musical sound. The phenomenon was explained by Rayleigh who pointed out that the fundamental factor of importance is the phase of heat supply relative to that of vibration of gas in the singing tube. In order to bring out the difference between this case and that of forced vibration, let us consider the equation of motion in case of forced vibration, viz.

$$\frac{d^2y}{dt^2}+2K.\frac{dy}{dt}+P^2y=f\sin nt. \tag{12.10}$$

were $2K$ is the damping factor, P is the natural frequency of vibration and n is the frequency of the impressed force.

Let $\quad y=A\sin(nt-\delta)$

then $\quad \dfrac{dy}{dt}=An\cos(nt-\delta)$. and $\dfrac{d^2y}{dt^2}=-An^2\sin(nt-\delta)$.

From equation (12.10)

$$-An^2(nt-\delta)+2K\,An\cos(nt-\delta)$$
$$+p^2A\sin(nt-\delta)=f\sin(nt-\delta+\delta)$$

Equating the coefficients of $\sin(nt-\delta)$ and $\cos(nt-\delta)$

$$A=\frac{f\sin\delta}{2Kn}\text{ and }\tan\delta=\frac{2Kn}{P^2-n^2}.$$

Hence $\quad y=\dfrac{f\sin\delta}{2Kn}\sin(nt-\delta)$.

For kinetic energy to be maximum, we must have $\sin\delta$ a maximum, i.e. $\delta=\dfrac{\pi}{2}$

Hence $\quad P=n$

and $\quad y=-\dfrac{f}{2KP}\cos pt$

but Rayleigh showed theoretically that heat must be supplied at the moment of greatest condensation and removed at the moment of greatest rarefaction in order to maintain vibrations. In case of stationary waves, the states of greatest condensation and rarefaction occur when the particles are at their maximum amplitude and it is evident that this is contradictory to what has been stated above with regard to forced vibration but the communication of heat may be regarded as either (1) replacing the impressed force of a forced vibration or (2) alternatively as altering the zero position of the vibrating point and consequently the value of the restoring force throughout the time until the next abstraction or communication of heat. Since in the present case, heat not being supplied periodically the first view cannot be accepted; on the other hand, heat is provided some what suddenly and the second view seems more acceptable. If the heat is supplied at the instant when the pressure amplitude is maximum, that is a, then the amplitude becomes $(a+\delta)$ due to application of heat. If there is no loss due to sound radiation and viscous forces then the amplitude would go on increasing by δ at each complete vibration and would reach a very large value. But due to presence of viscous forces and sound radiation, an equilibrium stage is reached when the increase of amplitude due to heat supply is completely balanced by the loss due to viscous forces and sound radiation. The theoretical predictions of Rayleigh were verified by Richardson experimentally.

12.21 SINGING ARC

It was observed that a continuous current arc if shunted by inductance L and capacity C in series would emit a musical sound of frequency $N=\frac{1}{2\pi}\sqrt{LC}$ for a certain value of inductance and capacity. The effect has been ascribed to the superposition of a.c. current with the d.c. current of arc with corresponding heating effects in the surrounding air. It has been observed that best effects are obtained if the d.c. resistance in series with the main supply compares favourably with the impedance of the L.C. circuit

12.22 GAUGE TONE

It was observed by Rijki that a sound of considerable intensity could be produced by a heated metallic gauge stretched across the lower part of a tube. Keeping the gauge hot by means of an electric current, the sound can be maintained continuously. This sound is called gauge tone and requires for its maintenance the variation of velocity of air through the gauge. The resultant air flow is due to a combination of continuous flow of air upwards due to convection together with the vibration of air near the heated gauge.

13

SOUND MEASUREMENT AND ANALYSIS

The three important factors which are characteristic of a sound wave at any point are the amplitude, frequency and phase of its various components into which it can be analysed. By amplitude is meant the displacement, or pressure or density which represents the condition of the medium at the particular point in question. It is rather difficult to measure the intensity of sound accurately and though many instruments have been devised to measure the intensity of a sound wave, it is sometimes necessary to make certain assumptions to convert their readings to absolute measure of intensity. Receivers have been found to be sensitive to different degrees in the different frequency ranges and so a single receiver cannot give the absolute measure of intensity throughout a wide range of frequency and their sensitivity is also dependent upon the nature of the medium in which they are placed. For comparison purposes, receivers may be used but it is preferable to get them calibrated so that their indications may be taken as a measure of sound intensity within prescribed limits of intensity and frequency.

The various apparatus that are employed in measuring the intensity of a sound wave are: (1) Rayleigh disc, (2) sound pressure radiometer, (3) hot wire microphone, (4) sound interferometers, (5) various electrical devices such as electromagnetic, electrodynamic or piezoelectric receivers.

13.1 MEASUREMENT OF INTENSITY

Reyleigh disc

When an ellipsodial obstacle is placed in a medium through which a sound wave is being propagated, the obstacle tends to set itself in such a fashion as to place its least axis in the direction of undisturbed flow and Konig (1891) showed that the couple which acts on the obstacle is given by

$$\tau = \frac{4}{3}\rho\, a^2 v^2 \sin 2\theta \tag{13.1}$$

where a is the radius of the disc, placed in a fluid of density ρ and θ is the angle made by the normal to the disc to the direction of motion of undisturbed flow and v denotes the velocity of the wave. This torque is maximum when $\theta = 45°$ and is independent of the direction of flow as v in the expression for τ occurs as a squared term. Hence

$$\tau_{max} = \frac{4}{3} \rho \, a^2 v^2 \tag{13.2}$$

Based on this principle, Rayleigh devised a simple instrument for comparing the intensities of sounds of definite pitch, the intensities being proportional to v^2, which is measured directly by the torque τ. A tube $3\lambda/4$ in length is open at one end and closed by a glass plate at the other end, where λ is the wavelength of sound. At an antinode distant $\lambda/4$ from the closed end, a light circular mirror is hung by a fine fibre at an angle of 45° to the axis of the tube. Light incident on the mirror and reflected from it is received by a scale at a distance of 1 m from the tube. When the tube is set in resonance by the incoming sound wave, the torque thus set up rotates the mirror which can be read on the scale outside and the deflection of the mirror thus becomes proportional to the intensity of the sound wave. The actual value of the torque may be determined by means of a torsion head which brings the mirror back to its previous position. Rayleigh's disc was improved further later on by Sivian (1928) in which the amplitude of sound wave to be measured is modulated with a frequency equal to that of the frequency of free vibration of the suspended disc. The measurement consists in reading the amplitude of oscillation corresponding to modulating frequency rather than a steady deflection of the disc. The disturbances caused by spurious air currents are thus eliminated.

Sound radiometer

Sound waves like light waves exert a pressure on the surface on which they are incident. Maxwell first calculated the pressure exerted by a beam of light and showed it to be equal to volume density of light energy in front of the surface and this was found to be so within the limits of experimental error. Prof. Poynting showed that this property of exerting pressure is a general property of wave motion and a very simple treatment is given by Larmor in calculating the pressure of sound radiation.

Let a sound wave of intensity E be incident on a perfectly reflecting wall which is pushed against the direction of wave motion with a velocity v to meet the advancing train of waves and let the velocity of advancing sound wave be v_s. In unit time the length of wavetrain incident on the wall is $(v + v_s)$ and on account of the approach of the reflecting wall this is compressed to $(v_s - v)$ Consequently the energy density in the reflected wave is increased in the ratio.

$$\frac{E + dE}{E} = \frac{v + v_s}{v - v_s} = 1 + \frac{2v}{v_s} \tag{13.3}$$

as v is small in comparison with v_s.

Hence $$dE = \frac{2\,vE}{v_s} \tag{13.4}$$

In the region of length v_s in front of the wall, the increase in total energy is $2\,VE$ and this must equal the total work done by the wall in compressing the radiation.

Hence if P is the pressure

$$PV = 2PE; \quad P = 2E \tag{13.5}$$

The radiation pressure is therefore equal to twice the mean energy density in front of the reflector. This simple treatment of the pressure of sound wave has been extended to a more accurate treatment by Rayleigh in which the gas is regarded as enclosed in a long cylinder of length l enclosed by a piston subjected to additional pressure due to sound waves reflected from it. The formula deduced by Rayleigh is

$$P = (\gamma + 1)\, E \tag{13.6}$$

and in case of a gas obeying Boyle's law $\gamma = 1$ the equation reduces to $P = 2E$ the same formula obtained earlier by Larmor. As the intensity I of the sound is given by $I = Ev$ where v denotes the velocity, we get from (13.5)

$$I = Ev = \frac{Pv}{(1+\gamma)} \tag{13.7}$$

The above principle of the calculation of pressure of a sound wave has been utilized by Altberg in determining the intensity of a sound wave. The apparatus consists of a loosely fitting piston which closes a small hole in the wall of a cube and is attached to the arm of a torsion pendulum, a balance weight (not exposed to radiation) being fixed at the opposite end. The arm was supported at the centre of gravity of the system by a fine torsion wire and a mirror with a lamp and scale indicates the movement of the piston. By means of a torsion head the spot of light was restored to its zero position. If the area of the piston be S at an effective distance γ from the point of suspension the torque T is given by

$$T = SP\gamma \tag{13.8}$$

This force is counterbalanced by the torsion of the suspension. If τ is the torque per unit twist and θ is the angular deflection then

$$SP\gamma = \tau\theta$$

$$P = \tau\theta / S\gamma \tag{13.9}$$

And from equation (13.7) and (13.8)

$$I = \frac{\tau\theta}{S\gamma} \cdot \frac{v}{(1+\gamma)} \tag{13.10}$$

The radiometer method of measuring the sound intensity has been employed by Langevin and Boyle in measuring the high frequency sound intensities under water. The torsion vane is a disc of metal of appropriate thickness supported from a fine phosphor bronze or steel wire. A piezoelectric quartz transmitter provides the source of sound and when these supersonic beams are incident on the vane it is deflected and the deflection was observed by means of a telescope and the vane was restored to its original position by means of the torsion head.

The sound radiometers are not very sensitive and they cannot be used for the detection of feeble sound but they respond to a great extent to sounds of high intensity and high frequency.

The hot air microphone

Richardo (1923) described a method of determining the intensity of sound wave by noting the drop in the resistance of a hot wire grid which was attached to the prong of a vibrating tuning fork. When the fork is in vibration, the grid is exposed to an oscillating air current whose velocity amplitude depends on the displacement amplitude of the tuning fork. As a result of the oscillating air current, the ohmic resistance of the hot wire grid falls and, by comparing this drop with that produced by steady air currents of various velocities, it has been shown that the drop in resistance for the oscillating grid is the same as that for a steady stream of air of velocity equal to the maximum velocity relative to air of the oscillating grid. Thus if the grid is calibrated in air streams of varying velocities v, then when the air surrounding the grid is in oscillation with an amplitude a, the value of a can be obtained from the relation $v = a\omega$ where $\omega = 2\pi f$, the frequency of the sound wave.

As the fall of ohmic resistance of the grid has been calibrated against v, noting the change of ohmic resistance for the particular experiment, the value of v can be obtained and the amplitude of oscillation a can be calculated. The velocities involved in ordinary waves in the open are much too small to be measured by this device but Richardson (1926) applied it for measurements in an organ pipe.

The hot air microphone was modified by Tucker and Paris (1921) by associating it with Helmholtz resonator but, as the sensitivity of the resonator is a function of the frequency, the increase of sensitivity has been obtained by a limitation of the range. The modified apparatus thus consists of three parts: (a) a platinum wire grid mounted in a circular mica plate and connected to the neck of the resonator; (b) the holder which consists of the neck of the resonator, the contact pieces and the terminals; and (c) the resonator itself.

The cylindrical neck of the resonator is made of brass and is soldered in the centre of a circular plate made of the same material which is provided with a terminal. A similar plate which is also provided with another terminal is placed in parallel with the first plate and in between the two the mica plate with the fine grid is rigidly fixed. Beneath the second plate is a rubber ring which rests on a block of ebonite to which the upper plate is fixed by means of a screw. When the upper place is fixed by the screw with the brass plate the mica plate with the grid is fixed between the two plates and a current can be sent by connecting the two terminals to a battery. As the resonator is cylindrical in shape the frequency of vibration is given by

$$f = \frac{v_s}{2\pi}\sqrt{\frac{S}{l v_0}} \tag{13.11}$$

where v_s is the velocity of sound, S = area of cross-section of the neck, l = length of the neck, and v_0 = volume of the resonator.

As the sound wave impinges upon the grid the change in its ohmic resistance takes place and it can be shown that the total change is due to (a) oscillatory change; and (b) steady change. The steady change can be measured by the ordinary Wheatstone bridge method but to measure the oscillatory change it has to be amplified. The sensitivity increases when, for a given intensity of sound, the amplitude of vibration of the air surrounding the grid increases and this achieved when, for the particular frequency, the air column in the resonator is also set into vibration. The method therefore suffers from the fact that it is limited by frequency, and for comparison of intensities of sounds of different frequencies different resonators are to be utilized. The sensitivity of the equipment is, however, considerably increased and Tucker and Paris were able to pick up signals of low frequency from distant sirens and found that quite inaudible sounds could be picked up even from a confused mass of other noises.

Sound interferometer

The principle of sound interferometer will be described in greater detail in the chapter on Ultrasonics but the basic idea can be outlined here. As in the case of formation of stationary waves in a Kundt's tube, nodes and antinodes are formed when sound waves combine after reflection from a perfectly reflecting wall with the progressive waves. If a probe can be moved along through the system of stationary waves, the positions of the maxima and minima can be located and the distance between the successive maxima or minima can give a measure of the wavelength and hence the velocity of the sound. This is the method adopted for the measurement of the velocity of ultrasonic waves. If A is the maximum amplitude of oscillation and if the reflector is a perfect one, the displacement at the antinode is $2A$ and that at the node is zero. Hence the measurement of maximum amplitudes at the antinodes gives a measure of the intensity of sound. Since it is difficult to measure the absolute amplitude, the method can be utilized for measurement of relative intensities of two sources.

An optical interferometric method has also been employed to measure the density amplitude of sound waves. The principle is based upon the fact that the refractive index of a gas is a function of its density and when a sound wave propagates through the medium there is an instantaneous change of density due to compression and a reverse change due to rarefaction. If μ is the refractive index and ρ the density when the sound wave is propagating through the medium and if μ_0 and ρ_0 are the original refractive index and density, then

$$\frac{(\mu - 1)}{\rho} = \frac{(\mu_0 - 1)}{\rho_0} \tag{13.12}$$

This change of refractive index will cause a change of optical path length and cause a shift in the interference fringes. The change in the optical path length is $l\,(\mu - \mu_0)$ where l is the geometrical length and from the above relation

$$l\,(\mu - \mu_0) = l\left[(\mu_0 - 1)\,\frac{(\rho - \rho_0)}{\rho_0}\right]$$

If n is the shift produced in the interferometer

$$n\lambda = l\,(\mu - \mu_0) = l\left[(\mu_0 - 1)\,\frac{(\rho - \rho_0)}{\rho_0}\right] = l\left[(\mu_0 - 1)\,\frac{\delta\rho}{\rho_0}\right].$$

Now if P_0 is the total pressure, $P_0 = A\rho_0^{\gamma}$ where A is a constant.

then
$$\frac{dP}{P_0} = \gamma . \frac{d\rho}{\rho_0}$$

$$\therefore \qquad n = \frac{l}{\lambda}\left[\frac{(\mu_0 - 1)}{\gamma}\frac{dP}{\rho_0}\right].$$

If the change of pressure dP can be regarded as the pressure amplitude,

$$dP = P = \frac{n\lambda\gamma P_0}{(\mu_0 - 1)\, l} . \tag{13.13}$$

Now, of the two beams of light which are made to interfere, one passes through an organ pipe and the other through air; there will be a shift of fringes when the organ pipe is set into vibration. The method was originally used by Toppler and Boltzman to determine the pressure amplitude in a sounding organ pipe.

Other methods

Besides the above methods some other devices have also been utilized for the measurement of intensity of sound waves. Gerlach and Schottkey used a light metallic ribbon suspended in a steady magnetic field. The ribbon is sufficiently light so that it can move freely up to a frequency of 4000 c/s in air and when sound waves are incident on it, it vibrates in the magnetic field and an induced high frequency voltage is set up in the ribbon. This alternating current can be amplified and measured. As the electrodynamic forces acting on the ribbon can be calculated the instrument can be used for absolute measurement.

13.2 MEASUREMENT OF FREQUENCY

The pitch of a sound wave which is almost analogous with frequency is another characteristic which can be measured by a number of methods.

(a) Seebeck's Siren: The siren was developed by Seebeck in 1841. In the present form the siren consists of a rotating disc with a circle of perforations which alternately opened and closed a similar ring of holes on the top of a cylindrical wind chest. At the upper part of the apparatus was added a counting mechanism with fingers and dials which recorded the number of rotations of the disc. These perforations are slanted in opposite direction so that the disc is driven forward by the air blast and its speed of rotation can be modified by varying the speed of wind. To determine the pitch we have to tune the siren to the note in question and observe the indications of the dial at the beginning and end of the timed period during which the siren is maintained at a constant pitch. Let N denote the frequency of the source and the wheel contains n holes and makes r complete turns in t seconds, then the frequency of the note is given by

$$N = \frac{nr}{t} \tag{13.14}$$

If one wishes to make a very exact determination of pitch it is better to observe beats between the two tones. The note whose frequency is to be determined should be maintained during the whole time of counting and to keep the siren the whole time beating with it, the beats being counted also. This delicate adjustment can be preserved by lightly touching the axle with a feather. Let the total number of beats be x in the counted time of t seconds. Let the total number of revolutions be r and n the number of holes. Then the frequency N of the note under examination is

$$N = \frac{nr - x}{t} \tag{13.15}$$

Another method that is also used for the determination and comparison of frequency of a source of sound is that done with the help of monochord. The assembly consists of a monochord, an auxiliary source of sound and the source whose frequency is to be determined. By counting the beats we get the difference of frequencies between the source under test and the auxiliary source. Also by finding the lengths of the string which at a given tension are in unison with the two sounds, we infer the ratio of their frequencies which are inversely as their lengths. Let the source under test and the auxiliary source have the frequencies N and N' respectively and let them be inunison with the lengths l and l' of the monochord and let the number of beats be n per second.

then $$N' - N = n$$

$$\frac{N'}{N} = \frac{l}{l'}$$

Hence $$N = \frac{nl'}{(l - l')}.$$

Besides these methods, for the determination and specially for comparison of frequencies, the stroboscopic method can also be employed.

(b) Determination with tuning forks: For determination of the absolute frequency of a source of sound, comparison with a tuning fork is usually adopted, for tuning forks are still regarded as the standards of frequency. The determination of the absolute frequency of tuning forks has been discussed in the chapter on the theory of vibration of bars. One of the earliest examples of the use of tuning fork as a standard of frequency is due to Scheibler who prepared a set of standard forks which constituted what is known as Scheibler's tonometer, and by careful tuning and counting of beats the absolute pitch of each fork was determined. Let two tuning forks be exactly tuned to an octave. Let the frequency of the lower fork be denoted by N, then that of the higher is $2N$. Now let a number of intermediate forks be prepared each making about four beats per second with the one below and one above it in the series. Let the exact number of beats per second between the adjacent forks in the series be denoted by b_1, b_2, b_3 etc., then

$$2N = N + b_1 + b_2 + b_3 + \ldots\ldots\ldots\ldots \quad \text{or} \quad N = \Sigma b$$

where the summation extends over the octave. Thus knowing N it is possible to determine the frequency of any other fork in the series. For it is apparent that if the frequency of the nth fork in the series beginning at the lowest is N_n then

$$N_n = N + b_1 + b_2 + b_3 + \ldots\ldots\ldots\ldots b_{n-1}$$

Konig produced a more elaborate series by using 154 forks covering the frequency range from 16 to 21845·3 c/s . The forks were provided with adjustable resonators and with sliding weights by means of which the frequencies can be adjusted.

An electrically-driven or a valve-maintained tuning fork (described in chapter 7 on the theory of vibration of bars) is regarded as a standard of frequency by comparison with which the frequencies of the other sources can be determined. For the precise determination of frequency and for the use of the tuning fork as a standard, the temperature variation of frequency has to be taken account of. In chapter 7 this effect has also been calculated.

Besides the tuning fork, magnetostriction oscillator can also be used as a standard of frequency. The use of the phenomenon of magnetostriction will be described in detail in a later chapter on ultrasonics (Chapter 16). Pierce suggested the use of a rod maintained in longitudinal vibration by magnetostriction as a standard of frequency. With a nichrome rod the frequency was shown to be independent of valve voltages and characteristics and to have a temperature coefficient of $-1{\cdot}07 \times 10^{-4}$.

The most widely used and precision standard source of frequency is the quartz oscillator and it is also used for stabilization of frequency in broadcasting stations. The principle of the use of quartz oscillator as a standard of frequency has been described in the chapter on reception of sound (Chapter 12).

13.3 DOPPLER'S PRINCIPLE

The frequency or pitch of a source of sound depends on the motion of the source, the observer and also upon the motion of the medium. It is a matter of common experience for an observer who is standing at a station to note that the pitch of the whistle emitted by an approaching locomotive increases gradually as it approaches him and drops suddenly when the train passes away from him. Similarly if a source of sound emitting a note is fixed in position and an observer approaches it the apparent pitch increases and it diminishes as the observer receds away from it. In 1842, Doppler considering the coloured light from the double stars showed that a motion of approach between the source and the observer would increase the frequency whereas an apparent decrease of frequency would occur with the motion of separation. He applied the principle to explain the colour of the star, the colour being attributable to the relative velocity of the star and the earth in the line of sight. If the two were approaching, the apparent frequency would increase and there will be decrease of wavelength and the star would appear blue whereas if the two were separating, the reverse effect would occur and the colour of the star would appear red.

The change of wavelength can be measured in a spectrograph which enables one to calculate the relative velocity between the star and the earth in the line of sight in terms of the velocity of light.

To calculate the apparent change of frequency, let us assume that the source, the medium and the observer are all moving in the same direction and the velocities are along the line joining the source and the observer. Let V_s be the velocity of sound, U_s the velocity of source and U_o the velocity of the observer, f the real frequency of the source, f' the apparent frequency and W is the velocity of the medium.

Let S (Fig. 13.1) be the original position of the source and S' the position one second later. If $SA = V_s + W$ then the waves emitted by the source in one second are contained within the distance $V_s + W - U_s$. Let O be the position

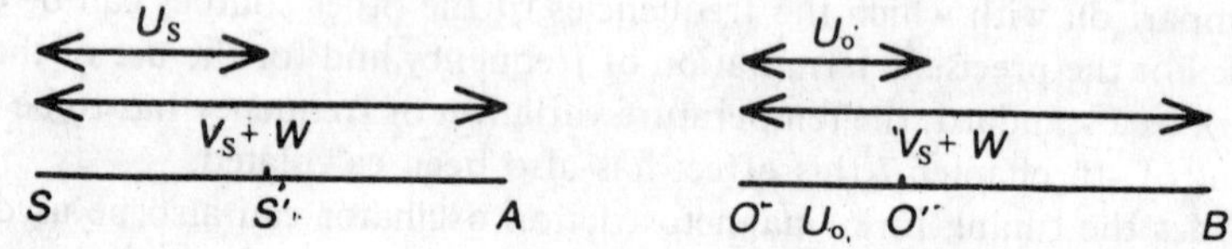

Fig. 13.1

of the observer at a given instant and O' the position a second later. Let $OB = V_s + W$ and $OO' = U_o$ then the waves received by the observer in one second are contained within the distance $V_s + W - U_o$. In the distance $V_s + W - U_s$ the number of waves contained is f; hence in the distance $V_s + W - U_o$ the number of waves contained is

$$\frac{f\,(V_s + W - U_o)}{(V_s + W - U_s)}$$

Hence the apparent frequency as it appears to the observer is

$$f' = f\,\frac{V_s + W - U_o}{V_s + W - U_s}$$

From this general formula, same specialised cases can be noted.

CASE 1: If the velocity of the source and that of the observer are the same, then the apparent frequency becomes equal to the real frequency and the motion of the medium has no effect. In this case the source appears stationary to the observer and the relative velocity between the two is zero.

CASE 2: The observer is stationary and the source moving with velocity U_s the velocity of the medium is assumed zero

$$f' = f\,\frac{V_s}{V_s - U_s}$$

CASE 3: The observer is moving but the source is stationary.

$$f' = f\,\frac{V_s - U_o}{V_s}$$

The relative direction of motion has to be taken into consideration in calculating the change of frequency.

CASE 4: If the source and the observer do not move in a straight line, as assumed, then the component of velocity in a particular direction has to be taken into consideration.

13.4 MEASUREMENT OF PHASE

A complex sound wave can be analysed by means of Fourier analysis which shows that it can be represented as a combination of a large number of components having different amplitudes, frequency and gradual change of phase. It is established that the quality of a musical note depends on the relative intensities of harmonics but the question whether the quality depends upon the relative phase has not been decided as yet. Helmholtz came to the conclusion that the relative phase is without effect on the quality. This conclusion has been disputed by Konig. An experiment was performed by Lloyd and Agnew using a telephone operated by a series of harmonically varying electric currents whose frequencies were in the ratio of the whole numbers. They changed the phases of the constituent currents and came to the conclusion that variation of the phase of the components is without influence on the quality of the complex note. This viewpoint has been disputed by Chapin and Firestone (1934).

It is clear that the relative phase difference produces different waveforms – hence differences in displacement curves – and it may influence the quality.

13.5 MUSICAL SOUND

When considering a musical instrument it is convenient to consider it as made up of three main divisions: (a) the exciter or the means of producing vibrations; (b) the vibrating system; and (c) the manipulative mechanism for the production of various notes of the scale. A musical sound possesses three definite characteristics and our sound sensations differ from one another in these three respects, namely intensity, pitch and quality.

13.6 INTENSITY, PITCH AND QUALITY

Intensity: The intensity of sound denotes its loudness and the intensity is proportional to square of the amplitude of vibration. In equation (5.18), we have deduced an expression for the total energy of sound wave per unit volume and is found to be $\frac{1}{2} \rho a^2 \omega^2$ where ρ is the density of the medium, a the amplitude and ω the angular frequency of the sound wave, and this quantity may be called the intensity of the sound wave. Thus the intensity of a sound wave is directly proportional to the square of the amplitude and also proportional to square of the frequency. The intensity of a sound falls off with distance from the source obeying the inverse square law. Let O be the source of sound and let Q denote the amount of sound energy emitted per second from the source in all directions. Imagine two spherical surfaces with radii r_1 and r_2 concentric with one another; then the amount of energy crossing per unit area of the spheres in one second is the intensity; then the intensity at P_1 is

$$\frac{Q}{4\pi r_1^2}$$

and intensity at P_2 is

$$\frac{Q}{4\pi r_2^2}$$

Hence
$$\frac{\text{Intensity at } P_1}{\text{Intensity at } P_2} = \frac{r_2^2}{r_1^2}$$

Thus intensity varies inversely as the square of the distance from the source.

Pitch: The pitch of a musical note is the physical cause which enables a hearer to distinguish between a shrill note from a brass note of the same intensity emitted from the same musical instrument. The cause which is responsible for the differentiation is due to difference of frequency between the two notes and a shrill note is due to higher frequency than the frequency of a brass note. As the pitch of a note is determined by its frequency it is the convention to express the pitch of the note by its frequency.

Quality: Besides amplitude and pitch, there is a third characteristic of musical sound which enables one to distinguish between two musical sounds of same pitch and intensity but arising from different musical instruments. Helmholtz discovered this third characteristic and he called it 'quality'. Helmholtz maintained that when a note of assigned pitch is produced by a musical instrument then the note is not pure but is a mixture of a predominant fundamental and some overtones which are harmonics of the fundamental but of lower intensity. He thus concluded that the quality of a musical note depends upon the number, order and relative strength of the harmonics but not upon their difference of phase. As to the quality the various musical tones have been divided into five classes: (a) those with full harmonic series of partials, i.e. including the fundamental; the relative frequencies are 1, 2, 3, 4, etc.; (b) those with harmonic partials but forming only the odd series of natural numbers, i.e. 1, 3, 5, 7, etc.; (c) tones with inharmonic partials; (d) simple tones, usually limiting cases of the foregoing three classes, in which the upper partials are indefinitely diminished or suppressed; and (e) tones with harmonic partials but whatever the pitch of the note, the partials near some fixed pitches specially reinforced, the others being somewhat relatively discouraged.

Musicians have thus regarded the three characteristics of musical sound, the intensity, quality and pitch which distinguish one musical sound from another. The quality of the musical sound from plucked, bowed and struck strings has been discussed in case of vibration of strings (vide chapter 6). The measurement of pitch or frequency has been dealt with in chapter 7 and the measurement of intensity has been taken up in this chapter.

13.7 CONSONANCE AND DISSONANCE

It is generally observed that when two or more notes are simultaneously sounded from the same instrument, a pleasant sensation is produced in the ear. The notes are said to produce consonance or concord. Sometimes it is also noted that when two or more notes are sounded together they produce a disagreeable sensation to the ear and the notes are said to be in dissonance.

It was noted by the Greeks long ago that consonance could be produced from various lengths of a given string and that between these lengths a very simple relation exists. This relation could be expressed by small whole numbers such as 1:2 or 2:3 and so forth. But if the lengths of the string do not bear a simple ratio the notes are said to produce dissonance. In 1862, Helmholtz published his researches in acoustics and he enunciated his theory of concord and discord which still holds the field. The theory in the bare outline states that dissonances and discords are due to unpleasant beats formed by the component tones. Consonance or concord is produced by two notes which fail to produce the unpleasant beats. Helmholtz maintains that unpleasantness of beats is due to the fact that during the loudest phase of the beats the ear is fatigued somewhat but during the feeblest phase the ear is rested and its sensitivity is restored. Hence in this specially sensitive state the recurrence of loud phase may be distressing. Another factor which is also responsible for the unpleasantness of the beats is that they should succeed each other at a frequency between certain limits and further it has been demonstrated experimentally that the roughness arising from the sounding of the two notes together depends in a complex manner on the magnitude of the interval between the two notes and on the frequency of beats produced by them.

13.8 MUSICAL SCALE

In a musical instrument such as piano or harmonium, a fixed number of notes are produced by the keys of the instrument with which it is provided. In an instrument like violin any number of notes can however be produced by the skill of the performer to suit a vocal music. The object of a musical scale is to determine the particular notes to be associated with the keys in the former class of instruments within an octave to be most suitable to vocal music.

13.9 MUSICAL INTERVAL

The absolute frequencies of the notes in a musical scale are not of much importance as they vary in different countries and have also undergone change in course of time. In passing from one musical note to another, the ear recognises the ratio in which their frequencies alter. The ratio between the frequencies of the two notes is called the interval between the two. If the notes having the frequencies m and n change in frequencies but retain the same value of the ratio (m/n) then the ear hardly recognises any distinction in passing from one note to the other.

In case of consonance we have noted that if the ratio (m/n) can be expressed as a simple number, then the notes are said to be in consonance whereas if the ratio cannot be expressed as a simple number then the notes are in dissonance. The former ratio is known as consonance interval whereas the latter is called the dissonance interval.

13.10 DIATONIC SCALE

The musical scale which is in general use for a long time is the diatonic musical scale. The scale comprises eight notes between the lowest of the series called the tonic and its octave. The various tones commencing from the tonic are usuall: known as:

Do, Re, Mi, Fa, Sol, La, Ti, Do

Helmholtz introduced a different notation and the notes are respectivel designated by

C D E F G A B C

A musical scale cannot be complete with these few notes only and the note which are respectively one octave higher are denoted with small letters

c d e f g a b c

The next higher scale is denoted by one dash above the small letters the nex higher one with two dashes and so on. The scale lower than *C-c* is denoted b; putting suffix 1 below the capital letters as

$C_1\ D_1\ E_1\ F_1\ G_1\ A_1\ B_1\ C_1$

The various notations are entered below for the diatonic scale and relative frequencies with the tonic as unity, and the last row gives the interval.

Usual notation	*Do*	*Re*	*Mi*	*Fa*	*Sol*	*La*	*Ti*	*Do*
Helmholtz	*C*	*D*	*E*	*F*	*G*	*A*	*B*	C^1
Frequencies	1	$\frac{9}{8}$	$\frac{5}{4}$	$\frac{4}{3}$	$\frac{3}{2}$	$\frac{5}{3}$	$\frac{15}{8}$	2
Interval	$\frac{9}{8}$	$\frac{10}{9}$	$\frac{16}{15}$	$\frac{9}{8}$	$\frac{10}{9}$	$\frac{9}{8}$	$\frac{16}{15}$	

13.11 ANALYSIS OF MUSICAL NOTES

In the chapter on vibration of strings we have carried out analytical treatment of notes emitted by different musical instruments employing either the plucked, struck or bowed strings. D.C. Miller carried out extensive researches on the analyses of notes given by common musical instruments. He has published results in case of clarionet and oboe. The vibrations produced by these instruments have been photographed and the results then plotted graphically where the intensity of sound has been plotted against the corresponding partial. Until these analyses were published it was commonly believed that the fundamental tone is by far the most intense and the higher harmonics form a series of rapidly diminishing intensity. These analyses, however, make it clear that this is by no means the case in every musical instrument. In case of oboe, the fundamental tone is relatively insignificant but has twelve or more partials among which the fourth and the fifth predominate and more than 66% of the total energy is carried in between them. In case of clarionet, the energy is mostly carried by the fundamental but the energy is distributed over a large number of partials. In case of violin there is disagreement between the findings of different observers. Diffraction gratings can be utilized for the analysis of intensities emitted by different musical instruments.

14

ACOUSTICS OF BUILDINGS

It is sometimes observed that a speech made in a certain hall or building or the sound produced in a cinema house is not audible at certain places in the hall or there is so much of interference that it is sometimes difficult to understand what is being spoken. It is in fact necessay to bear certain points in mind while a place of public speaking is being designed so that one can follow the utterances from every point clearly without any interference. Sabine put forward the following three points which are essential for the design of a good auditorium.

(1) The intensity of sound must be loud so that it can be distinctly heard from every place in the auditorium.

(2) The quality of sound must be unaltered, that is the relative intensities of the components of the complex sound must be preserved.

(3) The successive sounds of speech or music must remain distinct, that is there must not be any confusion due to overlapping of sound.

4.1 POSITION OF THE SPEAKER

rom a series of experiments it has been found that a sound which can be heard a distance of 100 ft. in front of the speaker is heard at a distance of 75 ft ı both sides and at a distance of 30 ft at the back of the speaker with equal tensity. Hence remembering this fact the seat of the speaker should be diciously selected. Consequently the seats should be so arranged that they e along the circumference of an ellipse with the ratio that semimajor axis to miminor axis ratio as 4:3.

4.2 LOUDNESS

big wall reflects the sound and thereby increases the loudness. A reflector aced at the back of the speaker reflects the sound to proceed further and ables him to be heard at a great distance, a parabolic reflector placed at the ıck of the speaker will reflect the sound in a parallel direction, provided the ›eaker is at the focus of the reflector. Thus placing parabolic reflectors at the ıck of the speaker will increase the intensity of sound.

4.3 REVERBERATION

he most important factor in the design of an auditorium is reverberation. It has been found that a sound made in a hall gradually reaches a maximum value and then dies abruptly, i.e. the sound persists for some time after it has been uttered and then dies in an abrupt fashion. The intensity of sound plotted against time gives a curve as shown in Fig. 14.1.

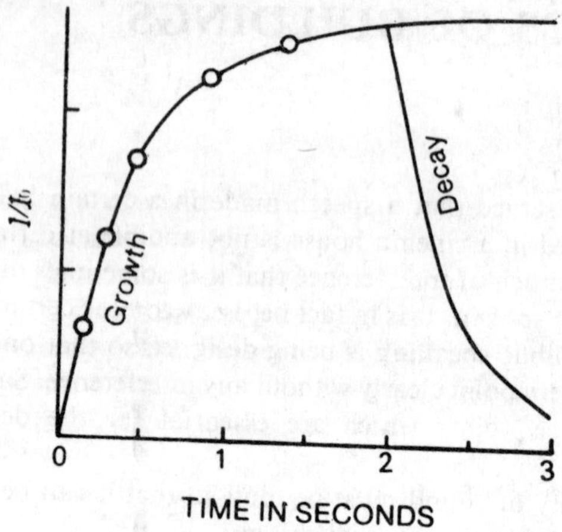

Fig. 14.1

This persistence of sound is due to large number of reflections in the surrounding wall. The persistence of sound due to successive reflections is called the phenomenon of reverberation. The phenomenon can be physically visualized thus. Suppose the sound uttered reaches the audience directly at a certain time t_1. The same sound reaches after suffering say a single reflection from the wall at a time t_2. The same sound will reach the audience after suffering more than one reflection at a time t_3 with diminished intensity and the process will continue until the intensity falls below the minimum audible value due to each reflection. The time of reverberation has been defined as the time taken for the sound intensity to fall to 10^{-6} of its original value and is denoted by T. It has been found that some amount of reverberation is good for music because it adds to brilliance but excessive reverberation is detrimental to speech. Prof. Sabine of Harvard University was faced with the problem of bad acoustics for the auditorium of the University where a speaker could hardly be understood by the audience. He found that in that auditorium, the sound uttered persisted for a period of 5½ seconds. During this interval more sounds would be uttered by the speaker and this combined with the persisting sound caused a great deal of confusion. He was able to reduce the time of reverberation to 1 second by bringing in cushions from outside which absorbed the sound. The confusion then disappeared. By plotting $1/T$ against the length of cushion introduced he obtained a straight line; the effect of cushions is to absorb the sound, and if A denotes the absorption then

$$A \propto \frac{1}{T} \tag{14.1}$$

By conducting experiments in rooms of different dimensions, Sabine found that time of reverberation is proportional to volume of the room, hence

$$T \propto V \tag{14.2}$$

from equations (14.1) and (14.2) we get

$$T \propto V/A$$

$$T = K\frac{V}{A}$$

where K is a constant.

If a = absorption coefficient per unit area, and s denotes a small area either of the walls of the room or that of an absorbing material we get,

$$T = K\frac{V}{\Sigma as} \tag{14.3}$$

and the experimental value of K, as determined by Sabine, is approximately equal to 0·05 and hence we get

$$T = \frac{0{\cdot}05\ V}{\Sigma as} \tag{14.4}$$

14.4 THEORETICAL CONSIDERATION

The theoretical consideration regarding reverberation was carried out independently by Jager, Buckingham, Watson and others. All theories assume that sound produced in a room undergoes three or four hundred reflections until the intensity becomes so small that it becomes inaudible, interference and similar effects being neglected.

Growth of sound

Let I denote the intensity of sound at an instant t and let A denote the fraction of the loss of the intensity due to each reflection. Let n denote the number of reflections suffered by the sound wave in unit time, then the loss of intensity dI in time dt is

$$dI = -AIn\ dt$$

By statistical analysis, Jaeger proved that

$$n = \frac{CS}{4V}$$

where C is the velocity of sound, S is the total surface area and V is the volume of the room.

Further if E denotes the rate of emission of energy from the source, then the rate of energy change per unit volume of the room,

$$\frac{dI}{dt} = \frac{E}{V} - \frac{IACS}{4V} = \frac{E}{V}\left[1 - \frac{ICAS}{4E}\right].$$

$$\frac{dI}{\left\{1-\frac{IACS}{4E}\right\}}=\frac{E}{V}dt.$$

Intergrating

$$\log\left\{1-\frac{IACS}{4E}\right\}\frac{4E}{ACS}=-\frac{E}{V}t+C_1$$

where C_1 is a constant.

When $\quad t=0,\ I=0$ and $C_1=0$

or $$1-\frac{IACS}{4E}=e^{-ACST/4V}$$

or $$I=\left[1-e^{\frac{-ACST}{4V}}\right]\frac{4E}{ACS}$$

This equation shows that the growth of sound energy in a room will be exponential and the experimental result (vide Fig. 14.1) supports the theoretical deduction.

Decay of sound

As the source has stopped sounding,

$$\frac{dI}{dt}=-\frac{IACS}{4V}$$

$$\frac{dI}{I}=-\frac{ACS}{4V}dt$$

$$\log I=-\frac{ACSt}{4V}+C_1$$

when $\quad t=0,\ I=I_{max}$

and hence $\quad C_1=\log I_{max}$

$$\therefore \quad I=I_{max}\,e^{-ACST/4V}$$

As T is defined as that time in which I becomes $I_{max}\times 10^{-6}$, we get

$$10^{-6}=e^{-ACST/4V}$$

$$T=\frac{6\times 4V\times 2\cdot 3}{CAS}=\frac{55\cdot 2V}{CAS}$$

Taking the velocity of sound as 1100 ft/s,

$$T=\frac{0\cdot 05V}{AS} \tag{14.5}$$

The same formula as was deduced by Sabine experimentally.

14.5 DETERMINATION OF TIME OF REVERBERATION

The method of Sabine has been regarded as one of the standard methods for the determination of the time of reverberation. As a source he took an organ pipe blown at a definite frequency and under a constant pressure. The instant of cutting off of the sound and the instant at which the observer considered it inaudible were recorded on a chronograph drum. In this type of measurement an accuracy of $\pm 0 \cdot 05$ s in the time of reverberation measurement was claimed. Two other important deductions were also made by Sabine from a series of measurements:

(a) The duration of reverberation was almost independent of the position of the source and of the observer in the room.

(b) The effect of any given amount of absorbant was also independent of its position in the room.

Appropriate times of reverberation are entered in table (14.2)

TABLE 14.2

Appropriate times of reverberation in seconds at 500 c/s

	10^4 *cu ft*	$1 \cdot 5 \times 10^4$ *cu ft*	2×10^4 *cu ft*	3×10^4 *cu ft*
Choir	1·0	1·0	1·2	1·25
Orchestra	0·8	0·85	0·9	1·0
Speech or music	0·6	0·65	0·7	0·75

14.6 DETERMINATION OF ABSORPTION COEFFICIENT

An audio frequency source of sound is taken and the time of reverberation T_1 was determined first in the empty room. If $\Sigma\, as$ denotes the absorption due to the walls of the room, the ceiling and the floor, then

$$T_1 = \frac{0 \cdot 05 V}{\Sigma\, as}$$

Then a certain amount of absorbing material of area S and absorption coefficient α was introduced into the room and the time reverberation T_2 again determined

$$T_2 = \frac{0 \cdot 05 V}{\Sigma\, as + \alpha\, s}$$

$$\text{Then } \frac{1}{T_2} - \frac{1}{T_1} = \frac{\alpha\, S}{0 \cdot 05 V}$$

$$\therefore \quad \alpha = \frac{0 \cdot 05 V}{s}\left[\frac{1}{T_2} - \frac{1}{T_1}\right]$$

Sabine used an open window as his standard unit of absorption expressing other results in terms of open window units. Values of absorption coefficients for some materials are given in table (14.1)

TABLE 14.1
Absorption coefficients of various materials

Material	*a* (absorption coefficient)
Treetax	0·49
Lime plaster	0·02–0·04
Hard plaster	0·01–0·03
Felt (½″ thick)	0·27
Red cloth	0·17
Absestos	0·146
Wood panelling	0·01–0·02
Porous rubber sheet	0·05–0·1
Acoustic plasters	0·27
Fibre boards ½″ thick	0·30–0·35
Audience per person	4·7
Chairs	0·17–0·21
Cushions 2¾ sq ft	1·5–1·8

14.7 OPTIMUM TIME OF REVERBERATION

After a series of observations regarding the time of reverberation, Sabine determined the optimum time of reverberation in halls of different dimensions for speech or music. Because it was observed that, whereas excessive reverberation is detrimental for speech, some amount of reverberation is good for music because it adds to its brilliance. For piano music, it was particularly observed that optimum time of reverberation should be of the order of 1·08 s. Eckhardt has theoretically discussed the optimum reverberation time for syllabic speech and observed that in a room of low absorbing power the syllables overlap seriously whereas in rooms of high absorbing power they are entirely separated.. Generally speaking, the optimum value appears to lie between 1 and 2·5 s for speech and for light music it tends towards the lower limit, whereas for orchestral and grand music it tends towards the higher value. Thus to correct a hall for acoustic purposes it is ascertained whether the hall has optimum time of reverberation. If it is already existing no change is made; but if it is far from the optimum value the requisite amount of abosrbing material is introduced into the hall until the time of reverberation approaches the optimum value.

14.8 NOISE

With the development of electrical and mechanical machinery such as railway locomotives, trams and motor cars and specially the high speed jet aeroplanes the problem of noise has become of such importance that special studies are now being undertaken to cope with this everincreasing problem. In order to study the physical as well as the psychological effect on human beings it is necessary to measure and analyse the noise and devise ways to keep the noise level to a bare minimum. Noise is a general term in physics which may mean sporadic and irregular emission of electrons in a vacuum tube or a background distrubance in a d.c. amplifier or a sensitive galvanometer or undesirable sound in acoustics. It may physically be defined as a disturbance of complex character with all kinds of irregular periods and amplitudes. In acoustics, the most important characteristic of noise is loudness and the unit of measuring noise is decibel. Since the sensation in our ear is a logarithmic function of the intensity it is customary to express noise in decibels above the threshold value of the standard tone of 1000 c/s. In order to find the noise level we have therefore to raise the intensity of the standard tone, till the noise and the standard tones are pronounced to have the same loudness, as judged by the ear, and then find the sound level of the standard tone, which is the noise level.

Though there are various methods for the determination of the noise level, the method adopted by Davis is simple and fairly accurate. A standard tuning fork is struck in a convenient manner and then held near the opening of the ear as close as possible without touching it. The time of striking is noted and the interval of time until the intensity of the fork is equal to the loudness of the surrounding noise is also noted. The time interval of the standard tone to decay upto the limit of bare audibility in the absence of noise is also noted. This part of the experiment has to be conducted in the same place when it is perfectly quiet and the tuning fork must be struck exactly in the same manner.

The intensity of the sound emitted by a tuning fork may be represented by the equation

$$I_t = I_o \, e^{-\alpha t}$$

where I_t is the intensity at t seconds, I_0 the initial intensity and α is a constant depending on the fork. Then log $I_0/I_t = 2\cdot34\ \alpha t$ which is the difference in intensity in time t measured in decibels, and decay in intensity is αt where α is a constant depending on the fork. Hence if t is the time in which the intensity of the fork decays to the loudness of the noise and N is this level and t_0 is the time interval after striking when the sound dies to threshold limit, then $N = \alpha\ (t_0 - t) + M$ where M is a small correction which varies a little with the nature and pitch of the noise but is fairly constant at 15-20 db. If the frequency of the fork is 1000 c/s, N is the noise level in db.

This method is subject to some shortcomings; first the method is subjective, secondly it cannot be used for a sound of very small duration, and thirdly it cannot be used for very intense sound also because the initial intensity of the tuning fork may not be sufficiently large in comparison with the noise to be measured.

The physiological effect of noise on human beings is being studied in great detail. It has been found that a prolonged sound of high intensity may cause deafness such as people working in modern workshops and appliances are now provided in most machines to reduce the noise level. A normal person is not usually subjected to intense sounds so as to cause a permanent injury to auditory systems. Noise levels for different types of vehicles are entered in table (14.3).

TABLE 14.3
Noise level in db

Type of noise	*Noise level*
Tram car	90
Motor lorry	70
Motor horn	80
Aeroplane	100
Ship's siren	95
Riveting machine	102

14.9 OTHER CONSIDERATIONS

In order that the speech of the observer or the music in a hall is not disturbed by sound from outside, the doors and windows as well as the walls of the room may be constructed of sound absorbing materials. Regarding the coefficients of absorption of different materials it has been found that absorption varies with frequency. As a general rule, it increases with frequency but sometimes the variation is of a complicated nature. Some substances used as absorbant absorb copiously at low frequencies and some at high frequencies. Some absorb to the same extent throughout the whole range of frequencies. Hence in case of music which, in general, consists of fundamental as well as higher partials, if an absorber which is effective at high frequencies is used it will have the effect of increasing the relative importance of fundamental tone and the emitted note will be pure. If an absorbant is used which is effective at low frequencies then the relative importance of high partials will be enhanced and it will add to the brilliance of the note. Depending upon the material of the walls there will be different amounts of absorption and a number of experiments have been performed to determine the coefficients of absorption of different samples over a wide range of frequencies. But it is obvious that the coefficient of absorption measured is not an exactly determined quantity. The size of the sample, its exact location in the hall and the method of mounting determine to a large extent the total effect. But in the actual design of the hall, the average value of the coefficient of absorption can be accepted taking into consideration the purpose for which the hall is to be ultimately used, that is whether it is for speech or for music.

The presence or absence of audience affects to a great extent the acoustic quality of an auditorium. Halls which have very bad acoustics when empty become quite good in acoustic quality when the audience is present. This is due to the fact that audience itself becomes a good absorber of sound and thereby changes the reverberation time of the hall. Two measurements are generally made. The time of reverberation is measured when the hall is full of audience and all doors and windows are closed and the second measurement consists in measuring the time of reverberation when the hall is empty and the doors and windows are gradually opened until the same time of reverberation is obtained. Sabine obtained a value of 4·7 sq ft of window per person and though the figure has been modified, still this value is taken in designing the hall for acoustic purposes.

15
RECORDING AND REPRODUCTION OF SOUND

In this chapter we shall discuss the methods of recording sound and reproducing it. The first sound records were made by Leon Scott in 1857. In 1877, Edison produced record of sound by indenting a trace of tin foil covering the face of a metal cylinder. In 1878, Alexander Graham Bell recorded sound on wax cylinders the material being cut out according to the amplitude of sound.

15.1 RECORDING IN DISCS

Leaving aside the earlier methods used for recording of sound waves in discs, it is necessary to describe the modern methods used for recording. With the development of microphone and distortionless amplification with the help of valve tubes, the energy for recording can be amplified as desired. The recording machine consists essentially of a heavy turn-table driven at a constant speed of rotation either by a synchronous motor or by means of a clockwork driven by a weight. The recording wax is a circular slab of 13″ in diameter and 1½″ thick which is composed of a metallic soap and has a highly polished plane surface. The recording stylus has a slow traverse across this long radius of the disc from the circumference to the centre. A block diagram of the method used for recording is shown in Fig. 15.1.

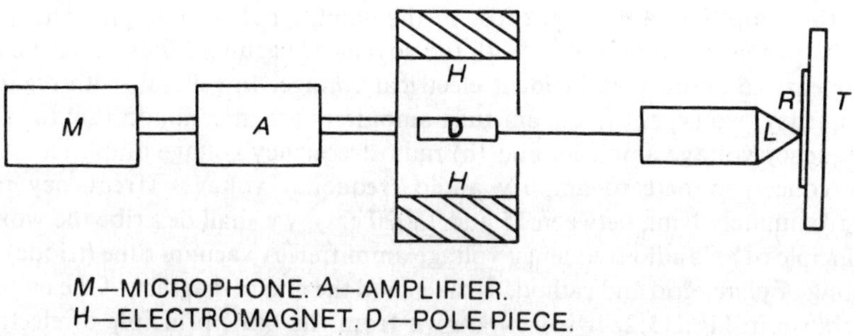

M—MICROPHONE. *A*—AMPLIFIER.
H—ELECTROMAGNET. *D*—POLE PIECE.
L—CUTTING STYLUS. *R*—RECORDING DISC
T—TURN TABLE.

Fig. 15.1

A microphone M converts the sound waves into a weak electric current. This current which is an electrical replica of the original sound wave is amplified by means of an amplifier A and fed to an electromagnet H. The amplified current thus produced when passed through the winding of the electromagnet H produces a magnetic field which varies in intensity in conformity with the output of the amplifier A. The varying magnetic field causes the soft iron pole piece D to be attracted in varying degree to the pole of the electromagnet. This in turn actuates the cutting stylus L and as a result a record of the original sound wave is made on the disc R. The energy of the needle in vibration as it passes round the groove of a record is proportional to the square of the amplitude multiplied by the square of the frequency. In order that this must be constant for all frequencies the amplitude should vary inversely as the frequency and hence the maximum velocity of the recording point must be constant for the same input energy for all the values of frequency. This is known as constant velocity recording and is most convenient for reproduction.

The different component parts of the recording system are as follows:

(a) Microphone *M*. The working principle of the microphone has been discussed in Reception and Transformation of Sound (Chapter 12). Either a condenser or a carbon granular microphone, preferably the latter, may be used. In modern recording systems, other types of microphones such as moving coil, or ribbon microphone or a crystal microphone may also be employed. However, most microphones show a directional effect which means that the output from the microphone depends not only upon the intensity of the sound but also on the direction from which sound waves are incident on the diaphragm of the microphone. The directional effect is due to diffraction and is specially marked for frequencies near about or above 8000 c/s. The responce curve showing the variàtion of the intensity of the output signal with frequency for different typès of microphone shows that the response is practically the same for frequencies below 8000 c/s for all the types, but shows a peak at 8000 c/s specially in case of condenser and carbon microphones. As noted earlier, the purpose of the microphone is to convert mechanical vibrations to corresponding electrical vibrations of the same frequency so that these may be amplified by an amplifier.

(b) Amplifier *A*. The purpose of the amplifier A is to amplify the output signal from the microphone. With the advent of vacuum tubes, it has become very easy to amplify an incident electrical voltage. In general, with regard to frequency two types of vacuum tube amplifiers are in common use: (a) audio frequency voltage amplifier and (b) radio frequency voltage amplifier. As we are concerned here to amplify audio frequency voltages (frequency range approximately lying between 15 and 15000 c/s), we shall describe the working principle of an audio frequency voltage amplifier. A vacuum tube (triode) consisting of plate, grid and cathode is taken and the circuit diagram of the amplifier is shown in Fig. 15.2. It is well known from the basic principle of electronic circuits that a small variation of the grid voltage causes a large change in the plate current of the tube. If this plate current is now allowed to flow through a resistance or load, an amplified voltage will develop across the load. The corresponding equivalent circuit is shown in Fig. 15.3. It can be shown that if i represents the instantaneous plate current due to variation v_g of the grid voltage, then

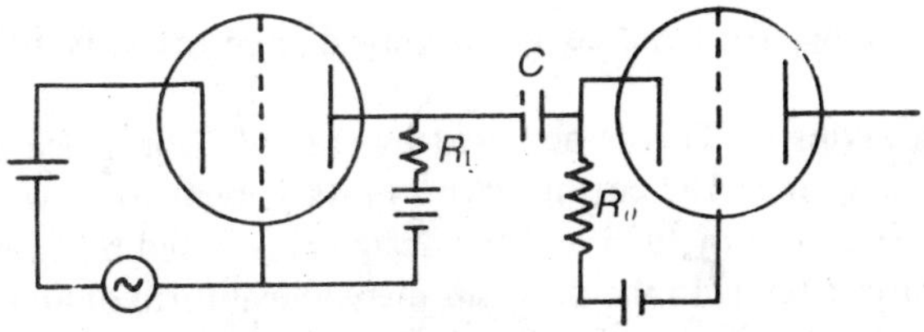

Fig. 15.2

$$i_a = av_a + gv_g \qquad (15.1).$$

where a is the plate conductance $a = 1/r_p$ where r_p is the plate resistance and g the mutual conductance of the tube and v_a is the instantaneous plate voltage.

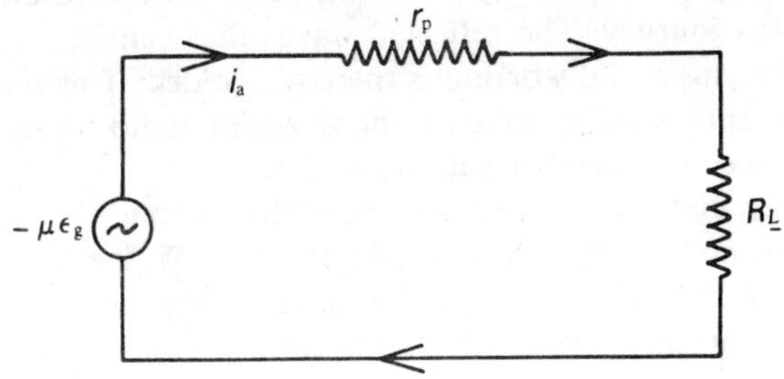

Fig.15.3

If R_L is the load resistance, $v_a = i_a R_L$ and as the grid voltage is out of phase with the instantaneous plate voltage by 180°, then

$$-\frac{v_a}{R_L} = av_a + gv_g$$

$$v_a\left[a + \frac{1}{R_L}\right] = -gv_g$$

or

$$\frac{v_a}{v_g} = -\frac{gr_p}{1+\gamma_p/R_L} = \frac{-\mu}{1+\gamma_p/R_L} \qquad (15.2)$$

where μ is called the amplification factor of the tube. This amplified voltage may be applied to the grid of the second tube through a condenser C such that no d.c. plate voltage is applied to the grid but only the amplified audio frequency voltage appears at the grid of the second tube. The system is known as cascade amplifier, and employing a number of tubes the desired amplification is obtained. One of the main advantages of R.C. coupled amplifier system is that the frequency response curve is linear over a wide range of frequencies. The combination of a microphone with an audio frequency amplifier is of general occurence in all systems of sound recording and reproduction and hence it has been described in some detail.

(c) The electromagnet. The audio frequency voltage thus amplified sends a current through the electromagnet which becomes energised according to the intensity of the sound wave incident on the microphone, that is upon the intensity of the speech or music. The soft iron pole piece D placed between the poles of the electomagnet is attracted in varying degree towards the pole of the electromagnet.

(d) Cutting stylus *L*. This is actuated by the soft iron piece *D* to which it is attached by a spring. The cutting stylus in its present form was invented by Maxfield and Harrison in 1926 and the design was based by comparison with an electrical filter circuit. In the previous mechanical form of acoustic recorder the response was not uniform over the whole of the frequency range and it showed a number of peaks at a considerable number of frequencies. Just as in the case of an electrical filter which is terminated by its characteristic impendance, the cutting stylus system is terminated by an equivalent mechanical impedance which usually consists of a rod of gum rubber about 25 cm long such that torsional waves transmitted by the stylus are dissipated in the mechanical impedance by its to and fro journey. The reflected waves thus cannot interfere with the motion of the stylus and distortion is thereby avoided. This in turn results in an almost uniform response curve for the whole of audio frequency range and the recording becomes smooth and perfect.

(e) Recording disc. The circular recording disc (about 13″ in diameter and 1½″ thick) is made from metallic soap. After recording, the wax surface is made conducting by a coat of graphite or by metal sputtering. From the record a negative is now produced by electrodeposition of copper.

Reproduction

In the process of reproduction, the microphone is replaced by the loudspeaker. A playback needle follows the grove cut in the disc, thereby causing the iron disc to move harmonically towards and away from the electromagnet *H*. As a result, a variable current will be induced in the magnet and this current being amplified by the amplifier can actuate the loudspeaker. The process is known as magnetic pickup.

In the process of crystal pickup, a crystal is placed in contact with the playback needle. When the needle vibrates a variable pressure is developed and due to piezoelectric effect an electric voltage is developed. This voltage amplified by means of the amplifier *A* may actuate the loudspeaker. Besides the magnetic and the crystal pickups, other forms of reproduction have been attempted. It is known, as in the case of carbon resistance microphone, that the resistance of carbon particles varies with the impinging pressure. Hence if the movement of the reproduction needle be used to change the resistance of carbon particles then a varying current flows through the circuit, the amplitude of which is proportional to the intensity of the recorded sound. This current flowing through a resistance develops a voltage which can be amplified by an audio frequency amplifier and then can actuate a loudspeaker.

In another form of reproduction, the movement of the needle changes the capacity of a condenser and a current flows through the circuit in porportion to the intensity of the original sound and the current or voltage can be amplified and fed to the loudspeaker.

One of the major advantages of electrical reproduction system is that output can be varied as one desires by varying the volume control attached to the amplifier whereas in case of mechanical reproduction, as was done previously, no control of volume was possible. Due to heavy pickup in case of mechanical system the wear and tear of the record was large but it has been considerably reduced by the modern method of electrical reproduction.

15.2 WIRE OR TAPE RECORDING

The method which is of comparatively recent development was first suggested by Poulson, a Danish engineer. Stille, a German engineer made certain improvements in the method and a schematic diagram of the system is shown in Fig. 15.4.

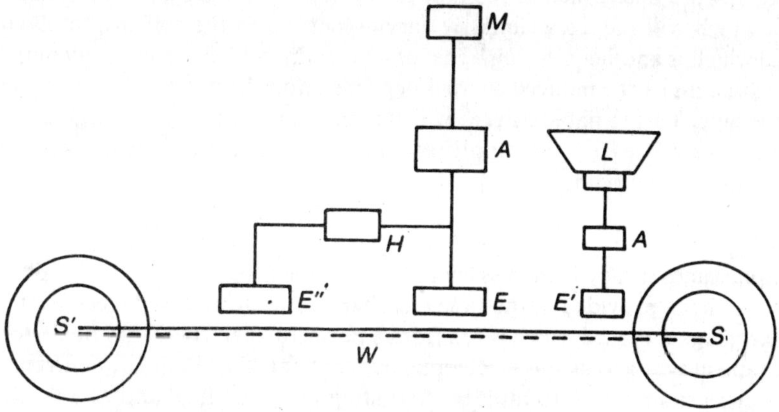

S.S′—SPOOLS. *W*—WIRE OR TAPE.
E—ELECTROMAGNET FOR RECORDING.
E′—ELECTROMAGNET FOR REPRODUCTION.
E″—ELECTROMAGNET FOR ERASING.
A AND *A′*—AUDIO FREQUENCY AMPLIFIER.
M—MICROPHONE. *L*—LOUDSPEAKER
H—HIGH FREQUENCY AMPLIFIER.

Fig. 15.4

S and *S′* are two spools. *W* is a steel wire which is usually made of tungsten magnet steel of high coercivity, 3 mm wide and about 0.07 mm thick, or a tape consisting of a base of cellulose acetate 0.5×10^{3}″ thick and ¼″ wide coated on one side with finely divided ferric oxide. By means of a motor drive the wire or tape *W* unwinds from *S* and winds itself around S′. The electromagnet *E* with a pointed head is actuated by a battery, and connected in series with the microphone *M* and the audio frequency amplifier *A*. As sound waves are incident on the microphone they are converted to corresponding electrical voltages and amplified by the amplifier *A*. This variable electric current flows through the electromagnet and the strength of the magnetic field is modified and thereby gives rise to varying magnetic field in the moving wire or tape. This means that the degree of induced magnetism in the tape is a replica of the original sound wave. Thus a permanent record is made of the sound wave on the tape.

The magnetisation may be longitudinal or parallel to breadth or depth. It has been found in practice that longitudinal magnetisation with a depth component is best. Consequently the pole pieces should be on the opposite sides of the tape. Instead of a steady current through the electromagnet, a high frequency current may be sent through which sets the particles of the magnetisable material vibrating and so make them more easily influenced by the varing magnetic field produced by the audio frequency current.

Reproduction

In order to reproduce the sound, the microphone is replaced by the loudspeaker. If the wire is now wound back in the first spool *S* and again caused to unwind itself, then as the tape moves it will produce a variable magnetic flux which will induce a similarly varying current in the coil of the playback head which is another electromagnet of an extremely high permeability material. The strength of the induced current depends upon the degree of magnetisation in the tape. This variable current which is an exact replica of the original sound wave is amplified by the amplifier and then fed to the loudspeaker which reproduces the original sound.

Erasing

Sometimes it may be necessary to erase a given record and rerecord it. This has also been provided in the tape recorder. To perform this function another electromagnet is used which is fed from a powerful high frequency oscillator. As the tape moves across this electromagnet carrying high frequency current, the particles are subjected to rapidly alternating magnetic field and as a result the tape becomes demagnetised and all previous records are obliterated.

Three switches are provided in the tape recorder which alternately connects the system either with recording electromagnet, or playback or eraser.-Tape recording has some definite advantages over the usual disc recording. (a) It is suitable for quick reproduction and for long programmes to be recorded in a single tape. (b) The records do not deteriorate with time and even after repeated reproduction. (c) The same tape may be used for a number of recordings by erasing the previous one.

15.3 RECORDING OF SOUND IN FILM

There are two principal methods by means of which sound is recorded in films. One is the variable density method and the other the variable area method. The experimental arrangement of the apparatus is as shown in Fig. 15.5 and is detailed in the following:

Variable density method

The output of the Microphone *M* is picked up by the amplifier *A* and connected through a transformer *T* to the glow lamp *G*. Such a lamp consists of a glass envelope equipped with two electrodes and containing a gas at a low pressure. When the voltage of the battery is raised to a certain value, curren

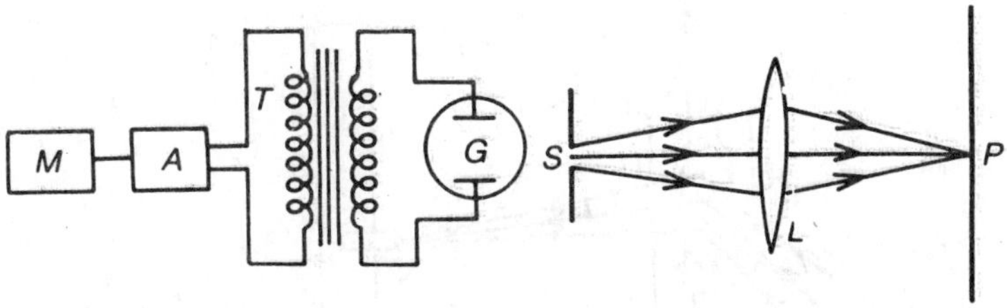

M—MICROPHONE. A—AMPLIFIER. T—TRANSFORMER.
G—GLOW LAMP. S—SLIT. L—LENS. P—PHOTOGRAPHIC FILM.

Fig. 15.5

passes through the glow lamp in the form of a luminous discharge the colour of the emitted light depending upon the nature of the gas. For sound recording a bluish or whittish glow is employed. The voltage of the battery is so adjusted that a discharge takes place and the intensity of the discharge depends upon the voltage. When the speaker speaks before the microphone, the amplified a.c. voltage modifies the voltage applied to the battery and thereby the intensity of the emitted light changes; thus sound waves are used to modulate the intensity of the light beam. This modulated light beam is allowed to pass through the slits and brought to a focus by means of a lens *L* to the moving photographic film *P*. By this means a photographic record is made of the modulated light beam.

Variable area method

An alternative arrangement in which the width the sound track is changed with the change of intensity of sound while the density of the track remains the same throughout has also been used. The schematic diagram of the arrangement is shown in Fig. 15.6. A strip of phosphor bronze in the form of a loop passes over a pulley and placed in a permanent magnetic field as shown. The ends of the phosphor bronze strip are connected to the microphone through the amplifier. A small reflecting *M′* mirror is attached to the phosphor bronze strip as shown and a beam of light from a source of constant intensity is incident on the mirror through a lens and then focussed on the slit *S′* behind which the photographic film *P* is moving vertically with a constant speed. The audio frequency voltage from the amplifier and the microphone sends equal and oppositely directed oscillatory current through the phosphor bronze. As the strip is placed in a magnetic field which is perpendicular to the length of the phosphor bronze strip, a couple is set up which rotates the mirror, the moment of the couple being proportional to the original audio frequency voltage. Accordingly, the slit is illuminated over varying width and a strip of variable area is obtained on the film.

In reproducing sound, the following experimental arrangement is used Fig. 15.7. The transformation of such a sound is accomplished by means of a photo cell, which is an electronic device by means of which light causes liberation of electrons from a specially prepared metallic surface. These liberated electrons are allowed to move under the action of an electric field which constitutes a

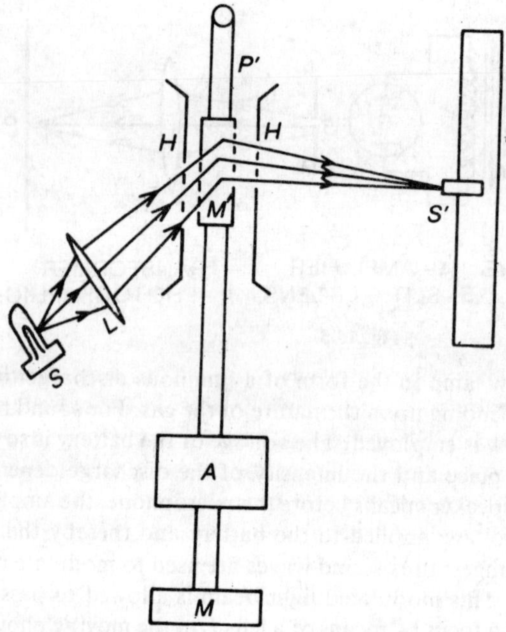

M—MICROPHONE. A—AMPLIFIER. S—SOURCE OF LIGHT. L—LENS. M'—MIRROR. P'—PHOSPHOR BRONZE STRIP. H—ELECTROMAGNET- OR A PERMANENT MAGNET. S'—SLIT. P—PHOTOGRAPHIC FILM

Fig. 15.6

current. This current can be amplified and caused to operate a loudspeaker. Light from the exciter lamp L is first passed through a slit S_1 and focussed by lens L_1 on to the sound track of moving photographic film. A second lens changes the light to a parallel beam which then enters the photo cell G and thereby sets a current in the circuit. The photographic lines constituting the sound track cause a variation of intensity of light incident on the photo cell. The resulting variable current can be put on to the amplifier A through a transformer T. The electrical output actuates the Loudspeaker L'.

The sound track in 35mm film is 2mm wide whereas in 16mm it is 1 mm wide.

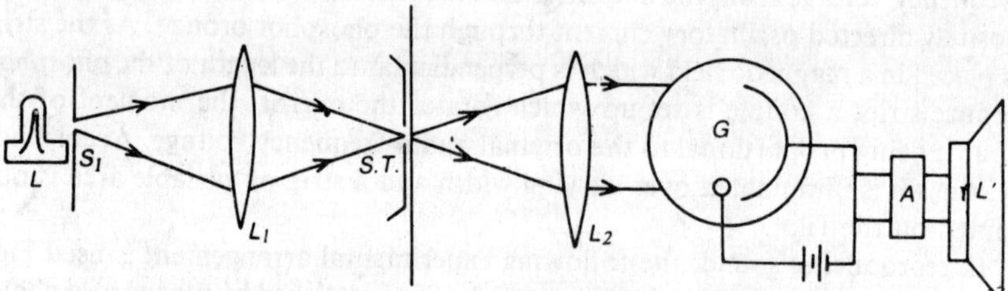

L—ARC LAMP S_1—SLIT. L_1-lens. S.T.—SOUND TRACK. L_2—LAMP. G—PHOTOCELL.. A—AMPLIFIER. L'—LOUD SPEAKER

Fig. 15.7

16

ULTRASONICS

In general, the human ear is capable of receiving sound waves having the frequency lying between 15 and 15000 c/s. Below and above this range, mechanical vibrations fail to produce any sensation in the human ear. Though there is no standard limit, the vibrations lying above 15000 c/s are known as ultrasonics. If the velocity of sound waves in air is taken as 331 m/s at 0°C, then the upper limit of wavelength of ultrasonic waves will be given by

$$\lambda = \frac{33100 \text{ cm}}{15000 \text{ c/s}} = 2.2 \text{ cm}.$$

Though the human ear is not capable of appreciating ultrasonic waves some of the animals such as dogs, bats and some kinds of birds are capable of receiving such waves.

16.1 GENERATION OF ULTRASONIC WAVES.

There are number of ways by which ultrasonic waves can be generated. The method to be employed depends upon the power output necessary and the frequency range to be covered. Generators of mechanical type such as tuning forks or Galton's whistle can be used up to 10,000 c/s.

Galton's whistle

To determine the limit of audibility, Galton devised a miniature organ pipe in the form of a whistle. At one end of the pipe there is a moveable plunger or reflector and its position can be varied by means of a micrometer screw. By this means the length of the air column within the pipe and consequently the pitch of the note can be varied. Edelman later designed the pipe which is blown from an annular nozzle fitted with a screw to vary its distance from the edge of the pipe. By adjusting this distance and the pressure of the air blast, the pipe is set into resonant vibration at a frequency corresponding to its length and diameter. Sounds of very high frequency can thus be produced; but for all practical purposes few of these mechanical methods are used for the generation of ultrasonics. The frequency range mechanically available is extremely limited and all high frequency ultrasonic waves are generated by methods described in the following.

16.2 THE PIEZOELECTRIC METHOD

The most widely used methods that are employed for the generation of ultrasonic waves are the piezoelectric method and the magnetostriction method. The theory of piezoelectric effect has already been discussed in chapter 12. As was shown therein, the effect was discovered by Curie brothers[1] in 1880 who found that certain crystals like quartz, tourmaline and rochelle salt will develop in electric charge when a mechanical pressure or tension is applied to the face of the crystal. Their experiments showed that there is a certain relation between the mechanical pressure applied and the nature of charge developed, and the sign of the charge changed when the pressure was changed to tension. This phenomenon is menifest in many crystals but is very distinctly marked in quartz and rochelle salt. Quartz crystals have been widely used for generating ultrasonic vibrations in solids and liquids since they possess a high mechanical impedance. When the impedance is low the ratio between the output and the charge applied to the crystal is too small for effective use. Professor Langevin was the pioneer worker in utilizing quartz crystal for ultrasonic work during the first world war, at the same time, A.M. Nikolson[2] of the Bell Telephone Laboratories did utilise rochelle salt for generation of ultrasonics. Though the effect is of greater intensity in rochellele salt than in quartz, the units are much softer and more subject to breakage and damage than quartz.

16.3 THE QUARTZ CRYSTAL

Natural quartz usually occurs in the shape of a prism of six sides with a pyramid attached to each end (Fig. 16.1). If the points of the pyramid are joined by a line, that line is defined as the optic axis of the crystal. If the opposite corners of the crystal are joined together then they are known as x-axes or they are

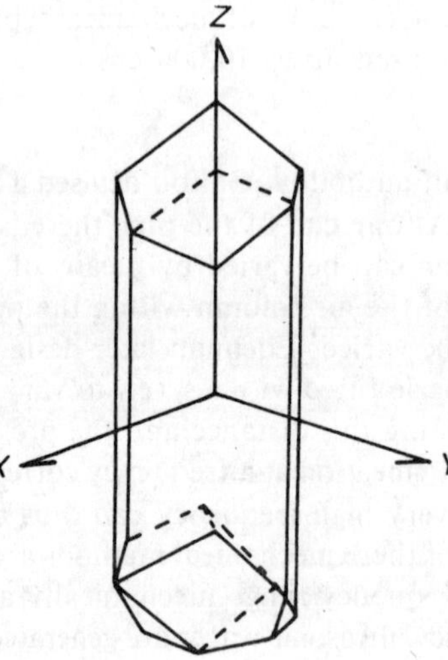

Fig.16.1

also called the electrical axes of the crystal. The y-axes are perpendicular to the sides of the crystal and both of these axes are perpendicular to the z-axes or the optic axis. The crystal must have parallel faces and be polished free of all kinds of chips or cracks. Otherwise they will not vibrate freely.

It was observed by earlier workers that when the tension is changed to pressure or vice versa, the sign of the effect changes. Hence if an alternating voltage is applied at high frequency to the crystal, and if the crystal is properly designed to oscillate at that frequency, it will follow the applied field. The faces of the crystal will move with respect to one another and if one face is pressed against the surface of a medium, ultrasonic waves will be produced and enter the medium and travel through it. Though the crystal will vibrate when a time varying electric field is applied to the crystal, whatever may be the frequency, the amplitude of vibration will be maximum when the frequency of the applied field will be equal to the natural frequency of the crystal and the amplitude of crystal oscillation at resonance is so large compared to its vibration at other frequencies that the crystal is generally made to oscillate at its resonance frequency.

16.4 DESIGN OF ULTRASONIC CRYSTAL

A crystal may be cut either along the x-axes or along the y-axes; it is called the x cut if it is cut along the x-axes and y-çut if it is cut along the y-axes. The x-cut is most generally used since it generates longitudinal or L waves. For the production of shear waves y-cut crystals are also used but for the propagation of this type of waves through a liquid or a gas the medium must have shear elasticity. In case of an x-cut crystal, the longitudinal vibration will occur along the thickness dimension of the crystal. If the crystal vibrates at its natural frequency, it can be shown that

$$t = \lambda/2,$$

where t is the thickness of the crystal and λ is the wavelength of ultrasonic wave. If the crystal is made of quartz, then the velocity of wave propagation is given by

$$c = \sqrt{\frac{E}{\rho}} = \sqrt{\frac{770 \times 10^9}{2.654}} = 540 \times 10^3 \text{ cm/s}.$$

If n = frequency of the wave, then

$$n = \frac{c}{\lambda} = \frac{540 \times 10^3}{2t} = \frac{2700}{t} \text{ kc}/s$$

If t is expressed in millimetres. In practice, the generated frequency is given by

$$n = \frac{2870}{t(\text{mm})} \text{ kc/s}$$

16.5 POWER FOR ULTRASONIC GENERATION

As the frequency of ultrasonic waves is generally higher than 20000 c/s it is natural that the electrical voltage supplied to the crystal must be obtained from a radio trequency oscillator. Any type of radio frequency oscillator such as Hartley or Colpitts oscillator may be employed. The variable frequency oscillator should be employed so that it should be continuously variable in the vicinity of the resonant crystal frequency so that it can be tuned to compensate for changes in the system such as cable lengths. A typical Hartley oscillator is shown in Fig. 16.2. If extreme frequency control is desired, then a crystal-controlled

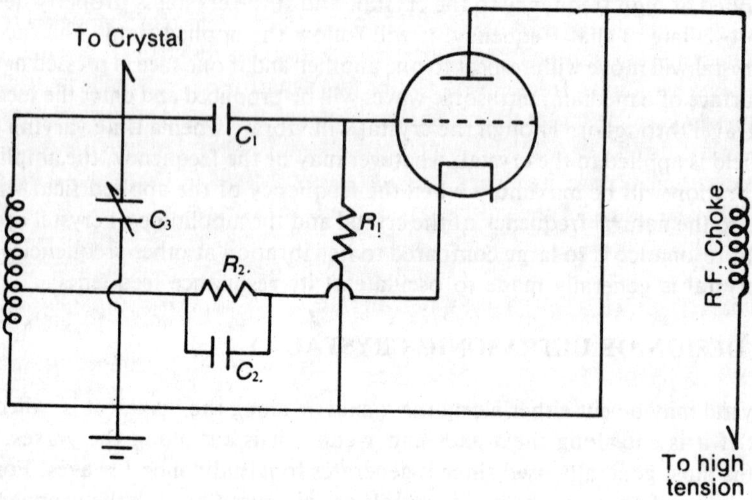

Fig.16.2

oscillator tube having an output of 10 W is generally used. The oscillator should be properly shielded so that no radio frequency voltage may be picked up by the receiver.

16.6 GENERATION OF ULTRASONIC VIBRATION BY MAGNETO-STRICTION

Besides the piezoelectric phenomenon, the most wide use has been made of the phenomenon of magnetostriction in the generation of ultrasonic waves. It was observed by Joule in 1847 that if a magnetic field is applied along the axis of a ferromagnetic material such as iron, cóbalt and nickel in the form of a rectangular box, then a change in the length of the bar occurs. In a direct field, this change is small, being only $1 \times 10^{-6}\ L$ in nickel where L is the length of the bar. If, however, the field becomes oscillating then the effect becomes much more pronounced because then the elastic forces of the bar no longer oppose the change, and only forces that are to be overcome come from the viscosity of the material; further if the oscillating field is resonant with the natural frequency of the bar, this effect becomes much more pronounced and it has been found that the change increases manifold.

The velocity of ultrasonic waves in a longitudinal bar is given by

$$c = \sqrt{\frac{Y}{\rho}}$$

where Y = Young's modulus and ρ = density of the material.

If l denotes the length of the bar, the fundamental wavelength of the bar is $2l$ and hence the frequency $f = \frac{c}{2l}$. Hence, in general $f = \frac{sc}{2l} = \frac{s}{2l}\sqrt{\frac{Y}{\rho}}$ or $l = \frac{s}{2f}\sqrt{\frac{Y}{\rho}}$ where s is the order of the harmonic. It can thus be seen from the above formula that at a frequency of 20000 c/s, the length of the nickel rod that will be resonant will be of the order of 5″ and this length will be smaller and smaller with higher frequencies so that the length will become very small at a frequency greater than 60,000 c/s; hence the usual range of a magnetostriction ultrasonic oscillator will be from 5000 c/s to 60,000 c/s. Magnetostriction has been used in laboratories to generate ultrasonic signals of frequency 2 Mc/s but at higher frequencies the output is so small that it cannot be utilized for any practical purposes.

16.7 MAGNETOSTRICTION OSCILLATOR

Pierce[3] who carried out extensive work on magnetostriction utilized various forms of circuits to generate the radio frequency power to excite the magnetostriction rod. In the simple form, the circuit is as shown in Fig. 16.3.

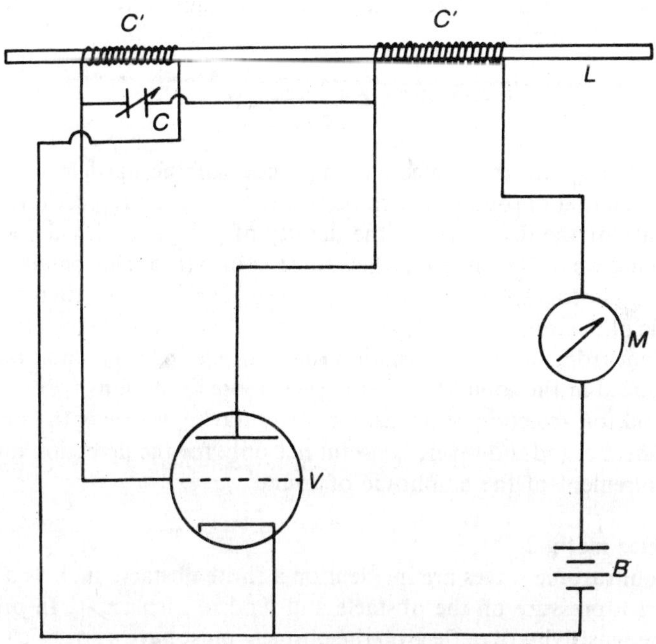

V—TUBE. L—MAGNETOSTRICTION ROD.
M—METER. B—HIGH TENSION.
C′—COIL. C—VARIABLE CONDENSER.

Fig.16.3

The magnetostriction rod is indicated by L in the figure and a coil is placed loosely around the rod. Oscillations are self-excited and under their influence the rod vibrates and this movement of the bar produces a voltage in the feed-back coil which is applied to the grid and oscillations are maintained. The meter in the plate circuit merely indicates the presence or absence of oscillations. The part of the rod in the plate side is driven by the output while the other section in the grid side couples part of the energy back into the tube and the two coils are connected regeneratively, i.e. the feed back voltage is subtracted from the input signal voltage and hence decreases the amplification.

16.8 DETECTION OF ULTRASONIC WAVES

The methods which are commonly used for the detection of sonic waves can be used for the ultrasonic waves as well except that the ear cannot be used. We shall discuss some methods for the detection of progressive ultrasonic waves in this section and the detection of stationary waves will be dealt in the next section when we shall consider the methods used for the measurement of the velocity of ultrasonic waves. We shall discuss some of the methods below.

Smoke method

When light solid particles or liquid drops are introduced in the field of a ound wave, the particles take up the motion the amplitude of which has been alculated by Kcnig as

$$\frac{y_1}{y_2} = \sqrt{1 + a^2} \text{ where } a = \frac{2}{g} \frac{\rho_1}{\rho_0 \lambda b^2}.$$

vhere y_1 and y_2 are the respective ampıtudes of the particle when set into ibration and that of sound wave respectively, b and ρ are respectively the radius nd density of the detectors, ρ_0 the density of the gas and λ the wavelength f the sound wave. The method then consists in introducing small particles in he field to photograph them with long time of exposure and then measure the mplitude of the motion of the particles which appear as streaks in the negative. t is evident from the above equation that particles of very small radius must e introduced in the sound field. However, these limitations forbid the use of he method for detection of ultrasonic waves having wavelengths smaller than 0 cm. The method, however, is useful not only for the detection but also for he measurement of the amplitude of sound wave.

Radiometer method

When ultrasonic waves are incident on a finite obstacle such as a solid disc hey exert a pressure on the obstacle and tend to displace it. In order to in-crease the sensitivity of deflection the obstacle must have a specific impedance natching with that of the fluid medium. Boyle and Lehmann used a disc suspended by a quartz fibre with torsion head and placed it in the field of the ultrasonic beam. When the force acted on the beam to deflect it, it was restored to its previous position by twisting the torsion head. As in the case of sonic beams, flames can also be used as detector of ultrasonic waves but it is difficult to make any quantitative measurements in this method.

Electrical detector

When ultrasonic waves propagate through a fluid, compressions and rarefactions take place in accordance with the adiabatic law. This principle has been utilized by Tucker and Paris by using the cooling of a hot wire by a sound wave in their hot wire microphone and the method has been extensively used by Richardson in measuring the amplitude of ultrasonic waves. A fine platinum or a nickel wire exposed to the ultrasonic beam suffers an oscillatory change of temperature and hence of resistance which is representative of a fraction of ultrasonic amplitude owing to lag in attaining equilibrium with a rapidly alternating field. Besides the oscillatory drop there is a steady drop which can be related however with the ultrasonic amplitude.

The oscillatory change of resistance causes a change of current flowing through the circuit which can be amplified and detected. The measure of the steady change can be obtained by obtaining the balance with a Wheatstone network.

Quartz crystal receivers

Just as quartz or rochelle salt crystals can be used for the generation of ultrasonic waves, they can be used as detectors of ultrasonic waves also. When ultrasonic waves are incident on a quartz or a rochelle salt crystal, alternating electromotive force of the same frequency as the ultrasonic wave is generated. This voltage is very small in magnitude and a radio frequency amplifier can be used to amplify the received signal, which may be detected by a superheterodyne receiver and displayed on the screen of an oscilloscope. This is the universal method for the detection of ultrasonics.

16.9 VELOCITY OF ULTRASONIC WAVES

In chapter 10, we have described methods for the determination of velocity of sound waves in liquids, gases and solids. It was a natural curiosity to think that as the frequency of the waves is increased manifold when we pass from ordinary sound waves to ultrasonic waves, the velocity of the ultrasonic waves might change and indicate a region of dispersion. The problem was quite interesting and many workers devoted their attention for the accurate determination of the velocity of ultrasonic waves.

Velocity in liquids

There are in general two methods for the determination of velocity of ultrasonic waves through a liquid and both these methods can be employed with slight modification in the case of gases. The two methods are: (a) diffraction method, and (b) interference method.

(a) Diffraction method. This method, first suggested by Brillouin, was developed by Debye and Sears[4]. According to Brillouin, when an ultrasonic wave passes through a liquid it gives rise to a periodic variation of density in a liquid and the structure of the liquid thus agitated can be simulated to that of a light diffraction grating. Consequently if a beam of monochromatic light be incident on such a simulated grating there should be visible the diffraction pattern in the transmitted light. The complete theory presents many difficulties and was worked out by Raman and Nagendranath[5]. Just as in the case of X-ray diffraction the theory can be worked out by considering the net effect as a resultant of a number of reflections from a series of parallel equidistant planes represented by the loci of maximum compression, and evidently these planes of maximum compression will be situated at a distance λ, the wavelength of the transmitted sound wave. The theory of optical grating can then be applied and if θ denotes the angle of diffraction maximum, then

$$2\lambda \sin \theta = n\lambda^*$$

where λ^* denotes the wavelength of the incident monochromatic light; when $n=1$ we get

$$\sin \theta = \pm \frac{\lambda^*}{2\lambda}$$

Consequently, if the frequency f of the crystal generating the ultrasonics be known, the velocity of the waves can be determined from the relation

$$v = f\lambda$$

The theory of the method is not so simple as deduced above and the differences in the intensities of the maxima were calculated by Raman and Nagendranath[5]. Further theoretical work was also done by Extermann and Wannier and also by Exterman. The experimental work was carried out by Parthasarathy[7] in a large number of organic liquids.

A quartz crystal generating ultrasonics is placed in a rectangular trough filled with the experimental liquid (Fig. 16.4). At right angles to the trough, a slit

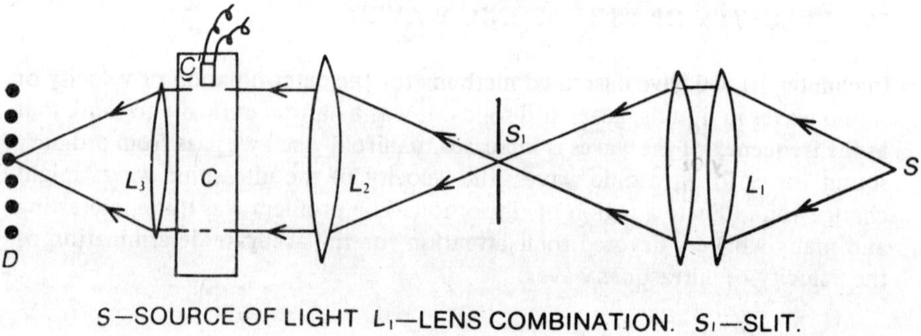

S—SOURCE OF LIGHT L_1—LENS COMBINATION. S_1—SLIT. L_2 & L_3—LENS. C—CELL CONTAINING LIQUID. C′—ULTRASONIC CRYSTAL D—DIFFRACTION SPECTRA.

Fig. 16.4

and lens are arranged so that plane monochromatic light waves are sent through the liquid approximately at right angles to the direction of propagation of waves. After transmission through the liquid the emergent light is observed across the focal plane of a telescope where besides the central image, a series of diffracted images can be observed. Even when λ is very small that is for high frequencies and θ is of the order of few degrees. Parthasarathy determined the velocity in a large number of organic liquids up to a frequency of 7 Mc/s, but no dispersion in velocity could be ascertained. Further work in this direction was carried out by Lucas and Biquard[6] who also did not observe any change of velocity with frequency. The same method was also applied with slight modification in case of gases. The change in velocity with frequency cannot be observed in the frequency region of ultrasonic waves investigated experimentally but dispersion was observed indirectly through the measurements of the wavelength change in the case of hyperfine structure in the Rayleigh scattering in liquids, specially in the case of viscous liquids such as glycerine and castor oil. This hyperfine structure in the case of Rayleigh scattering is known as Brilliouin spectra after Brillouin who explained satisfactorily the shift of the line as due to propagation of hypersonic vibrations through the liquid. The frequency of such vibrations lies in the range of 10^{10} to 10^{12} c/s and the experimental results in the case of viscous liquids were explained by Sen[7] by utilizing the general equation of wave propagation after Lamb, with the incorporation of the idea of complex viscosity of Maxwell.

(b) Interference method. A new method was devised by Pierce[8] which can be utilized for the measurement of velocity of ultrasonic waves in both liquids and gases, and is known as 'interference method'. The schematic diagram of the apparatus is shown in Fig. 16.5. The source of ultrasonic waves is a quartz

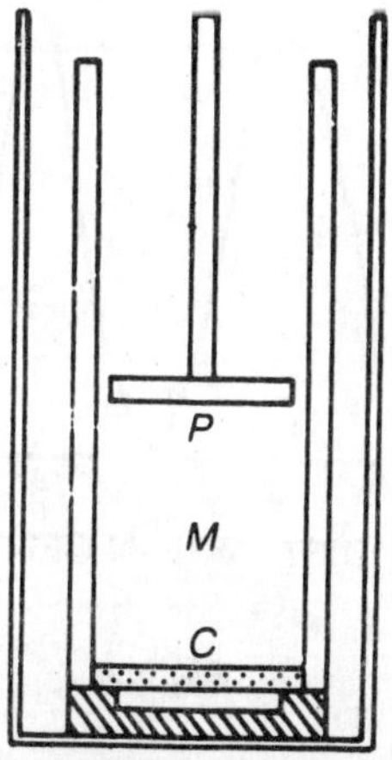

P—REFLECTOR PLATE.
C—CRYSTAL.
M—MEDIUM (Liquid or Gas)

Fig. 16.5

crystal excited by a radio frequency oscillator in the usual way. The dimension of the crystal plate is large compared with the wavelength of the sound in the liquid. The crystal plate is placed at the bottom of the metallic container either of rectangular or cylindrical cross-section. At the other end of the container a metallic piston moves with the help of the micrometer screw. Due to reflection from this reflector a system of stationary waves is formed with nodes and antinodes. The prime criterion for the experiment is that the two surfaces, that of the reflector and that of the crystal should be optically parallel to one another and the parallelism should be within 1 or 2 fringe widths with a monochromatic source of light. The reflected waves react on the quartz source and thereby change the plate current or the tank current of the oscillator supplying the voltage to the quartz crystal. It is natural that the plate current or the tank current will depend upon the amplitude of vibration of the crystal. Depending upon the position of the reflector, the vibrations will arrive at the crystal after reflection and either damp or augment the vibrations of the crystal according as the vibrations after reflection are out of phase or in phase with the vibrations of the crystal. This will be seen in the change of either plate or tank current of the oscillator. Consequently the plate or tank current will go through a cycle of values as the reflector plate is moved through half a wavelength. A curve is plotted Fig. 16.6 between the change of plate or tank current and the position

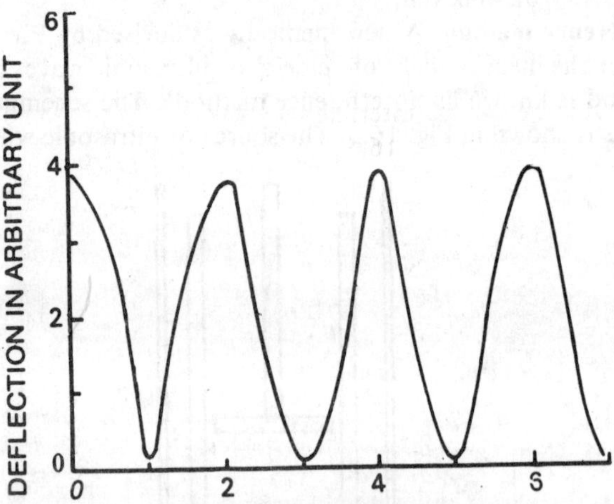

Fig. 16.6

of the piston as noted in the micrometer screw. From the positions of successive maxima or minima, the value of $\lambda/2$ can be obtained and the velocity v determined from the relation $v=f\lambda$ where f is the frequency of the wave. As is evident, the interferometer method of measuring the velocity of ultrasonic waves can be utilized for measurements in both liquids and gases. Thus the method was utilized by van Itterbeck and Verhacam[9] for measurements of velocity at very low temperature and Pitt and Jackson[10] utilized it in case of liquid oxygen and hydrogen.

16.10 ABSORPTION AND DISPERSION OF ULTRASONIC WAVES

When ultrasonic waves pass through a medium there are three main causes for the dissipation of energy, namely (a) viscosity, (b) heat conduction, and (c) heat radiation.

When the waves pass through the medium, there is a relative motion between different parts of a medium which is opposed by the viscous forces in the medium. The energy which is necessary to oppose these viscous forces is supplied by the incoming ultrasonic waves and as a result, the mechanical energy is converted to heat.

The second cause for the dissipation of energy is due to heat conduction. When layers of air are compressed during the propogation of waves, their temperature is raised while the temperature of neighbouring layers which are in a state of rarefaction is correspondingly lowered. Consequently heat flows from the compressed to the rarefied layers and thus a portion of energy is dissipated. This dissipation can be avoided if the compressions and rarefactions take place so rapidly that there is no time for the transfer of heat to take place. It has been observed that the changes are adiabatic when the frequency is small and it may be remembered in this connection that Laplace theoretically obtained the correct value of the velocity of propagation by assuming that the changes are adiabatic; Hertzfield and Rice showed that the rate of conduction is proportional to temperature gradient and for a given amplitude of wave inversely proportional to the square of the wavelength and therefore directly proportional to square of the frequency, but when the frequency of sound waves becomes very high, the adiabatic conditions may be only partly fulfilled and interesting cases of absorption and dispersion may occur.

The third cause is the radiation of heat from the compressed to the rarefied layers, with consequent dissipation of energy.

Based on above considerations, Stokes and Kirchoff developed the theory of absorption and dispersion of ultrasonics in a fluid. Let ρ_0 denote the density of the fluid before the ultrasonic waves are incident on the medium and let W denote the flow velocity and P the pressure of the liquid. Then from the fundamental equation of hydrodynamics,

$$\rho_0 \frac{\partial W}{\partial t} = \text{div } P \tag{16.1}$$

In an idealised nonviscous fluid, only hydrostatic pressure exists. A uniform hydrostatic pressure would not give a resultant force on any part of the liquid. Thus a force results only when a difference of pressure exists and evidently the resultant force on a volume element dv is $-\text{grad } P.\, dv$.

For a less idealised fluid, however, it is necessary to describe the stresses in the liquid by a more complicated quantity than the hydrostatic pressure, namely by a symmetrical stress tensor P_{ij} just as in the theory of elasticity. Such a symmetrical tensor will have three normal components such as P_{xx}, P_{yy} and P_{zz} and also three shear components $P_{xy} = P_{yx}$, $P_{xz} = P_{zx}$, $P_{yz} = P_{zy}$ and for an idealised fluid

$$P_{xx} = P_{yy} = P_{zz} = P$$
$$P_{xy} = P_{yz} = P_{zx} = 0$$

The force evidently due to these shear stresses is given by div P'. Hence we get div $\bar{P} = -$ grad $P +$ div P'

Consequently from equation (16.1) we get

$$\rho_0 \frac{\partial w}{\partial t} = -\text{ grad } P + \text{div } P' \tag{16.2}$$

Consequently in the general equation of motion of fluid the stress stensor $\bar{P}$ is made up of two parts, the negative hydrostatic pressure P and the viscosity term P' Stokes further showed that if P'_{xx}, P'_{yy} and P'_{zz} are the three components at P' and if further P'_{xx} is a linear function of the gradient of velocity,

$$P'_{xx} = 2\eta \left\{ \frac{\partial U}{\partial x} - \frac{1}{3} \frac{\partial U}{\partial x} \right\}$$

where U is the x-component of W; then, considering the flow in one direction only

$$\rho_0 \frac{\partial U}{\partial t} = -\frac{\partial P}{\partial x} + \frac{4}{3} \eta . \frac{\partial^2 U}{\partial x^2} \tag{16.3}$$

If y is the displacement, then $U = \dfrac{dy}{dt}$ and the excess pressure $P = -K.\left(\dfrac{dy}{dx}\right)$ where K is the bulk modulus. Then, from equation (16.3).

$$\rho_0 \frac{d^2 y}{dt^2} = K . \frac{d^2 y}{dx^2} + \frac{4}{3} . \eta . \frac{d^2 U}{dx^2} .$$

$$\rho_0 \frac{d^2 y}{dt^2} = K . \frac{d^2 y}{dx^2} + \frac{4}{3} . \eta . \frac{d^3 y}{dx^2 . dt} . \tag{16.4}$$

Let us assume $y = ae^{J\omega (t - x/v)}$

then from equation (16.4)

$$-\rho_0 \omega^2 = -K . \frac{\omega^2}{v^2} - \frac{4}{3} . \eta . \frac{\omega^2}{v^2} . J\omega .$$

or

$$\frac{\rho_0}{K} = \frac{1}{v^2} \left\{ 1 + \frac{4}{3} \frac{J\omega\eta}{K} \right\} .$$

or

$$\frac{1}{v} = \sqrt{\frac{\rho_0}{K}} \left[1 - \frac{2}{3} \frac{J\omega\eta}{K} \right] = \frac{1}{v_0} - \frac{2}{3} J\omega \frac{\eta}{K v_0}$$

Hence

$$y = ae^{J\omega \left(t - \frac{x}{v} + \frac{2}{3} \frac{J\omega\eta}{K v_0} x \right)}$$

$$= ae^{-\frac{2}{3} \omega^2 \frac{\eta}{K v_0} x} \; e^{J(\omega t - \beta x)}$$

where $\beta = \dfrac{2\pi}{\lambda}$ phase difference per centimetre.

Putting $\nu = \frac{\eta}{\rho_0}$ where ν is called the kinematic viscosity

$$y = ae^{-\frac{2}{3}\omega^2 \frac{\nu}{v_0^3} x} \quad e^{J(\omega t - \beta x)}.$$

Putting it in the form $y = ae^{-\alpha_1 x} \, e^{J(\omega t - \beta x)}$

we get $$\alpha_1 = \frac{2}{3}\,\omega^2 . \frac{\nu}{v_0^3} \tag{16.5}$$

Thus it is observed that the effect of addition of a term of viscosity has two effects on the velocity of sound waves. In the first instance, an absorption term denoted by the attenuation constant α appears and secondly, the velocity of propagation v_0 is changed to a value, given by $\frac{1}{v} = \frac{1}{v_0}\left[1 - J.\,\frac{2}{3}\,\omega\,\frac{\eta}{K}\right]$. Thus the velosity becomes a function of frequency but in the particular case of viscous damping the effect on velocity is negligible. The effect on amplitude is given by $y = y_0\, e^{-\alpha_1 x}$ and the amplitude will fall to $1/e$ of its value $x = 1/\alpha_1$.

Then $$\alpha_1 = \frac{3v_0^3}{2\omega^2\nu} = \frac{3\lambda^3 f}{8\pi^2\nu}.$$

Effect of heat conduction

The effect of heat conduction was treated first by Stokes and later by Kirchoff and Rayleigh. Considering the picture of a sound wave at a given time, the density crests will have temperature above the average, and the density troughs temperature below the average. Heat conduction will tend to equate the temperature; accordingly the compressed region upon re-expanding returns less work than was expanded in compressing them. A similar statement applies to re-compression of the rarefied region. The net result is a loss and hence there is absorption of sound. In this case the effect may be similarly expressed by a relation of the form

$$y = y_0\, e^{-\alpha_2 x}$$

where the value of α_2 has been calculated as

$$\alpha_2 = \frac{2\pi^2 f^2}{v_0^3}\left(\frac{\gamma - 1}{\gamma}\right) K' \tag{16.6}$$

where K' is the thermometric conductivity.

$$= \frac{\text{Heat conductivity}}{\text{Heat capacity per unit volume}}$$

$$= K/C_v\rho_0$$

where K is the heat conductivity, C_v the specific heat at constant volume, ρ_0 is the density and γ is the ratio of the specific heats. But from the kinetic theory, $K = f'\eta C_v$ where η is the viscosity, and f' is a constant, different for different gases. Then we get,

$$\alpha_1 = \frac{2\pi^2 f^2}{v_0^3} \frac{4\nu}{3}$$

and
$$\alpha_2 = \frac{2\pi^2 f^2}{v_0^3} \frac{\gamma - 1}{\gamma} \frac{K}{C_v \rho_0} = \frac{2\pi^2 f^2}{v_0^3} \frac{\gamma - 1}{\gamma} f' \nu$$

Thus
$$\alpha_1 : \alpha_2 = \frac{4}{3} : \frac{\gamma - 1}{\gamma} f' = 1 : \frac{3}{4} \cdot \frac{\gamma - 1}{\gamma} f'$$

as
$$f' = 1 \cdot 78 \text{ for air, } \alpha_1 : \alpha_2 = 1 : 0 \cdot 38$$

so that conduction of heat contributes less than that due to viscosity. The total attenuation constant

$$\alpha = \alpha_1 + \alpha_2 = \frac{2\pi^2 f^2}{v_0^3} \left[\frac{4\nu}{3} + \frac{\gamma - 1}{\gamma} f' \nu \right]$$

$$= \frac{2\pi^2 f^2 \nu}{v_0^3} \left[\frac{4}{3} + \frac{\gamma - 1}{\gamma} f' \right] \tag{16.7}$$

Effect of heat radiation

Besides viscosity and heat conduction, energy is lost also due to radiation. An expression for the loss of amplitude has been given by Stokes in the form

$$y_x = y_0 \, e^{-\alpha_3 x}$$

or
$$y_x = y_0 \, e^{-\left(\frac{\gamma - 1}{\gamma}\right) \left(\frac{q}{2v_0}\right) x}$$

where γ is the ratio of specific heats, v_0 the velocity of sound, q is the rate of cooling at constant volume of a mass of the gas. If θ_t is the excess temperature at time t and θ_0 is the excess temperature at $t = 0$, then

$$\theta_t = \theta_0 \, e^{-qt}$$

The value of q can be determined experimentally for a number of gases. In case of air, Rayleigh observed that a mass of air contained in a sphere of diameter 35 cm, the excess temperature was reduced to half in 26 s.

there
$$\frac{1}{2} = e^{-q.26} \quad \text{or} \quad q = 0 \cdot 027.$$

Then, in case of air,

$$\frac{\gamma - 1}{\gamma} \cdot \frac{q}{2v_0} = 1 \cdot 14 \times 10^{-7}$$

In case of other gases also the value can be determined experimentally. Thus we have deduced the following three expressions for the attenuations constants α_1 due to viscosity, α_2 due to heat conduction and α_3 due to heat radiation.

$$\alpha_1 = \frac{8}{3} \cdot \frac{\pi^2 f^2}{v_0^3} \nu$$

$$\alpha_2 = \frac{2\pi f^2}{v_0^3} \left(\frac{\gamma - 1}{\gamma} \right) K'$$

$$\alpha_3 = \left(\frac{\gamma - 1}{\gamma}\right) \cdot \frac{q}{2\nu_0}$$

The attenuation due to viscosity and heat conduction is a function of frequency whereas that due to heat radiation is independent of frequency. Consequently, leaving aside the attenuation due to heat radiation, we find

$$\alpha_1 = \frac{8}{3} \cdot \frac{\pi^2 \nu}{\nu_0 \lambda^2} = \frac{\alpha_1'}{\lambda^2}$$

$$\alpha_2 = \frac{2\pi^2 K'}{\nu_0} \frac{(\gamma - 1)}{\gamma} \frac{1}{\lambda^2} = \frac{\alpha_2'}{\lambda^2}.$$

Hence the amplitude of a sound wave when it proceeds through a distance x is given by

$$y = y_0\, e^{-\frac{(\alpha_1' + \alpha_2')}{\lambda^2} x}$$

$$= y_0\, e^{-\alpha' x/\lambda^2}$$

In an actual experiment instead of amplitude, intensity is measured and if I is intensity at a distance x and I_0 is the intensity at $x=0$, $I = I_0\, e^{-\mu x}$. as I is proportional to y^2, $y^2 = y_0^2\, e^{-2\alpha' x/\lambda^2}$.

Many workers have studied the absorption of sound in gases and liquids and a representative set of results is given in Table 16.1 for a few gases, as collected by Bergman. The last column gives the value of α/f^2 instead of α'/f^2.

TABLE 16.1

Values of absorption of sound (α/f^2) for a few gases

Air	*Frequency (kc/s)*	*α/f^2 (measured)*	*α/f^2 (Calculated)*
Air Gas	132-415	2·94-3·99	1·45
O_2	655-1220	3·47-1·90	1·78
CO_2	64	277	1·60
Ar	612	0	2·0

The measurement of velocity and absorption in different gases was done by Abello, Kneser and Grossman and the results showed that while the velocities in diatomic and monatomic gases at N.T.P. were the same as at low frequencies, and the absorption as represented by the above theoretical formula only slightly greater than that indicated by the theory, yet a number of triatomic gases such as carbon dioxide exhibited a rising velocity with the increase in the frequency and absorption many times the classical value.

In case of liquids we have noted that no dispersion in velocity occurs specially for ultrasonic frequencies which are capable of being generated in the laboratory. Indirect evidence of the dispersion of velocity has been obtained specially in case of viscous liquids by the study of Brillouin spectra. But the experimental determination of absorption denoted by α/f^2 has shown that it far exceeds the theoretical value, specially in liquids like carbon disulphide, carbon tetrachloride and benzene, but in most of the liquids α/f^2 is a constant at a particular temperature; only in the case of acetic acid α/f^2 decreases with increasing frequency. Table 16.2 gives the theoretical and experimental values α/f^2 in some common organic liquids.

TABLE 16.2

Values of α/f^2 (Experimental and theoretical for liquids)

Liquid	$(\alpha/f^2)\times 10^{15}$ *(Exptl)*	$(\alpha/f^2)\times 10^{15}$ *(Theoretical)*	*Frequency range Mc/s*
Water	0·5	0·08	0·1 to 200
Acetone	0·6	0·07	0·2 to 54
Chloroform	2·0	0·12	2 to 16
Carbon tetrachloride	4·0		0·2 to 105
Carbon disulphide	50·0	0·05	0·2 to 105
Benzene	8·0	0·09	0·2 to 165
Toluene	1·0	0·08	0·4 to 75
Chlorobenzene	1·7	0·1	3 to 30
Nitrobenzene	0·8	0·16	6 to 15
Acetic acid	12·0	0·17	0·5 to 70
Formic acid	2·0		4 to 10
Methyl alcohol	0·9	0·14	7 to 250
Ethyl alcohol	0·4	0·3	0·2 to 220
Probyl alcohol	0·7	0·3	3 to 16
Amyl alcohol	1·0	0·64	3 to 16
Cyclohexane	2·0	0·1	0·7 to 25
Normal hexane	0·8	0·1	3 to 16
Ether	3·5	0·57	4 to 20
Glycerine	0·4	0·09	8 to 40
Mercury	30·0	0·055	

Thus it is evident that the experimental values obtained for absorption are many times greater than the theoretical values calculated from Stokes-Kirchoff formula. It indicates that there are further sources of loss besides viscosity, heat conduction and heat radiation which have not been taken into consideration in deducing the theoretical formula and the question is still an open one. As our knowledge regarding the nature of the liquid state is still far from satisfactory further work is needed to settle the problem.

16.11 PROPAGATION OF ULTRASONICS THROUGH LIQUID HELIUM

The propagation of sound through liquid helium presents some interesting results and it is worth while to mention the same, in brief, here. The critical temperature is 5·2K and the boiling point 4·2K and at these temperatures some quantum effects become predominant. At 2·18K the liquid undergoes a transition from the comparatively normal high temperature modification He 1, to the very abnormal low temperature modification He 2. At this point, which is called the λ-point there are anomalies in the variation of specific heat and coefficient of expansion. X-ray and neutron diffraction experiments, however, reveal that no detectable change in spatial structure occurs. Another characteristic property of liquid He 2 is its ability to flow readily through very narrow channels whereas the flow of normal He 1 is imperceptible. To explain this behaviour Tisza[11] assumes that the total density of the liquid can be divided into two parts

$$\rho = \rho_s + \rho_n.$$

where for the superfluid component ρ_s has negligible viscosity and ρ_n is associated with the normal type of viscosity. As the liquid is supposed to be an admixture of two parts, the superfluid and the normal components, two types of wave propagation with different velocities are possible in liquid helium. First sound or ordinary sound occurs when the superfluid and normal components oscillate in phase with one another and normal periodic density variation is produced. Second sound is a temperature wave which results when the two components oscillate out of phase so that the cold superfluid component collects at a point of low temperature while the normal component collects at a point of high temperature half a wavelength apart.

The velocity of first sound at oK is 239 m/s. The attenuation of first sound as a function of temperature is shown in Fig. 16.7. The part of the curve above

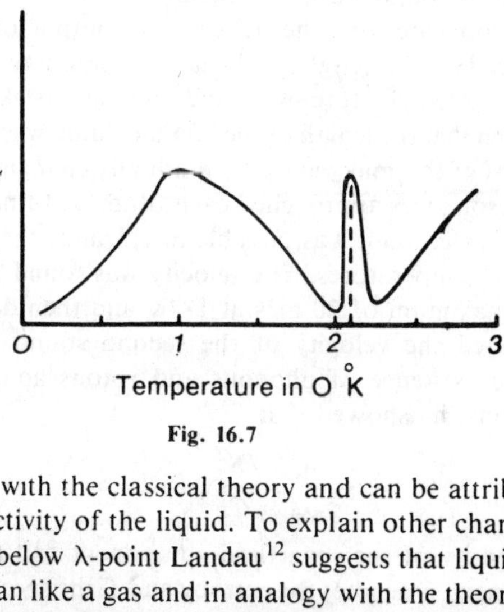

Fig. 16.7

3K is in agreement with the classical theory and can be attributed to viscosity and thermal conductivity of the liquid. To explain other characteristic property of liquid helium below λ-point Landau[12] suggests that liquid helium behaves more like a solid than like a gas and in analogy with the theory of specific heat developed by Debye, he assumes the elementary excitations as analogous to longitudinal and transverse sound waves in solids. As liquids cannot support transverse vibrations he retains only the logitudinal waves and introduces a new type of excitation called rotons corresponding to rotational motion of the molecules. He assumed a certain form of variation of energy of excitation with momentum. The elementary excitations of small energy which are longitudinal sound waves are called phonons and their energy is given by $\epsilon = vP$ where v is the velocity of ordinary sound and P is the momentum. From the nature of the energy-momentum curve, with higher values of P, there is a minimum corresponding to

$$\epsilon = \Delta + \frac{(P - P_2)^2}{\mu}$$

where μ is the effective mass of roton, and this part of the energy curve corresponds to roton as introduced by Landau.

The absorption characteristic of the first sound can be explained in terms of the relaxation mechanism which gives rise to absorption of sound in a diatomic gas when the rotational and vibrational energy levels of the molecule are not able to adjust themselves immediately to the changes in temperature accompanying the adiabatic compressions and rarefactions of the sound wave. When liquid helium 2 is compressed adiabatically the number of rotons and phonons have to adjust themselves to the new conditions of density and temperature but can only do so after a characteristic relaxation time determined by the rate of collisions by which new phonons and rotons are created. The existence of a finite relaxation time indicates a phase lag which manifests itself as an absorption peak at a temperature of the order of 1K. Experimental investigation of the velocity of second sound was made by Lane and Fairbank[13]. The apparatus consists of a lucite tube closed by a microphone at one end and by a carbon strip resistance thermometer at the other end. The whole assembly is kept inside a dewar vessel. A sound wave of frequency 1000 c/s from the transmitter was allowed to propagate into the helium, the output of the detector was amplified and recorded. The length of the liquid column remained substantially constant during this temperature sweep and resonance peak occurred whenever the velocity was such that the length of the liquid column was an integral number of half wavelengths of thermal waves. By gradually changing the temperature, they found that resonances approached each other and finally disappeared at the λ-point. By this method it was possible to calculate the velocity of second sound at a series of temperatures. The velocity was found to be zero at the λ-point, reached a maximum of 20 m/s at 1·7K and then decreased up to 1K.

Landau calculated the velocity of the second sound (U_2) based on his assumption of the existence of phonons and rotons and, using the hydrodynamical equations, he showed that

$$U_2^2 = \frac{\rho_s}{\rho_n} \cdot \frac{TS^2}{C} \tag{16.8}$$

where ρ_n is the density of the superfluid component and ρ_n is the density of the normal component, S denotes the entropy and C the specific heat. The variation of this velocity with temperature is as shown in Fig. 16.8. At 1K, U_2 is consistent with known values of ρ_s, ρ_n, S and C. Below 0·5K, only phonons need be considered and it can be shown that equation (16.8) reduces to $U_2 = U_1/\sqrt{3}$ where U_1 is the velocity of sound, which is assumed to be the same as the velocity of phonons. It can be seen from Fig. 16.8 that U_2 has a tendency to approximate the value $U_1/\sqrt{3}$ near about 0·5K, but at still lower temperatures it appears to rise towards a value U_1.

The attenuation of second sound is very large near the λ-point, falls to a minimum near 1·8K and then rises rapidly as the temperature is lowered further. At temperatures below the minimum, the attenuation can be explained

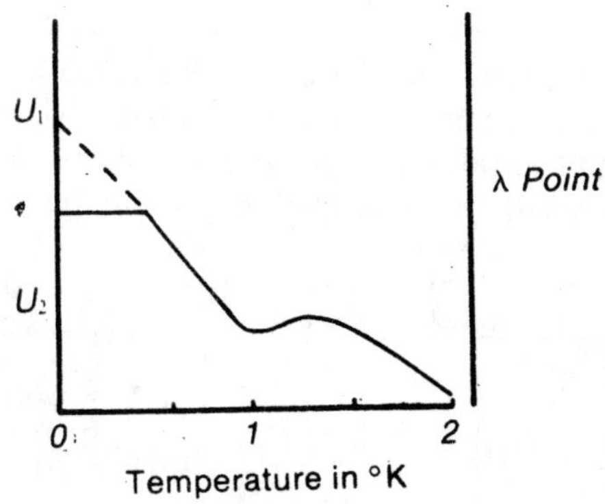

Fig. 16.8

in terms of viscosity of the normal component and the relaxation effects which occur in first sound and a type of thermal conductivity in the phonon-roton gas

16.12 APPLICATION OF ULTRASONICS

The importance of ultrasonics lies in the fact that it is a very useful tool in the hands of physicists and chemists because from the nature of the absorption and dispersion of ultrasonics in liquids and gases much information can be obtained regarding the structure of molecules. The propagation of ultrasonics through liquid helium has provided useful data regarding the superconducting state. Besides these purely theoretical considerations, the technical applications of ultrasonics are large and varied. We shall consider some of these applications here.

(a) Ultrasonic signaling

Because of their small wavelength, ultrasonics can propagate in the form of a beam. Hence signaling and locating the presence of objects can be carried out with beams of ultrasonics. Either pulsed or continuous beam can be used. The signaling is usually carried out in sea, in locating the depths of ocean. In atmospheric signaling, low frequency ultrasonics (20 to 30 kc/s) are usually used; but unfortunately there is large absorption in the atmosphere and also other associated losses due to scattering, so that even with very powerful sources and parabolic reflectors the range is not usually greater than 1000 ft. With the increase of frequency, the depth of penetration decreases because the absorption increases and hence for signaling purpose low frequency ultrasonic waves are used.

(b) Ultrasonic flaw detector

In metals specially there may arise the presence of a foreign material, or there may be a crack or crevice inside the body of the metal which is not visible to the naked eye. The presence of these discontinuities may seriously hamper the construction of equipments from these metal parts. Ultrasonics finds a very useful application in detecting these flaws and irregularities. In 1933, Malhauser first published an account of testing the defect of metals by sending an ultrasonic beam through the material under test. In the simplest set-up (Fig. 16.9) a tramsmitter denoted by *T* and the receiver denoted *R* were used. The transmitter *T* sends a beam of ultrasonics through the material under test. In absence of a flaw in the specimen, the intensity of the transmitted beam will be the same

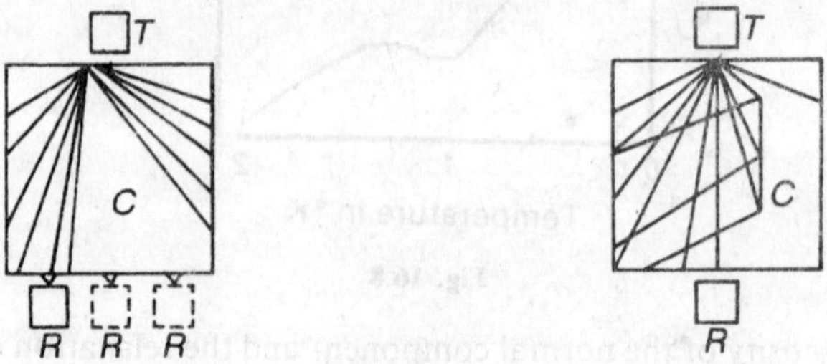

Fig. 16.9

for almost all positions of the receiver *R* but if a flaw *F* exists within the specimen, then the waves will be reflected back and the corresponding recorded intensity in the receiver will be very feeble. Similarly if there is a crack in the specimen, the waves will be referred back from the crack and the transmitted intensity will be extremely small. The method therefore consists in probing the surface of the crystal with the receiver and detect any marked change of intensity. Sokolov carried out extensive investigation of flaw detection by ultrasonics and he noted that if thin layers of a liquid are placed both in the transmitter and receiver side of the specimen, then coupling of ultrasonic energy to the specimen under test is greatly enhanced. In his later work he actually was able to obtain an actual image of the flaw inside the specimen. The frequency range used for this purpose generally lies between 20 kc/s and 20 Mc/s. The actual frequency to be used depends upon the dimension of the flaw. The flaws or holes, to be detected, must be larger than the natural discontinuities or changes in the grain size within the material.

Instead of a continuous beam, a pulsed ultrasonic beam can also be utilised. The length of the pulse can range from 1 to 10 μ s and the frequency can vary from 100 kc/s to 30 Mc/s.

(c) Heating by ultrasonics

It was observed by early workers that when ultrasonic energy is concentrated in various materials considerable amount of heat is produced, and there is a definite ratio between the heat produced and the ultrasonic energy absorbed. With the increase of frequency of ultrasonic waves the heat generated increases due to increased absorption.

(d) Production of fog and mist

When ultrasonic beams of very high energy are incident on the interface between a liquid and air, a jet of liquid is thrown up and a fine mist or fog is produced. The intensity of the fog depends upon the surface tension of the liquid and the incident power of the ultrasonic beam.

(e) Biological effects

The effect of ultrasonics on vaiious forms of life such as frogs, animals and fish has been extensively studied and the results indicate that these small animals may be either killed or a great damage caused to them particularly if the beam is of strong intensity. The effect may be utilized to destroy the harmful germs or bacteria. The body or skin temperature of animals is susceptible to exposure to a strong beam of ultrasonics.

(f) Medical uses

In modern surgery ultrasonics has a dominant role to play; ultrasonics has been used for the treatment of arthritis and other similar diseases. The use of ultrasonics for measuring the rate of flow of blood has been suggested. Location of tumor and gallstone has been done with ultrasonics.

(g) Chemical effects

Many chemical changes take place in presence of ultrasonics which in their absence do not occur. Oxidation and iodine reactions occur more rapidly in presence of ultrasonics. Both dispersive and coagulative effects take place rapidly under ultrasonic irradiation and oscillations varying from 20 to100 kc/s are generally used. High polymers break up under the effect of ultrasonics at a frequency of 600 kc/s and above.

REFERENCES

1. Curie P. and Curie J. (1880) *Compt. Rend.* **91**, 383.
2. Nikolson A.M. (1919), *Proc. Am. Inst. Elec. Engrs.* **38**, 1315.
3. Pierce G.W. (1928), *Proc. Am. Acad. Sci.* **63**, 1.
4. Debye, P. & Sears, F.W. (1932) *Proc. Natl. Acad. Sci.* **18**, 410.
5. Raman, C.V. and Nagendranath, (1936; 1938) *Proc. Indian Acad. Sci.* **2**, 406, 413, **8**, 499.
6. Lucas, R. & Biquard, P. (1933) *Compt. Rend.* **194**, 2132.
7. Sen, S.N., (1960) *Proc. Phys. Soc.* (London) **75**, 612.
8. Pierce, G.W. (1925) *Proc. Am. Acad. Sci.* **60**, 271.
9. Van Iterbeck, A. & Verhacgan, L. (1949) *Physica*, **15**, 624.
10. Pitt, A. & Jackson, W.J. (1935) *Can. J. Res.* **12**, 686.
11. Tisza, L. (1942), *Phys. Rev.* **61**, 531.
12. Landau, L. J. (1941 & 1944), *Phys. U.S.S.R.* **5**, 71, **8**, 1.
13. Lane, H.A. & Fairbank, H.A. (1947) *Phys. Rev.* **71**, 600: **72**, 645.

17

HYPERSONIC VELOCITY IN VISCOUS LIQUIDS AS REVEALED FROM BRILLOUIN SPECTRA

The work regarding the dispersion of ultrasonic velocity in a large number of liquids was experimentally investigated by a number of workers. The change in velocity with frequency cannot be observed in the frequency region of ultrasonic waves investigated experimentally but dispersion was observed indirectly through the measurement of wavelength change in the hypersonic structure in the Rayleigh scattering in liquids. This hyperfine structure in the case of Rayleigh scattering is known as Brillouin Spectra. With the analysis of experimental data in some viscous liquids and with the help of standard mathematical formula Sen* (1959) was able to explain the experimental data which shows the existence of dispersion of ultrasonic waves in viscous liquids.

17.1 INTRODUCTION

The brillouin scattering of light in liquids produces a method of determining the velocity of hypersonic vibrations which are supposed to be the cause of the appearance of hyperfine structure in the case of Rayleigh scattering. The shift in frequency is given by

$$d\nu = \pm\, 2\nu \frac{v}{c/\mu} \sin\frac{\theta}{2} \qquad \text{...(17.1)}$$

where ν is the original frequency of light, v is the velocity of sound in the liquid, μ is the refracting index of the liquid at the light of frequency ν, c the velocity of light and θ the angle between the incident light and the direction of observation. Thus, it is clear that the velocity of sound waves causing the Brillouin Spectra can be obtained if the frequency shift can be measured. The wavelength and consequently the frequency of these acoustical waves can be obtained from the relation.

$$\lambda_0 = 2\lambda_s \mu \sin\frac{\theta}{2} \qquad \text{...(17.2)}$$

* The new chapter (Chapter 17) has been prepared mainly with the help of the research paper published by S. N. Sen in the Proceedings of the Physical Society, London, Volume LXXV, p. 612, 1960.

where λ_0 is the wavelength of the incident light and λ_s the wavelength of the sound wave.

From equation (17.2) it can be shown that for almost all the liquids studied the frequency of these acoustical waves lies within the range 10^9 to 10^{10} cycles/sec whereas the maximum frequency of ultrasonic waves at which the experimental observations have been carried out is of the order of 10^6 cycles/s. The Brillouin spectrum of light scattered provides us with a method of ascertaining whether any dispersion of sound velocity actually occurs as we pass from ultrasonic (10^6 cycles/s) to the hypersonic range (10^9 cycles/s or higher). The first systematic observations in this range were made by Venketeswaran[1] and Sunandabai[2] and later by Rank et al[3]. They have confirmed that in case of liquids which are mobile at ordinary temperatures no dispersion occurs as we pass from ultrasonic to hypersonic range but in the case of viscous liquids, such as glycerine and castor oil, Venketeswaran[1] found that there actually occurs a dispersion and the same was noted by Rank et al.[3] in the case of acetone at a temperature of –78°C. The results obtained by Venketeswaran for glycerine and castor oil which are highly viscous at ordinary temperatures are shown in Table 17.1.

TABLE 17.1

Hypersonic Velocity as Measured from Brillouin Spectra

Liquid	*Glycerine*	*Castor oil*
Temperature of observation (°C)	26	28
Velocity from Brillouin spectra (m/sec)	2500	1626
Ultrasonic velocity (m/sec)	1957	1508

Venketeswaran has tried to explain the dispersion on the assumption that for these high frequency waves, the viscous liquids possess the properties of solids and the velocity of wave propagation is given by $v = \left\{\left(K + \frac{4n}{3}\right)/\rho\right\}^{1/2}$ instead of ultrasonic velocity $(K/\rho)^{1/2}$ where K is the adiabatic bulk modulus, n is the supposed modulus of rigidity of the liquid and ρ is the density of liquid. He further maintains that whereas in the case of crystals the central component is weak and modified components are strong, in the case of viscous liquids the reverse is true and the intensity falls with the increase of viscosity, so these liquids are more akin to amorphous solids like glass than to crystals.

Another point which has been raised is that acc[illegible]ding to classical thermodynamics, plane sound waves propagated through a liquid of high viscosity suffer a diminution in its amplitude in the ratio e^{-1} in traversing a number of wavelengths of sound given by $3\,v\lambda_s/8\pi^2\eta$ where v is the velocity of sound wave, λ_s is the wavelength of sound wave and η is the coefficient of viscosity of the liquid. If $\lambda = 4722$ Å then for glycerine and castor oil these would not have any significance at all and so the corresponding components would not have been observed because for these two liquids this factor comes out to be a small fraction of unity. Venketeswaran thus maintains that the appearance of these components signifies that thermal sound waves are propagated as if kinematic viscosity has little or no influence on them at all. Bearing these facts in mind the theory of propagation of sound of high frequency through a viscous liquid has been reexamined and the present chapter deals with the propagation of sound waves through glycerine and castor oil which have been studied by Venketeswaran.

Theoretical Calculation

The object of the present chapter is to show that the observed dispersion can be explained if the theory of Lamb[3] regarding the propagation of sound through viscous liquids is extended further with the idea of Maxwell regarding the occurence of complex viscosity in the case of viscous liquids. Lamb[3] (Hydrodynamics 1953) has provided the expression for the amplitude of a plane sound wave in a viscous liquid.

$$U = \nu_0 \exp i\omega\left(t + \frac{mx}{i\omega}\right) \qquad \text{...(17.3)}$$

where

$$m = \leq \pm \frac{i\omega}{\sqrt{\frac{K}{\rho}\left(1 + \frac{4i\omega\eta}{3K}\right)}} \qquad \text{...(17.4)}$$

where x is the direction of propagation, ω the angular frequency of the sound wave, η the coefficient of viscosity, K the adiabatic bulk modulus and ρ the density of the liquid.

From equation (17.3) the velocity of wave propagation is given by

$$\nu = \frac{i\omega}{m} = \sqrt{\frac{K}{\rho}}\left(1 + \frac{4i\omega\eta}{3K}\right)^{1/2} \qquad \text{...(17.5)}$$

In the case of ordinary sound wave the quantity $\omega\eta/3K$ is very small compared with unity and so for all practical purposes the velocity of sound wave can be taken as

$v = \sqrt{\frac{K}{\rho}}$ but when we are dealing with hypersonic vibrations of frequency (10^{10} cycles/sec) and liquid of high viscosity we cannot neglect this term. Further, according to Maxwell[5] (1868), the behaviour of a liquid under a shearing strain is given by

$$\frac{dS}{dt} = \frac{1}{n}\frac{dF}{dt} + \frac{F}{\eta}$$

where S is the shearing strain, F the corresponding stress, t the time, n the modulus of rigidity and η the coefficient of viscosity. If the deformation is constant, $\frac{dS}{dt} = 0$, so the solution of the above equation is

$$F = F_0 \exp(-t/\tau) \qquad \text{...(17.6)}$$

where $\tau = \eta / n$ ... (17.6)

τ has been defined by Maxwell as the time of relaxation. Meson et al.[4] (1948) have measured the mechanical properties of long chain molecules of polyisobutylene by means of shear and longitudinal waves in the ultrasonic range. The shear waves show that these liquids behave as Maxwell relaxing liquids at high frequencies. They consider that the effect of shear can be represented as the action of a compliance in parallel with a viscous resistance. At low frequencies, the liquids behave in flow as viscous liquids but at sufficiently high frequencies, a movement of one part of it is transmitted as shear wave. Hence if it is assumed that the fluid possesser an acoustical resistance in the Maxwellian sense and a complex viscosity as has been assumed by Schallamach[8] (1949) such that

$$\eta = \frac{\eta_0 [1 - i\omega\tau]}{1 + \omega^2 \tau^2} \quad \text{... (17.7)}$$

then we get from equation (17.5)

$$v = v_0 \left[1 + \frac{4i\omega}{3K} \cdot \frac{\eta_0 (1 - i\omega\tau)}{1 + \omega^2 \tau^2} \right]^{1/2}$$

$$= v_0 \left[\left\{ 1 + \frac{4\omega^2 \tau \eta_0}{3K (1 + \omega^2 \tau^2)} \right\}^2 + \frac{16\omega^2 \eta_0^2}{9K^2 (1 + \omega^2 \tau^2)^2} \right]^{1/4}$$

where $v_0 = (K/p)^{1/2}$ ... (17.8)

It is clear that in order to calculate τ, the time of relaxation of the liquid it is necessary to know n, the rigidity modulus of the liquid. Frankel[2] (1946) from his kinetic theory of liquids has given an expression for n which is

$$n = \frac{6KT}{d^3} \quad \text{... (17.9)}$$

where d is the distance between the two molecules, K is the Boltzman constant and T is the absolute temperature. If it is assumed that $d = a$, the radius of the molecule then

$$n = \frac{6 \times 4\pi\, KTN\rho}{M} = \frac{24\pi\, KTN\rho}{M} \quad \text{... (17.10)}$$

where M is the molecular weight of the liquid, N the Avogadro's number, ρ is the density of the liquid.

If calculations are carried out for Glycerin and Castor oil then Table 17.2 gives the value of n for those liquids. The third row gives the values of τ and the fourth row gives the values of τ obtained by Venketeswaran (1942, *a*).

TABLE 17.2

Calculation of Rigidity Modulus and The Time of Relaxation of Liquids

Liquid	*Glycerine*	*Castor oil*
Value of n dynes cm^{-2}	2.545×10^{10}	0.168×10^{10}
Time of relaxation τ (sec)	3.748×10^{-10}	36×10^{-10}
τ obtained by Venketeswaran (sec)	4.2×10^{-10}	33×10^{-10}

As castor oil is a mixed glyceride an appropriate estimate of its molecular weight has been made assuming it contains 87.5% of receonilic acid and the molecular weight has been taken as 927.3. Inserting the values of the time of relaxation of these liquids in equation (17.8) the velocity of hypersonic vibrations has been calculated and entered in Table 17.3.

TABLE 17.3

Hypersonic Velocity as Calculated from Equation (17.8)

Liquid	(1)	(2)	(3)	(4)	(5)	(6)	(7)
Glycerine	9.9×10^{10}	9.54	3.748×10^{-10}	4.83×10^{10}	2548.3	2500	1957 at 28°C
Castor oil	6.28×10^{10}	6.04	36×10^{-10}	2.18×10^{10}	1601.2	1626	1508 at 18°C
Acetone	4.784×10^{9}	3×10^{-3}	1.180×10^{-12}	1.053×10^{10}	1153.3	1139	1153.3 at 28°C

Indications in Table 17.3

1. was calculated from equation (17.2)
2. η (Poise)
3. relaxation time τ (sec)
4. bulk modulus (dynes cm^{-2})
5. calculated velocity (m/sec)
6. measured velocity Venketeswaran 1942 (b)
7. ultrasonic velocity (m/sec).

Discussion

From the above calculation we see that if the theory of Lamb regarding the propagation of high frequency sound waves through viscous liquids is extended further with the idea of Maxwell that these viscous liquids possess a complex viscosity, then the theoretical value of the velocity of sound waves agrees well with the experimental a observation of Venketeswaran. As ordinary mobile liquids have a low value of viscosity it is clear from equation (17.8) that their velocities will not be much effected; that this is the case has been shown by the experimental results of Rank et al.[7] (1949) and Venketeswaran[10] for all mobile liquids. The theoretical value of velocity for acetone has been calculated and entered in Table 17.3. This equation is just seen to be a general one and holds for all liquids whether mobile or viscous. Though Frankel[2] in his kinetic theory of liquids had observed that his expression for n, the rigidity modulus is only approximate, the value obtained by his expression and those obtained by Venketeswaran by assuming the liquid as a solid for these high frequency vibration show agreement not only in order of magnitude but also in actual value. This formula shows that the region of dispersion of sound for almost all the liquids will lie beyond the range of 10^{10} cycles/sec and so up to the present time no direct experimental proof has been furnished regarding the positive dispersion of sound velocity in these liquids.

With the introduction of the idea of complex viscosity the propagation of high frequency waves in liquids can be accounted for. In that case the number of wavelengths after which the amplitude will fall to $1/e$ of its original value will be given by

$$\frac{3\nu\lambda}{8\pi^2\eta_0}\cdot\frac{1+\omega^2\tau^2}{1-i\omega\tau}=\frac{3\nu\lambda}{8\pi^2\eta_0}\left(1+\omega^2\tau^2\right)^{1/2}\ \exp(i\omega\tau)$$

which becomes a number many times greater than unity. It is therefore concluded that if the assumptions regarding the complex viscosity is accepted then the dispersion of sound velocity as well its propagation in viscous liquids can be accounted for.

REFERENCES

1. Bhagabantam, S. and Rao, J., 1939, Proc. Indian Acad. Sci., A, **9,** 312.
2. Frenkel, J., 1946, Kinetic Theory of Liquids (Oxford Clarendon Press), p. 199.
3. Lamb, H., 1953, Hydrodynamics (Cambridge), p. 647.
4. Mason, W.P., Baker, W.O. Mc Skimin, H.J. and Heiss, J.H., 1948, Phys Rev. **73**, 1074.
5. Maxwell, J.C., 1868, Phil. Nag. **35**, 133.
6. Rank, D.H., Mc Cartney, J.S. and Szasz, G.J., 1948, J. Opt. Soc., America, **38**, 287.
7. Rank, D.H., Shull, E.R. and Fixford, D.W., 1949 Nature, 164, 67.
8. Schallamach, A., 1949, Proc. Phys. Soc B. **62**, 70.
9. Sunanda Bai, K.S., 1942, Proc. Ind. A, **15**, 349.
10. Venketeswaran, C.S., 1942, A Proc. Ind. Acad. Sci., A, **15**, 362.
11. Zachoval, M.L., 1939 a. C.R. Acad. Sci. Paris, **208**, 265.
12. Zachoval, M.L., 1939, b. J, Physique, **10**, 350.

PROBLEMS

1. A body is executing a simple harmonic motion of periodic time 3 s. If the amplitude of displacement is 8 cm, calculate the maximum velocity and acceleration.
2. A vertical U-tube of uniform cross-section contains water up to a height of h cm. Show that if water on one side is depressed and then released, its motion up and down the tube is simple harmonic and calculate the time period. *(Punjab University, 1965)*
3. A body of mass 50 g is executing a simple harmonic motion of periodic time 3 s and amplitude 10 cm, calculate the force per unit displacement and the maximum kinetic energy of the body.
4. Calculate the resultant vibration when two simple harmonic motions of different amplitudes and frequencies in the ratio 2 : 1 and phase difference $\pi/4$ are compounded together. Deduce the result when the phase difference is $\pi/2$.
5. Two tuning forks produce Lissajous figure. The figure changes inform from a parabola to a figure of 8 and again to a parabola, the whole cycle occupying 6 s. If the frequency of one fork is 100, find the possible frequencies of the other.
6. Compound, analytically, two rectangular simple harmonic vibrations whose amplitudes as well as the periods are in the ratio 1 : 2 and phase difference 90°.
7. A mass M is attached to the end of a spring of mass M' and the restoring force per unit displacement is S. Show that if the mass M is displaced from its mean position, then the system will execute a simple harmonic motion of angular frequency
$$\omega = \sqrt{\frac{S}{(M + M'/3)}}.$$
8. Considering the earth to be a sphere of uniform density, show that a particle dropped into a tunnel bored so that it joins any two points on the surface will execute a simple harmonic motion and hence calculate the time period of oscillation.
9. Two open pipes are sounded together, each note consisting of its fundamental together with two upper harmonics. One fundamental note has 256 vibrations per second, the other 170. Would there be any beats produced? If so how many per second?
10. A pendulum of length 100 cm has an iron sphere of radius 8 mm. at its end and is executing simple harmonic motion. Taking into consideration the damping force as equivalent to viscous drag in air (given by Stoke's law) calculate the time in which the amplitude of oscillation will fall to 10% of the undamped amplitude.
11. Find an expression for the acceleration of a damped mechanical oscillator driven by a force $F \cos pt$ and hence calculate the frequency at which the acceleration will become a maximum.
12. An L.C.R. circuit is acted on by an alternating electromotive force $E_0 \sin \omega t$. Show that the frequency at which the voltage across the condenser becomes maximum is given by
$$\omega = \omega_0 \left[1 - \frac{1}{Q_0^2}\right]^{1/2} \quad \text{where } Q_0 = \frac{\omega L}{R}.$$
13. Three equal masses are placed on a weightless string of length l and under a tension T_1 at equal distances from each other. Deduce the resultant motion and calculate the frequency of normal vibration.

14. If a generator delivers maximum power when the load equals its internal impedance, show how an ideal transformer may be used as a device to match a load to the generator.
15. Utilizing the principle of coupled oscillation in a string deduce the equation of transverse vibration in a string.
16. Calculate the average amplitude of a sinusoidal sound wave in air of a frequency of 1 kc/and average intensity of 10^{-6} w/cm^2. Velocity of sound in air is 334 m/s and density of air is 0.001293 g/cc.
17. Calculate the velocity of sound in air at N.T.P., density of air is 0.001293 g/cc.
18. If the tension of a string is raised by 20 lb, the frequency of vibration becomes 2.5 times the original; calculate the tension.
19. Two wires of the same material are stretched with the same load. Their lengths are 40 cm and 60 cm and their diameters are 1.2 mm and 1.5 mm respectively. The first string resonates with a tuning fork of 384. Calculate the frequency of the other.
20. Four violin strings all of the same length and material but of diameters in the ratio 4 : 3 : 2 : 1 are to be stretched so that each gives a note whose frequency is 3 times that of preceding string. If the stretching force of the first string is 2.048 kg wt, calculate the tensions in the other strings.
21. A stretched string fixed between two points is plucked at a point which divides the string in the ratio 3 : 1. Give reason for the absence of certain higher harmonics.
22. A harp string is plucked so that the initial conditions are given by

$$y_0 = \frac{20\,hx}{9\,l} \text{ from } 0 < x < \frac{9l}{20}$$

$$y_0 = \frac{20\,h}{9}\left(\frac{l}{2} - x\right) \text{ from } \frac{9l}{20} < x < \frac{11l}{20}$$

$$y_0 = \frac{20\,h}{9}\,(l - x) \text{ from } \frac{11l}{20} < x < l$$

Discuss the nature of vibrations produced.
23. A sonometer is arranged to emit a note of frequency n. How must the tension be varied to increase the frequency of the note to 5 n/3. If the tension of the wire be maintained constant in what other way could the same change in frequency be made?
24. A weight is hung from the wire of a sonometer. When the vibrating length of the wire is adjusted to 80 cm, the note it emits when plucked is in tune with a standard fork. On adding a further weight of 100 g the vibrating length has to be altered by 1 cm in order to restore the unison. What is the initial tension of the wire?
25. In a falling plate experiment to determine the frequency of a tuning fork, the distance of 8.2 cm contains first 20 waves and distance of 12.6 cm contains the next 20 waves. Calculate the frequency of the fork.
26. Two pipes, one open at both ends and the other open at one end and closed at the other, are sounded together and they produce 10 beats per second. If the length of the open pipe is 40 cm, calculate the change that has to be made in the length of the other pipe so that both may have the same frequency; velocity of sound in air is 330 m/s.
27. Calculate the natural frequency of a Helmholtz resonator of volume 1000 cc, the area of cross-section and the length of the neck of the resonator being 2 sq. cm and 1.5 cm respectively. How will the frequency be affected if the resonator is filled with hydrogen?
28. Show that the change of velocity of sound in air is about 0.6 m/s per degree rise of temperature. *(Osmania, 1966)*

29. If the velocity of sound in hydrogen at 0°C is 4200 ft/s what will be the velocity of sound at the same temperature in a mixture of two parts by volume of hydrogen to one of oxygen. Density of oxygen is 16 times that of hydrogen. *(Punjab, 1958)*

30. A brass rod of 3 cm. is clamped at the centre. It emits a note of frequency 600 when it vibrates longitudinally. If the density of brass is 8.3 g/cc, calculate the Young's modulus. *(Punjab, 1953)*

31. The density of hydrogen at N.T.P. is 0.0893 g/litre and the ratio of the specific heats is 1.408. Calculate the velocity of sound in hydrogen at 30°C, taking the normal pressure to be 10^6 dynes/cm^2.

32. The sound of an enemy fire is heard at the same instant on two locating stations A and C and 3 s sooner at another station B. If A, B and C are in the same straight line and 2 miles apart, locate the position of the cannon, temperature of the air being 25°C. (Velocity of sound in air at 0°C is 332 m/s).

33. The velocity of sound through hydrogen at 0°C is 1286 m/s at N.T.P. What information can be obtained regarding its molecular structure? Density of hydrogen is 0.089×10^{-3} g/cc.

34. If two sound waves, one in air and another in water, are equal in intensity what is the ratio of pressure amplitude in air to that in water. If the amplitudes are equal calculate the ratio of the intensities.

35. Calculate the reflection and transmission coefficient when sound wave is incident from air to water (*a*) for normal incidence (*b*) for incident angle of 30°.

36. Calculate the intensity (in W/cm^2) of a sound wave in air having the frequency of 5000 c/s and amplitude of vibration 10^{-10} cm. Density of air is 0.00129 g/cc. and velocity in air is 330 m/s.

37. Two loudspeakers of output intensity 1.5×10^{-4} W and 2.0×10^{-4} W and emitting sound of frequency 1 kc/s are in phase and situated at a distance 10 m from one another. Calculate the phase and intensity at a point P at a distance 6 m from one and 4 m from the other.

38. Calculate the time taken by a sound wave to travel a distance of 10^8 cm upwards from the surface of the earth, assuming the temperature to be 20°C at the surface of the earth and drops at a constant rate to –38°C at the height stated.

39. A plane wave of length 75 cm is passing through a point where the intensity is 10^{-4} W. Calculate the amplitude of vibration of air particles at that point (velocity of sound = 332 m/ and density of air 1.293×10^{-3} g/cc).

40. Calculate the increase of pressure when a sound wave produces an energy flow 0.1 μW per second per unit area. Velocity of sound 332 m/s and density of air 1.293×10^{-3} g/cc.

41. Two express trains travelling at a speed of 50 miles/hr pass one another. The whistle of one of them is being sounded continuously. If the frequency of the note emitted is 900 c/s, calculate the apparent frequency to be noted by a passenger (*a*) before the trains meet, (*b*) after they have passed each other.

42. A train approaches a station with a velocity of 15 miles/hr whistling all the time with a frequency of 250 c/s. The note of reflection from the station building produces beats. Find the frequency of the beats heard by the engine driver (velocity of sound 1100 ft/s). *(Calcutta University, 1962)*

43. A spectrum line of wavelength 4000 Å in the spectrum of light emitted from a star is found to be displaced towards the red end of the spectrum by 1 Å. Calculate the velocity of the star along the line of sight. *(Agra University, 1946)*

44. A guided misile approaches a target and gives rise to a tone of 800 c/s. If the speed of the missile is 0.8 times the velocity of sound calculate the apparent frequency of the sound as will be noted by the observers near the target.
45. If the reverberation time for an empty hall is 2.5 s, calculate the time in which the intensity of the sound in the room will diminish by absorption to 1/20th of the original value.
46. An auditorium has a time of reverberation of 1.5 s. Calculate the time interval during which the intensity of the sound will diminish from 40 db to 20 db.
47. Calculate the reverberation time in a hall in which the sound decays to 1/3rd of its intensity in 0.04 s.
48. A beam of monochromatic radiation of $\lambda = 6000$ Å is incident on a liquid excited by ultrasonics of frequency 1.5 Mc/s. If the first diffracted maximum occurs at an angle of 30 min., calculate the velocity of the ultrasonic wave through the liquid.
49. Diffraction pattern is observed when a beam of monochromatic radiation of $\lambda = 5893$ Å is incident on a liquid excited by ultrasonics. If the velocity of propagation is 1200 m/s. calculate the angle at which the first diffraction maximum occurs.
50. In an ultrasonic interferometer maximum in the plate current is observed at a distance of 0.165 cm. If the frequency of excitation is 500 kc/s, calculate the velocity of ultrasonic waves through the liquid.
51. Obtain an expression for the displacement of a stretched string of finite length in transverse vibration.
52. Show that in case of forced vibration the average rate of work done by the external force is equal to average rate of dissipation of energy.
53. Explain the terms "phase velocity" and "group velocity" and deduce a relation between them.
54. In case of a string excited by plucking, if the plucked point divides the string in the ratio 1 : 2 and its initial displacement be 'h', find the amplitudes of vibration of the first three harmonics.
55. Calculate the average energy per unit volume for a plane progressive sound wave travelling through a medium.
56. Calculate the velocity of sound in nitrogen gas at N.T.P. given that nitrogen molecules are diatomic and molecular weight of nitrogen = 28 and volume of 1 gram molecule of the gas is 22.4 litres.
57. Obtain an expression for the total energy per unit length of a transverse wave in a stretched string.
58. A source emitting a frequency of 8000 c/s is approaching a stationery observer with a velocity of 86 km/hr. What is the change in frequency of the note as it goes past the observer?
59. A weight is hung from the wire of a sonometer. When the vibrating length of the wire is adjusted to 80 cm, the note it emits when plucked is in tune with a standard fork; on adding a further weight of 100 g the vibrating length has to be altered by 1 cm in order to restore to unison. What is the initial tension in the wire?
60. A body is being acted upon simultaneously by two simple harmonic forces at right angles to one another and of equal amplitude and frequency, but 90° out of phase. Calculate the resultant motion.
61. Determine the resulting wave amplitude at a certain point if two waves of same frequency arrive at that point with amplitudes in the ratio 3 : 2 and phase difference of 45°.

62. A violin string is 50 cm long and is kept fixed at both its ends. The string is excited by bowing and the vibrations are transverse to the length of the string. If the velocity of transverse waves is 506 m/s, what are the five lowest frequencies that will be produced?

63. Show that the intensity of a plane sound wave is the product of energy per unit volume and the speed of propagation of the wave disturbance.

64. Show that the intensity of a sound wave is given by

$$I = P^2/2\rho v$$

where P is the pressure amplitude and ρ is the standard density of air and v is the speed of the wave.

65. Two identical piano wires have the same fundamental frequency of 500 c/s. They are kept under the same tension. By how much the tension of one wire must be changed so as to hear 10 beats/s when both are sounded together?

66. A flexible string of length l is stretched with a tension T and fixed between two rigid supports; the mass of the string per unit length is ρ. The string is set into vibration with a hammer blow which imparts a velocity v to a small segment of length lying between x and $x + dx$, where x-axis is along the length of the string; calculate the amplitudes of the three lowest frequencies.

67. Express Y as a function of t by Fourier's theorem, given that from $t = 0$ to $t = T/2$, $y = 0$ and from $t = T/2$ to $t = T$, $y = 2K$.

68. A small ball is hung by a fine silk thread of length l cm to a large mass which is itself suspended by a strong wire of length L cm. They are initially at rest; the large mass is struck by a hammer so that it begins to oscillate with an amplitude of a cm. Write the equations of motion of the two masses and solve for displacements of the two masses.

69. It has been found that the temperature coefficient of variation of frequency of a steel tunning fork is 1.12×10^{-4} per degree celsius and the coefficient of linear expansion 1.2×10^{-4}. Calculate the temperature coefficient of variation of Young's modulus of steel.

70. The quartz crystal used to excite ultrasonic waves has the modulus of elasticity as 7.7×10^{11} dynes/cm^2 and density 2.654 g/cc. Calculate the thickness of the crystal for generating a frequency of 25000 c/s.

71. A plane wave of wavelength 65 cm passing through a point where the intensity is 10^{-5} W; calculate the amplitude of vibration of air particles at that point (velocity of sound is 332 m/s and density of air $1.293/10^{-3}$ g/cc).

72. Calculate the increase of pressure when a sound wave produces an energy flow of 0.1 μW/s per unit area; velocity of sound 332 m/s and density of air 1.293×10^{-3} g/cc.

73. A harmonic wave of frequency 50 c/s and amplitude 2 mm travels along a string of density 10 g/cm. The string is stretched under a tension of 4×10^{-4} dynes. Find the wavelength, velocity, period, and average kinetic and potential energies per cm of the wave.

74. Utilizing Lagrange's equation deduce the equation of motion of a vibrating string and obtain its solution.

75. If a copper foil of thickness 3×10^{-3} cm and density 3.8 g/cc is stretched over a metal frame of 3 cm. radius and the radial tension of 5×10^{6} dynes, what are the frequencies of the symmetrical modes?

76. A steel bar is 30 cm in length and is clamped at one end. If the area of cross-section is 2 sq cm, what will be the lowest three frequencies of vibration?

77. A square membrane of density 2 g/cc is under a tension of T dynes per cm. If the membrane is to respond to a frequency of 250 c/s, calculate the value of T.

78. The circular membrane of kettle drum has a radius of 40 cm and a density of 0.2 g/sq cm. It is under a tension of 10^6 dynes; calculate the fundamental frequency.
79. A Helmholtz resonator has a neck of cylindrical cross-section of 2 sq. cm and length 1 cm. If the resonating vessel is spherical in shape what must its radius be to have the resonance frequency of 500 c/s?
80. Calculate the velocity of sound in an area where an explosion has occurred so that the pressure has risen to hundred times the atmospheric pressure and the temperature is 2000°C.
81. A circular membrane of steel 5 cm in diameter and 0.003 cm thick is stretched to a certain tension. Under a uniform static pressure of ½ atm applied to one side of the membrane the central deflection is 0.01 cm. Calculate the first three natural frequencies for the normal symmetrical mode of vibration.
82. A spherical resonator has a volume of 400 cc and a circular neck of radius 2 cm. Calculate its natural frequency (velocity of sound is 332 m/s).
83. A plane wave of sound strikes a boundary of water/air at an incident angle of 45°. Investigate the properties of the reflected and transmitted waves.
84. Three masses each of mass m are placed at equal distances in a string of length $4l$. Calculate the resultant frequencies and displacements.
85. An office room is 20 ft high, 30 ft wide and 40 ft long. The walls of the room are covered by a sound absorbing material of coefficient 0.03. Calculate the reverberation time.
86. Calculate the velocity of sound in a gas in which two waves of wavelength 100 cm and 102 cm produce 8 beats per second.
87. A tuning fork A of frequency 256 c/s produces 4 beats/s with another tuning fork B: when the prongs of tuning fork A are loaded with a 1 g wt the number of beats is 1/s and when loaded with 2 g. wt the number of beats is 2/s. What is the frequency of the tuning fork B?
88. If two organ pipes sounded together produce 3 beats/s, find their frequencies if one of the pipes is 33 inches long and the other 33.5 inches long.
89. Three strings of equal length but stretched with different tensions are made to vibrate. If the masses per unit length are in the ratio 1 : 2 : 4 and the frequencies are the same, calculate the ratio of the tensions.
90. A hall of volume 60,000 cu ft is found to have a reverberation time of 3 sec. If the area of sound absorbing surface is 8000 sq ft, calculate the average absorption coefficient.
91. A stretched string of length l is struck a blow so that its initial velocity is zero from $x = 0$ to $x = l/2$. $4v/x\,(x - l/2)$ from $l/2$ to l. Discuss the motion of the string.
92. A steel bar of radius 0.6 cm has a length of 1 m. What is its fundamental frequency for free-free transverse vibration?
93. In problem 92 if the bar is clamped at one end what will be its frequency for longitudinal vibration and what weight must be attached to its free end so as to decrease the frequency by 50 per cent.
94. A circular membrane of radius 30 cm and density per unit area of 2g/cm² is stretched to a tension of 10^8 dynes/cm. Compute the frequencies of the four lowest vibrations.
95. A plane sound wave is travelling from oil to air. If the velocity of sound in oil is 1500 m/s and density of oil 1.2 g/cc, calculate the critical angle of incidence.
96. In a room having length, width and height as 15 ft, 12 ft and 20 ft respectively, the reverberation time is 5 s. What is the effective sound absorption coefficient of the walls?

97. Calculate the fundamental frequency of a 4 mm thick X-cut quartz crystal.

98. An ultrasonic wave is being propagated through a liquid which is illuminated by radiation of wavelength 5893 Å. If the frequency of ultrasonic waves is 25×10^3 c/s and the velocity is 800 m/s, calculate the first order angle of diffraction.

99. In an ultrasonic interferometer, an ultrasonic wave having a frequency of 30 kc/s is propagating. If the interferometer is filled with a gas having the velocity of propagation of sound as 450 m/s, calculate the distances at which the recording meter will show maximum deflections.

100. Calculate the attenuation coefficient of a sound wave of frequency 50 kc/s, when propagating through a liquid having a coefficient of viscosity of 0.1 cP (velocity of sound through the liquid as 1320 m/s).

INDEX

Abello, 215
Acceleration of particle, 43
Acoustics of buildings, 185-92
Agnew, 181
Air cavity, vibrations in, 121-21
Air columns, vibrations of, 115-22
 air cavity, 121-22
 conical pipe, 119
 cylindrical pipe, 115-18
 examples of, 118-21
 Galton's whistle, 120
 high frequency pipe, 120
 organ pipe, 118-19
 reed pipe, 119
Airy, 142
Altberg, 174
Amplitude of vibration, 2, 5
Amplitude resonance, of forced vibration, 23-25
Application of ultrasonics in, 219-21
 biology, 221
 chemical, 221
 flaw detector, 219-20
 heating, 220
 medicine, 221
 production of fog and mist, 220-21
 signaling, 219
Audible range, 1

Bars, vibration of,
 boundary conditions for, 84-85
 conditions of ends for, 85-87
 energy of, 88-89
 general equation for, 85
 transverse vibration of, 82-84
 tuning fork and, 90-95
Bergman, 2, 5
Bessel function, 105
Bell, Alexander Graham, 156, 193
Biological effect of ultrasonics, 221
Biquard, 209
Boltzman, 177
Bowed string, 70-75
Boyle, 140, 152, 206
Boyle's law, 123, 174
Brillouin, 207
Brillouin spectra, 209, 215
Brown, S.G., 157
Buckingham, 187
Buildings, acoustics of, 185-92
 decay of sound, 188
 growth of sound, 187-88
 loudness, 185
 noise, 190-91
 position of speaker, 185
 reverbration, 185-90
Butterworth, 93

Campbell, 132
Carbon microphone, 164-65
Chapin, 181
Chemical effects of ultrasonics, 221
Chladni, 90, 110, 170
Chronograph, 93
Circular membrane, vibration of, 104-10
Colpitts oscillator, 204
Combination of tones, 144-47
 existence of, 147
Components of recording system, 194-96
Condenser microphone, 162-64
Conical pipe, 119-20
Consonance and dissonance, 182-83
Cook, 132
Coupled oscillation, theory of, 29-42
 and electrical coupled circuits, 41
 examples of, 37-41
 general equation for, 29-32
 general solution for, 32-34
 natural modes of, 38-39
 special cases of, 34-37
Curie, 158, 202
Cylindrical pipe,
 vibration of air columns in, 115-18

Damped vibration, 17-21
  special cases of, 20-21
Davis, 191
Debye, 207, 217
Detection of ultrasonic waves, 206-07
  electrical detector, 207
  quartz crystal receiver, 207
  radiometer method, 206-07
  smoke method, 206
Diatonic scale, 183-84
Diffraction grating, 151
Diffraction of sound, 147-52
  experiments for, 151-52
  through circular aperture, 150-51
  through slit, 148-50
Discs, recording of sound on, 193-96
Dissonance and consonance, 182-83
Dixon, 132
Doppler's principle, 179-81

Eccles, 92
Echoes, 140-41
  harmonic, 141
  musical, 141
Eckhardt, 190
Edelman, 201
Edison, 193
Edser, 147
Einthovan string galvanometer, 126
Elastic vibration in solids, 47-49
Electrical coupled circuits, and coupled oscillations, 41
Electrically maintained tuning fork, 92-93
Electrodynamic receiver, 150
Electromagnetic receiver, moving iron type, 150-57
Energy,
  form of, 1
  of forced vibration, 28
  of particle in simple harmonic vibration, 7
  of plane wave of sound, 45-46
  of vibrating membrane, 103-04
  Equation of motion, of a vibrating body, 17
  Esclangon, 126
  Essen, 160
  Exterman, 208
  Extermann, 208

Fairbank, 218
Falling plate method, for frequency of tuning fork, 93-95
Fechner, 154
Film, recording of sound in, 198-200
Firestone, 181
Fitzgerald, Lorentz, 160
Fixed coil type loudspeakers, 168
Fog and mist, production of by ultrasonic, 220-21
Forced vibration,
  amplitude of, 23-25
  energy of, 28
  phase of, 23
  velocity response, 25-26
Fourier's theorem, 13-16
Frequency of sound, measurement of, 177-79
Frequency of tuning fork, measurement of, 91-95
Frequency of vibration, 2

Galton's whistle, 120, 201
Gas, velocity of sound in, 123-26
Gange tone, 171
Generation of ultrasonic waves, 201-06
  by magnetostriction, 204-05
  by piezo-electric method, 202
  power for, 203-04
  quartz crystal, 202-03
Gerlach, 177
Grossman, 215

Harmonic echoes, 141
Harrison, 196
Hartman, 120
Hartley oscillator, 204
Hearing, theories of, 154
Hebb, T.C., 127
Helmholtz, 59, 63, 70, 117, 122, 131, 147, 166, 175, 181-84
  intensity theory of, 145
Helmholtz resonator, 121
Hertzfield, 211

Horn loudspeakers, 168-69
Hot air microphone, 175-76
Hot wire microphone, 165-66
Hugén, 144
Huggins, 170
Hughos, 164
Human ear, 153-54
Huyghen's principle, 148, 150
Hydrophone, 166

Intensity of sound, 3, 155-56, 172-77, 181-82
Intensity theory of Helmholth, 145
Interference of sound, 144-47
Isochornous oscillation, 5

Jackson, 210
Jager, 187
Joule, 204

Kauffman, 59
Kettledrum, 107-10
Kinetic energy of, vibrating membrane, 106
Kirchhoff, 131, 211, 213
Kneser, 215
Konig, 90, 172, 181, 206
Kundt's tube, 128-32, 134, 136, 176

Lagrane, 145
Lamb, 209
Landan, 217-18
Lane, 218
Langevin, 174, 202
Laplace, 124
Larmor, 173
Laws of vibrating string
    experimental verification of, 53-54
    law of length, 53
    law of mass, 53
    law of tension, 53
Lehman, 140, 206
Liquids, velocity of sound in, 132-35
Lissajou's figures, 13-14
Lloyd, 181
Longitudinal waves, in solid, 47-49
Loudness, sensation of, 154-55
Loudspeakers, 166-69
Lucas, 209

Magnetostriction oscillator, 205-06
Maintenance of sound by heat, 169
Marti, 133
Mathews, 134
Maxfield, 196
Maxwell, 173
Medical uses of ultrasonics, 221
Membranes, vibration of, 97-110
    circular, 104-10
    energy of, 103-04
    initial conditions for, 100
    kinetic energy of, 106
    nodal lines for, 100-02
    potential energy of, 107
    rectangular, 97-102
    square, 102-04
    stretched, 97
Methods of producing vibration in strings, 55-75
    bowed string, 70-75
    plucked string, 55-59
    struck string, 59-70
Michelson, A.A., 127, 147
Microphones, 162-66, 194
    carbon, 164-65
    condenser, 162-64
    hot wire, 165-66
Miller, D.C. 184
Moving coil loudspeaker, 167-68
Musical echoes, 141
Musical interval, 183
Musical notes, analysis of, 84
Musical scale, 183
Musical sound, features of, 2-3, 181

Nagendranath, 208
Newton, 123
Nikolsan, A.M. 202
Noise, 2-3, 190-92

Ohm, G.S. 155
Ohm's law, 155
Open air, velocity of sound in, 126-27
Organ pipes, 118-19

Paris, 175-76, 207
Parker, 132

Parthasarathy, 208-09
Partial fourier series, 16
Particle,
  energy of in simple harmonic vibration, 7
  velocity, 43
Period of vibration, 2
Phase of sound, 181
Phase of vibration, 2
Phonic wheel method for frequency of tuning fork, 95
Piano string, 63-70
Pierce, G.M., 162, 179, 205, 209
Piezoelectric phenomena, 158-62
  crystal, 159
  receivers, 161-62
  standards of frequency, 160
Pitch, 2, 181-82
Pitt, 210
Plane wave,
  energy of, 45-46
  power of source emitting, 46-47
  of sound, 45-46
Plucked string, 55-59
Potential energy of vibrating membrane, 107
Poulson, 197
Power, of source emitting plane wave, 46-47
Poynting, 173
Propagation of ultrasonic waves,
  through liquid Helium, 216-19

Quartz crystal, 202-03
  as frequency stabilizer, 160-61

Raman, 75, 142, 208
Ramsay, 130
Rayleigh, U., 84-85, 90, 117, 121, 130, 140-42, 170-72, 209, 213
Rayleigh disc, 172-74
Receiver of sound, 156-66
  electrodynamic, 158
  electromagnetic, 156-57
  magnetosfriction, 161-62
  piezo-electric, 161-62
  thermal, 165-66
Reception of sound, 153-56
  electrodynamic receiver, 158
  electromagnetic receiver, 156-57
  jets, 156
  magnetostriction receiver, 162-65
  piezoelectric receiver, 161-62
  receiver, 156-71
  sensitive flame, 156
  thermal receiver, 165-66
  through human ear, 153-54
  underwater receiver, 166
Recording of sound,
  components of, 194-97
  in film, 198-200
  on discs, 193-96
  on tape, 197
  on wire, 197
Rectangular membrane, 97-102
Reed pipe, 119
Reflection of sound,
  at boundary of two media, 137-39
  boundary conditions, 138-39
  echoes and, 140-42
  from plate of finite, thickness, 139-40
  phase change on, 139
  total internal, 143
Refraction of sound, 142-44
  effect of temperature, 144
  effect of wind, 143-44
  in upper atmosphere, 142-43
Reid, 152
Resonance and forced vibration, 17-28
Resonance air column, velocity of sound by, 131-32
Resonator, theory of, 121-22
Reverbration of sound,
  decay, 188
  growth, 187-88
  time of, 189-90
Rice, 211
Richarson, 175
Rideout, 156
Rijki, 171
Rings, vibration of, 110-14
Rucker, 147

Sabine, 186, 188, 190, 192
Sandhauss, 122, 142
Scheibler, 178
Schottkey, 177
Scott, Leon, 193
Sears, 207
Seeback, 177
Seeback's strings, 177-78
Simple harmonic motion
composition of, 8-13
energy of particle in, 7
experiments, 13
Fouriers's theorem, 13-16
phase of, 6-7
requisite conditions for, 4-6
Singing arc, 171
Singing flames, 170-71
Sivian, 173
Slit, diffraction of sound through, 148-50
Solids,
elastic vibrations in, 47-49
velocity of sound in, 134-36
Sonometer, 53-54
Sorge, 144
Sound,
acoustics of buildings, 185-92
diffraction of, 147-52
energy of plane wave of, 45-46
frequency of, 177-81
intensity of, 3, 155-56, 172-77, 181-82
interference of, 144-97
loudness of, 3, 154-56
maintenance of, 169
measurement of, 172-84
musical, 2-3
noise, 2-3, 190-92
phase of, 181
pitch of, 181-82
propagation of, 1-2, 142-43
quality of, 3, 181-82
receivers of, 156-69
reception of, 153-77
recording of, 193-200
reflection of, 137-42
refraction of, 142-44
reproduction of, 193-200
transmission of, 123-36
use of resonator in sound analysis, 122
velocity of, 2, 123-36
Sound interferometer, 176-77
Sound radiometer, 177-74
Source emitting plane wave, power of, 46-47
Special cases of coupled oscillations, 34-37
loose coupling, 34
resonance, 34-37
Square membrane, vibration of, 102-04
Stationary waves, formation of, 51-52
Stevens, 132
Stille, 197
Stokes, 211, 213
Stretched membranes, 97
Strings, vibration of,
energy of, 80-81
experiments, 53-54
laws of, 53
methods of producting, 55-75
reflection, 51-53
sonometer, 53-54
special cases in, 75-80
transverse, 50-51
wave equation of, 54-55
Struck string, 59-70

Tape recording of sound, 197-98
Tartine, 144-45
Theory of forced vibration, 17-28
Tomlinson, 160
Toppler, 177
Transverse vibration
of bar, 82-84
of string, 50-51
Travelyan's rockers, 169-70
Trolle, 120
Tuning fork, 90-95, 178-79
determination of frequency of, 93-95
electrically maintained, 92-93
frequency of, 91-95
temperature effect on frequency of, 91-92
Tucker, W.S., 166, 175-76, 207
Tynall, 156

Ultrasonic flaw detector, 219-20
Ultrasonic signaling, 219
Ultrasonics, 201-21
  absorption of, 211-16
  application of, 219-21
  cystal for, 203
  detection of, 206-07
  dispersion of, 211-16
  effect of heat conduction on, 213-16
  Galton's whistle, 120, 201
  generation of, 201-06
  heating by, 220
  propagation of, 216-19
  velocity of, 207-10

Value maintained tuning fork, 92-93
Velocity of sound,
  by resonance air column, 131
  contained in tubes, 127-31
  effect of humidity on, 125-26
  effect of pressure on, 124-25
  effect of temperature on, 125
  effect of wind on, 126
  in gas, 123-26, 132-33
  in liquids, 132-35
  in open air, 126-27
  in solids, 134-36
Velocity of ultrasonic waves, 207-10
  by diffraction method, 207-09
  in liquids, 207-10
  interference method, 209-10
  liquids, 207-10
Velocity of wave propagation, 43-45
Velocity of response of forced vibration, 25-27
Verhacam, 210
Vibrating bar, energy of, 88-89
Vibration,
  of air column, 115-22
  of bars, 82-96
  demped, 17-21
  elastic, 47-49
  energy of plane wave of sound, 45-46
  forced, 20-28
  in extended medium, 42-49
  in solid, 47-49
  logarithmic decrement, 18-20
  longitudinal, 47-49
  of membranes, 97-110
  methods of producing, 55-56
  plane wave, 42-43, 45-46
  reflection, 51-53
  resonance, 17-28
  of rings, 110-14
  of strings, 50-81
  theory of forced, 17-28
  transverse, 50-51, 82-84
  velocity of wave propagation, 43-45
  velocity response of, 25-27

Wannier, 208
Warburg, 130
Watson, 187
Wave equation of string, general solution of, 54-56
Wave propagation, velocity of, 43-45
Wavelength, 2
Weber, 154
Weber Fechner law, 154-55
Wente, 163
Whispering gallery, 141-42
Wire recording of sound, 197-98
Wood, 13, 134, 160

Young, Thomas, 58, 145
Young's theorem, 75

Zone of silence, 143